American
Civil War
Almanac

American Civil War Almanac

Kevin Hillstrom
and
Laurie Collier
Hillstrom

Lawrence W. Baker, Editor

AN IMPRINT OF THE GALE GROUP

DETROIT · SAN FRANCISCO · LONDON
BOSTON · WOODBRIDGE, CT

American Civil War: Almanac

Kevin Hillstrom and Laurie Collier Hillstrom

Staff

Lawrence W. Baker, *U•X•L Senior Editor*
Carol DeKane Nagel, *U•X•L Managing Editor*
Tom Romig, *U•X•L Publisher*

Rita Wimberley, *Senior Buyer*
Evi Seoud, *Assistant Production Manager*
Dorothy Maki, *Manufacturing Manager*
Mary Beth Trimper, *Production Director*

Michelle DiMercurio, *Art Director*
Cynthia Baldwin, *Product Design Manager*

Shalice Shah-Caldwell, *Permissions Specialist*
Pamela Reed, *Imaging Coordinator*
Leitha Etheridge-Sims, *Cataloger*
Robert Duncan, *Senior Imaging Specialist*
Michael Logusz, *Imaging Specialist*
Randy A. Bassett, *Image Database Supervisor*
Barbara J. Yarrow, *Imaging and Multimedia Content Manager*

Marco Di Vita, Graphix Group, *Typesetting*

Library of Congress Cataloging-in-Publication Data

Hillstrom, Kevin, 1963–
    American Civil War. Almanac / Kevin Hillstrom and Laurie Collier Hillstrom ; Lawrence W. Baker, editor.
        p. cm.
    Includes bibliographical references and index.
    Summary: Describes and interprets the era of the Civil War, its events, and topics with viewpoints, definitions, report topics, chronologies, sidebars, and statistics.
    ISBN 0-7876-3823-4
        1. United States—History—Civil War, 1861–1865—Juvenile literature. 2. United States—History—Civil War, 1861–1865—Miscellanea—Juvenile literature. 3. Almanacs, American—Juvenile literature. [1. United States—History—Civil War, 1861–1865.] I. Title: American Civil War. II. Hillstrom, Laurie Collier, 1965– III. Baker, Lawrence W. IV. Title.

E468.H556 1999
973.7—dc21   99-046918

Cover photographs reproduced courtesy of the Library of Congress and the National Archives and Records Administration.

Copyright © 2000 — U•X•L, an imprint of The Gale Group
27500 Drake Road • Farmington Hills, MI 48331-3535

Printed in the United States of America

10 9 8 7 6 5 4 3 2 1

Contents

Advisory Board xi

Reader's Guide xiii

American Civil War Timeline xvii

Words to Know xxxiii

People to Know xxxix

Research and Activity Ideas xlv

Chapter 1—Slavery and the American South 1

    Slavery in Early America 2
    Slavery and the Constitution 3
    "King Cotton" 6
    Life as a Slave 7
    Two Different Economies 11

Chapter 2—The Northern Abolitionist Movement 15

    Early Abolitionists 16
    African Colonization 16

The Rise of the Abolitionists 17
Resistance to Abolitionism in the North 20
Support for Abolishing Slavery Grows 21
The Underground Railroad 25
Uncle Tom's Cabin 28

Chapter 3—1800–1858:
The North and the South Seek Compromise. 31

Federal Authority and States' Rights 32
Missouri Compromise 34
Slavery and the War with Mexico 36
Compromise of 1850 37
Fugitive Slave Act 42
Kansas-Nebraska Act 44
The Fight over Slavery in "Bleeding Kansas" . . . 45
Legislation Triggers Political Upheaval 48

Chapter 4—1857–1861:
The South Prepares to Secede 51

Dred Scott's Bid for Freedom 52
North-South Tensions Grow 54
Lincoln Challenges Douglas. 55
The Lincoln-Douglas Debates 56
John Brown Leads the Raid at Harpers Ferry . . . 59
Brown's Death Further Divides America 61
The 1860 Presidential Campaign 61
Lincoln Wins the Election 65
South Carolina Secedes, Other Southern
States Follow. 67

Chapter 5—1861: Creation of the Confederacy 69

The Crittenden Compromise 70
Formation of the Confederate States
of America. 71
The Confederacy Selects Its First President 72
Lincoln Signals Determination to Preserve
the Union 74
The Controversy over Fort Sumter. 76
Lincoln Attempts to Send Supplies 77
Southern Forces Attack Fort Sumter 80

Undecided States Join the Confederacy 81
The Union Fights to Keep Other Border States . . 84
Lincoln Silences Maryland Secessionists 84
The Union Struggle to Keep Missouri
and Kentucky 85

Chapter 6—Europe's View of the War **87**
European Concerns about the Rebellion 88
The South Hopes for Support 89
South Uses Cotton as a Weapon 90
The "Trent Affair" 93
Europe Considers Confederate Successes 96

Chapter 7—1861: The War Begins **99**
Celebrations of the Impending War 100
The North Builds Its Army 101
The South Struggles to Provide for
Its Soldiers 103
North and South Scramble for Military
Leadership 104
Amateur Officers and West Pointers 106
The Northern Strategy 108
The Southern Strategy 109
Lincoln Makes a New State Out of
Western Virginia 110
The Union Army Moves South 111
The First Battle of Bull Run 112
The South Spoils the North's Grand Picnic . . . 114
Southern Confidence and Northern Anger . . . 114

Chapter 8—1862: Near Victory for the Confederacy . . **117**
The Calm Before the Storm 117
Grant Leads Union Victories in the West 120
The Battle of Shiloh 120
Preparation for the Attack on New Orleans . . . 122
Farragut Devises a Bold Plan 124
The Confederacy Passes the Conscription Act . . 124
Lincoln Grows Impatient with McClellan 126
McClellan Begins His Advance on Richmond . . 127
Stonewall Jackson's Shenandoah Campaign . . . 128

Lee Stops McClellan's Advance 129
Lincoln Makes Changes in the Union
Military Leadership 130
The Second Battle of Bull Run 130
Confederate Victories in the West 131
Lee Advances into the North 132
Antietam—the Bloodiest Day in American
Military History 133
Lincoln's Emancipation Proclamation 134
Lincoln Fires McClellan 136
The Battle of Fredericksburg 136

Chapter 9—1863: The Tide Turns **139**

Rosecrans and Bragg Duel in the West 140
Lincoln Signs the Emancipation Proclamation . 143
Burnside's "Mud March" 143
Hooker Prepares for Battle 144
The Battle of Chancellorsville 145
Lee's Greatest Triumph 148
Lee Invades Pennsylvania 149
The Battle of Gettysburg 149
Lee Orders "Pickett's Charge" 151
Grant's Fight for Possession of the
Mississippi River 154
The Siege of Vicksburg 155
Lincoln's Troubles on the Home Front 156
Rosecrans Occupies Chattanooga 157
The Battle of Chickamauga 160
Federal Victory at Chattanooga 160

Chapter 10—Women in the Civil War **165**

A Time of Hardship and Grief 166
Women's Roles in the War 168
Nurses and Aid Workers 169
Spies, Scouts, Couriers, and Saboteurs 173
Changes in Attitudes after the War 175

Chapter 11—1864: The North Tightens Its Grip **177**

Grant Takes Control 178
The North Launches Twin Offensives 179

Battle of the Wilderness 179
The Battle of Spotsylvania 181
Two Wounded Armies 181
The Battle of Cold Harbor 183
Grant Targets Petersburg 185
Northern Disillusionment with
Grant's Campaign 185
Sherman Chases Johnston 185
Hood Assumes Command in the West 187
Democrats Nominate McClellan
for President 187
Farragut Captures Mobile Bay 188
Atlanta Falls to Sherman 190
Northern Confidence Returns 192
Sheridan Goes to the Shenandoah Valley 192
Total Warfare 194
Lincoln Wins Reelection 196
Sherman Begins His "March to the Sea" 198
Thomas Crushes Hood in Tennessee 199

Chapter 12—Blacks in the Civil War **201**

Northern Blacks Want to Join the Fight 202
Prejudice Leads to Race Riots in the North . . . 204
Blacks in the Confederacy 205
Word of Emancipation Spreads in the South . . 206
Escaped Slaves Move North 207
Union Army Finally Accepts Black Soldiers . . . 210
Blacks' Wartime Service Breaks Barrier
of Discrimination 215

Chapter 13—1865: Victory for the North **217**

Last Days of the Confederacy 217
Lee Remains Trapped in Petersburg 218
Sherman Moves Through South Carolina 219
Desperation in the Confederacy 220
The Confederacy Considers Using Blacks
as Soldiers 222
Passage of the Thirteenth Amendment 223
Grant Increases Pressure on Petersburg 223
Grant Captures Petersburg and Richmond . . . 224
Lee Surrenders to Grant 224

Union Celebrates Victory 227
Lincoln Is Assassinated 227
Davis Is Captured and Imprisoned 229

Chapter 14—1865–1877: Reconstruction **233**

End of the War Raises New Issues 235
Lincoln's Wartime Reconstruction Policies . . . 237
President Johnson's Reconstruction Policies . . . 237
Discrimination Continues in the South 239
Congress Takes Control of Reconstruction . . . 241
The Fourteenth Amendment 242
New Hopes of Equality 243
"Radical Reconstruction" 244
President Johnson Faces Impeachment 245
Reconstruction Unravels 248
Violence Against Blacks Increases 249
The Election of 1876 Ends Reconstruction . . . 250

Where to Learn More . . . . **xlvii**

Index . . . . **liii**

Advisory Board

Special thanks are due to U•X•L's Civil War Reference Library advisors for their invaluable comments and suggestions:

- Deborah Hammer, Former Librarian, Queens Borough Public Library, Jamaica, New York

- Ann Marie LaPrise, Librarian, Detroit Public Library, Elmwood Park Branch, Detroit, Michigan

- Susan Richards, Media Specialist, Northwest Junior High School, Coralville, Iowa

Reader's Guide

American Civil War: Almanac presents a comprehensive overview of the Civil War. The volume's fourteen chapters cover all aspects of the conflict, from the prewar issues and events that divided the nation to the war itself—an epic struggle from 1861 to 1865 that changed the political and social landscape of America forever. The chapters are arranged chronologically, beginning with "Slavery and the American South" and ending with "1865-1877: Reconstruction." Interspersed are two chapters that cover two unique groups during the Civil War: women and blacks.

Each chapter of the Almanac includes "Words to Know" and "People to Know" sections that define important terms and individuals discussed in the chapter for easy reference. In addition, each chapter features informative sidebars containing brief biographies, excerpts from memoirs and speeches, and interesting facts about the issues and events discussed in the main body of the text. More than ninety black-and-white photos and maps illustrate the work.

The Almanac also includes an "American Civil War Timeline" of important events, "Words to Know" and "People to Know" sections that combine those terms from individual chapters, and a list of "Research and Activity Ideas" with suggestions for research efforts, oral and dramatic presentations, and group projects. *American Civil War: Almanac* concludes with a bibliography of sources for further research and a comprehensive index.

American Civil War Reference Library

American Civil War: Almanac is only one component of a three-part American Civil War Reference Library. The other two titles in this multivolume set are:

- *American Civil War: Biographies:* This two-volume set presents profiles of sixty important figures from the Civil War era. The essays cover such key people as politicians Abraham Lincoln and Jefferson Davis; military figures Robert E. Lee, Ulysses S. Grant, David Farragut, and Braxton Bragg; and nurse Clara Barton, spy Rose O'Neal Greenhow, and photographer Mathew Brady. The volumes are filled with photographs, individual "Where to Learn More" sections, and an index.

- *American Civil War: Primary Sources:* This title presents fourteen full or excerpted speeches and written works from the Civil War. The volume includes an excerpt from Harriet Beecher Stowe's *Uncle Tom's Cabin,* President Abraham Lincoln's Emancipation Proclamation and Gettysburg Address, and the letters between Union general William T. Sherman and Atlanta, Georgia, city leaders. Each entry includes an introduction, things to remember while reading the excerpt, information on what happened after the work was published or event took place, and other interesting facts. Photographs, source information, and an index supplement the work.

- A cumulative index of all three titles in the American Civil War Reference Library is also available.

Acknowledgments

The authors extend thanks to Larry Baker and Tom Romig at U•X•L for their assistance throughout the production of this series. Thanks, too, to Christine Alexanian for her

quick and thorough copyediting and Amy Marcaccio Keyzer for lending her considerable editorial talents in the form of proofreading. The editor wishes to thank Marco Di Vita at Graphix Group for always working with common sense, flexibility, speed, and, above all, quality. Admiration, love, and a warm hug go to Beth Baker for her year of bravery. And, finally, a very special hello goes to Charlie and Dane, whose decision to move up their pub date made the Summer of '99 so very interesting.

Comments and suggestions

We welcome your comments on *American Civil War: Almanac* and suggestions for other topics in history to consider. Please write: Editors, *American Civil War: Almanac,* U•X•L, 27500 Drake Rd., Farmington Hills, Michigan 48331-3535; call toll-free: 800-877-4253; fax to 248-414-5043; or send e-mail via http://www.galegroup.com.

American Civil War Timeline

1775 Philadelphia Quakers organize America's first antislavery society.

1776–83 English colonies' War for Independence against Great Britain ends with the formation of the United States.

1788 The U.S. Constitution is ratified, providing legal protection to slaveowners.

1793 Eli Whitney invents the cotton gin, which will dramatically increase Southern cotton production.

1803 President Thomas Jefferson purchases the Louisiana Territory from France.

1775
"Yankee Doodle"
is written.

1789
George Washington
takes office as the first
U.S. president.

1800
The Library of
Congress is
established.

| 1775 | 1789 | 1800 |

1816 The American Colonization Society is formed with the idea of settling free blacks back in Africa.

1820 Congress passes the Missouri Compromise, which maintains the balance between slave and free states in the Union.

1828 Congress passes the so-called "Tariff of Abominations" over the objections of Southern states.

1831 Slave Nat Turner leads a violent slave rebellion in Virginia.

1832–33 The "Nullification Crisis" in South Carolina ends after tariffs on foreign goods are lowered.

1833 The Female Anti-Slavery Society and the American Anti-Slavery Society are founded.

1837 Abolitionist Elijah P. Lovejoy is murdered by a proslavery mob in Illinois.

1845 Texas is annexed by the United States over the objections of Mexico, which regards it as part of its country.

1848 The Mexican War ends with the United States acquiring five hundred thousand square miles of additional land in western North America.

1850 The Compromise of 1850, including the controversial Fugitive Slave Act, becomes law.

1852 Harriet Beecher Stowe's novel *Uncle Tom's Cabin* is published, increasing support for the abolitionist movement in the North.

1854 The Kansas-Nebraska Act is passed, returning decisions about allowing slavery back to individual states.

1818
Congress adopts
a U.S. flag.

1825
The New York
Stock Exchange
opens.

1844
Samuel F. B. Morse
transmits the first
telegraph message.

1853
Potato chips
are invented.

1818　　　　　　　　　　1825　　　1844　　　1853

1857   The U.S. Supreme Court issues its famous *Dred Scott* decision, which increases Northern fears about the spread of slavery.

1858   Illinois senate candidates Abraham Lincoln and Stephen Douglas meet in their famous debates over slavery and its future place in America.

1859   Abolitionist John Brown leads a raid on Harpers Ferry, Virginia, in an unsuccessful effort to start a slave revolt across the South.

5/18/1860   The Republican Party nominates Abraham Lincoln as its candidate for president.

11/6/1860   Abraham Lincoln is elected president of the United States.

12/20/1860   South Carolina secedes from the Union.

1/9/1861   Mississippi secedes from the Union.

1/10/1861   Florida secedes from the Union.

1/11/1861   Alabama secedes from the Union.

1/19/1861   Georgia secedes from the Union.

1/26/1861   Louisiana secedes from the Union.

1/29/1861   Kansas is admitted into the Union as the thirty-fourth state.

2/1/1861   Texas secedes from the Union.

2/8/1861   The Confederate Constitution is adopted in Montgomery, Alabama.

2/9/1861   Jefferson Davis is elected provisional president of the Confederacy.

2/18/1861   Jefferson Davis is inaugurated as the president of the Confederacy.

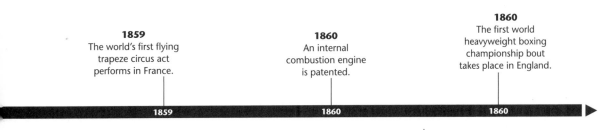

1859
The world's first flying trapeze circus act performs in France.

1860
An internal combustion engine is patented.

1860
The first world heavyweight boxing championship bout takes place in England.

1859   1860   1860

3/4/1861 Abraham Lincoln is inaugurated as the sixteenth president of the United States.

3/6/1861 The Confederacy calls for one hundred thousand volunteers to join its military.

4/12/1861 South Carolina troops open fire on Fort Sumter, marking the beginning of the American Civil War.

4/13/1861 Major Robert Anderson surrenders Fort Sumter to the Confederates.

4/15/1861 President Abraham Lincoln calls for seventy-five thousand volunteers to join the Union army.

4/19/1861 President Abraham Lincoln orders a blockade of Southern ports.

5/6/1861 Arkansas secedes from the Union.

5/7/1861 Tennessee forms an alliance with the Confederacy that makes it a Confederate state for all practical purposes.

5/13/1861 Queen Victoria proclaims British neutrality in the conflict between America's Northern and Southern sections.

5/20/1861 North Carolina secedes from the Union.

5/23/1861 Virginia secedes from the Union.

6/3/1861 Stephen A. Douglas dies in Chicago, Illinois.

6/10/1861 Napoleon III declares French neutrality in the American Civil War.

6/11/1861 Counties in western Virginia resist Virginia's vote to secede and set up their own government, which is loyal to the Union.

7/20/1861 Confederate Congress convenes at the Confederate capital of Richmond, Virginia.

1861
American inventor Elisha G. Otis patents a steam-powered elevator.

1861
English novelist Charles Dickens's *Great Expectations* is published.

1861
The United States introduces the passport system.

1861   1861   1861

7/21/1861 Confederate forces win the First Battle of Bull Run, the war's first major battle.

7/25/1861 U.S. Congress passes the Crittenden Resolution, which states that the North's war aim is to preserve the Union, not end slavery.

7/27/1861 General George McClellan assumes command of Federal forces in Washington.

8/30/1861 Union general John Frémont proclaims martial law in Missouri, which is torn by violence between pro-Union and pro-Confederate forces.

11/6/1861 Jefferson Davis is elected to a six-year term as president of the Confederacy.

11/8/1861 Union captain Charles Wilkes seizes two Confederate officials traveling on the *Trent,* a British vessel. The incident triggers deep outrage in England.

11/20/1861 The Union organizes the Joint Committee on the Conduct of the War in order to review the actions and qualifications of the North's military leadership.

11/27/1861 Confederate officials seized from the *Trent* are released from custody with apologies.

2/6/1862 Union general Ulysses S. Grant captures Fort Henry on the Tennessee River.

2/16/1862 Ulysses S. Grant captures Fort Donelson on the Cumberland River.

2/22/1862 Jefferson Davis is inaugurated as president of the Confederacy.

2/25/1862 The Confederates abandon Nashville, Tennessee, to oncoming Union forces.

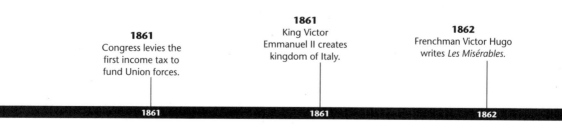

1861
Congress levies the first income tax to fund Union forces.

1861
King Victor Emmanuel II creates kingdom of Italy.

1862
Frenchman Victor Hugo writes *Les Misérables.*

1861   1861   1862

3/9/1862 The Union ship *Monitor* battles the Confederate ship *Virginia* to a draw at Hampton Roads, Virginia.

4/6–7/1862 Union and Confederate forces battle in the inconclusive Battle of Shiloh in Tennessee.

4/16/1862 The Confederate Congress passes a conscription act requiring most able-bodied men between the ages of eighteen and thirty-five to sign up for military service.

4/25/1862 The Union fleet under the command of Admiral David Farragut captures New Orleans.

6/1/1862 General Robert E. Lee assumes command of Confederate forces defending Richmond, Virginia.

6/6/1862 Union forces take control of Memphis, Tennessee.

6/17/1862 Confederate forces led by Stonewall Jackson leave the Shenandoah Valley after a successful military campaign.

6/25/1862 The Seven Days' Battles begin between George McClellan's Army of the Potomac and Robert E. Lee's Army of Northern Virginia.

7/2/1862 President Abraham Lincoln calls for three hundred thousand enlistments for three-year periods in order to further strengthen the Union army.

7/29/1862 Confederate commerce raider *Alabama* leaves England and starts attacking Northern trading vessels.

8/29–30/1862 The Second Battle of Bull Run ends in a disastrous defeat for the Union.

9/5/1862 General Robert E. Lee leads the Army of Northern Virginia into Northern territory for the first time, as his force enters Maryland.

1862
The Homestead Act encourages settlement of Western land.

1862
"Taps" is composed.

1862
British crops fail and hunger is widespread.

1862   1862   1862

9/15/1862 Stonewall Jackson's army captures twelve thousand Union troops at Harpers Ferry, Virginia.

9/17/1862 George McClellan's Army of the Potomac and Robert E. Lee's Army of Northern Virginia fight at Antietam in the bloodiest single day of the war. Neither side registers a conclusive victory, but the draw convinces Lee to return to Virginia.

9/22/1862 President Abraham Lincoln issues his preliminary Emancipation Proclamation, which will free slaves in Confederate territory.

10/8/1862 Confederate invasion of Kentucky ends after the Battle of Perryville.

11/7/1862 President Abraham Lincoln removes General George McClellan from command of the Army of the Potomac, replacing him with General Ambrose Burnside.

12/13/1862 General Robert E. Lee's Confederate forces hand the Union a decisive defeat at the Battle of Fredericksburg.

1/1/1863 President Abraham Lincoln issues the Emancipation Proclamation, which frees all slaves in Confederate territory.

1/2/1863 Union victory at the Battle of Stones River stops Confederate plans to invade middle Tennessee.

1/23/1863 General Ambrose Burnside's new offensive against Robert E. Lee's Army of Northern Virginia sputters to a halt in bad weather. Burnside's "Mud March" convinces President Abraham Lincoln to replace him with General Joseph Hooker.

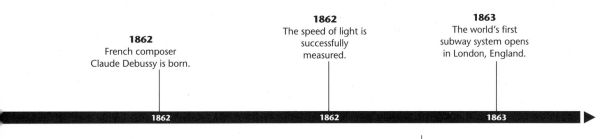

1862
French composer
Claude Debussy is born.

1862
The speed of light is
successfully
measured.

1863
The world's first
subway system opens
in London, England.

1862   1862   1863

3/3/1863 U.S. Congress passes a conscription act requiring most able-bodied Northern men to sign up for military service.

4/2/1863 Bread riots erupt in Richmond, Virginia, as hungry civilians resort to violence to feed their families.

5/2/1863 General Robert E. Lee and the Confederates claim a big victory at Chancellorsville, but Stonewall Jackson is killed during the battle.

5/22/1863 General Ulysses S. Grant begins the siege of Vicksburg, Mississippi, after attempts to take the Confederate stronghold by force are turned back.

6/20/1863 West Virginia is admitted into the Union as the thirty-fifth state.

7/1–3/1863 The famous Battle of Gettysburg takes place in Pennsylvania. Union general George Meade and the Army of the Potomac successfully turn back General Robert E. Lee's attempted invasion of the North, doing terrible damage to Lee's Army of Northern Virginia in the process.

7/4/1863 Vicksburg surrenders to General Ulysses S. Grant and his Union force after a six-week siege of the city.

7/9/1863 Union troops take control of Port Hudson, Louisiana. The victory gives the North control of the Mississippi River.

7/13/1863 Antidraft mobs begin four days of rioting in New York City.

8/21/1863 Confederate raiders led by William C. Quantrill murder 150 antislavery settlers and burn large sections of Lawrence, Kansas.

9/2/1863 Union troops take control of Knoxville, Tennessee.

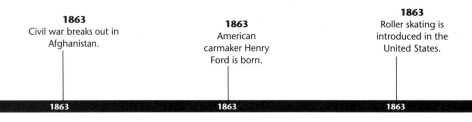

1863
Civil war breaks out in Afghanistan.

1863
American carmaker Henry Ford is born.

1863
Roller skating is introduced in the United States.

1863   1863   1863

9/9/1863 Union forces take control of Chattanooga, Tennessee, after the city is abandoned by General Braxton Bragg's army.

9/20/1863 The two-day Battle of Chickamauga ends in a major defeat for the Union.

9/23/1863 General Braxton Bragg begins the Confederate siege of Chattanooga.

10/17/1863 General Ulysses S. Grant is named supreme commander of Union forces in the west.

11/19/1863 President Abraham Lincoln delivers his famous Gettysburg Address at a ceremony dedicating a cemetery for soldiers who died at the Battle of Gettysburg in Pennsylvania.

11/25/1863 The three-day Battle of Chattanooga results in a major victory for the North, as Union troops led by General George Henry Thomas scatter General Braxton Bragg's Confederate army.

12/8/1863 President Abraham Lincoln proposes his Ten Percent Plan, which says that seceded states can return to the Union provided that one-tenth of the 1860 voters agree to form a state government that is loyal to the Union.

12/27/1863 General Joseph Johnston takes command of the Confederate Army of Tennessee.

3/12/1864 General Ulysses S. Grant is promoted to leadership of all of the Union armies.

3/18/1864 General William T. Sherman is named to lead Union armies in the west.

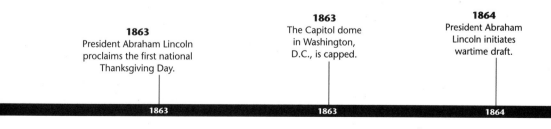

1863
President Abraham Lincoln proclaims the first national Thanksgiving Day.

1863
The Capitol dome in Washington, D.C., is capped.

1864
President Abraham Lincoln initiates wartime draft.

1863   1863   1864

4/12/1864 Confederate troops led by Nathan Bedford Forrest capture Fort Pillow, Tennessee, and are accused of murdering black Union soldiers stationed there.

4/17/1864 General Ulysses S. Grant calls a halt to prisoner exchanges between North and South, further increasing the Confederacy's manpower problems.

5/5/1864 General Robert E. Lee's Army of Northern Virginia and General Ulysses S. Grant's Army of the Potomac battle in the Wilderness campaign.

5/9–12/1864 General Robert E. Lee stops the Union advance on Richmond at the brutal Battle of Spotsylvania.

6/3/1864 The Union's Army of the Potomac suffers heavy losses in a failed assault on Robert E. Lee's army at Cold Harbor, Virginia.

6/18/1864 General Ulysses S. Grant begins the Union siege of Petersburg, which is defended by Robert E. Lee's Army of Northern Virginia.

6/23/1864 Confederate forces led by Jubal Early begin a campaign in the Shenandoah Valley.

7/11/1864 Confederate troops commanded by Jubal Early reach outskirts of Washington, D.C., before being forced to return to the Shenandoah Valley.

7/17/1864 General John Bell Hood takes command of the Confederate Army of Tennessee.

8/5/1864 Admiral David Farragut leads the Union Navy to a major victory in the Battle of Mobile Bay, which closes off one of the Confederacy's last remaining ports.

8/29/1864 The Democratic Party nominates General George McClellan as its candidate for president of the United

1864
President Abraham Lincoln is nominated for a second term.

1864
"In God We Trust" first appears on U.S. coins.

1864
The Red Cross is established.

1864   1864   1864

States and pushes a campaign promising an end to the war.

9/1/1864 General William T. Sherman captures Atlanta, Georgia, after a long campaign.

9/4/1864 General William T. Sherman orders all civilians to leave Atlanta, as a way to hurt Southern morale.

9/19–22/1864 Union troops led by Philip Sheridan defeat Jubal Early's Confederate army in the Shenandoah Valley.

10/6/1864 Philip Sheridan's Union troops begin a campaign of destruction in the Shenandoah Valley in order to wipe out Confederate sympathizers and sources of supplies.

10/19/1864 Philip Sheridan's army drives Jubal Early's Confederate force out of the Shenandoah Valley.

10/31/1864 Nevada is admitted into the Union as the thirty-sixth state.

11/8/1864 Abraham Lincoln is reelected to the presidency of the United States by a comfortable margin.

11/15/1864 General William T. Sherman begins his famous March to the Sea, in which his Union army destroys a large area of Georgia on its way to the port city of Savannah.

12/16/1864 Union forces under the command of General George Henry Thomas crush John Bell Hood's Army of Tennessee at the Battle of Nashville.

12/21/1864 William T. Sherman's Union army completes its March to the Sea by taking control of Savannah, Georgia.

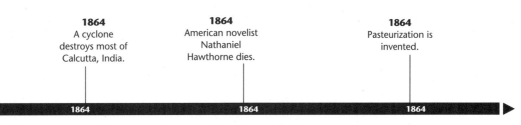

1864
A cyclone destroys most of Calcutta, India.

1864
American novelist Nathaniel Hawthorne dies.

1864
Pasteurization is invented.

1864   1864   1864

1/31/1865 The U.S. Congress submits the Thirteenth Amendment, which abolishes slavery, to the individual states for passage.

2/17/1865 General William T. Sherman's army occupies the South Carolina capital of Columbia.

2/18/1865 Union forces seize control of Charleston, South Carolina.

2/22/1865 Confederate president Jefferson Davis returns command of the Army of Tennessee to General Joseph Johnston in a desperate attempt to stop William T. Sherman's advance into North Carolina.

3/2/1865 Remaining Confederate troops in Shenandoah Valley go down to defeat at the hands of Philip Sheridan.

3/4/1865 President Abraham Lincoln is inaugurated for a second term of office.

3/13/1865 The Confederate Congress authorizes the use of slaves as Confederate combat soldiers.

4/1–2/1865 Ulysses S. Grant's Army of the Potomac successfully breaks through Confederate defenses at Petersburg, forcing Robert E. Lee's Army of Northern Virginia to evacuate the city and give up their defense of Richmond, Virginia.

4Union troops take control of Richmond, Virginia, and prepare for a visit from President Abraham Lincoln a day later.

4/9/1865 Trapped by pursuing Federal troops, General Robert E. Lee surrenders to General Ulysses S. Grant at Appomattox in Virginia.

1865
Lewis Carroll writes *Alice's Adventures in Wonderland.*

1865
Civil War balloonist Thaddeus Lowe invents the ice machine.

1865
Ku Klux Klan is founded in Tennessee.

1865   1865   1865

4/14/1865 President Abraham Lincoln is shot by John Wilkes Booth while attending a play at Ford's Theatre in Washington, D.C.

4/15/1865 Vice president Andrew Johnson becomes president after Abraham Lincoln dies.

4/18/1865 Confederate General Joseph Johnston surrenders his Army of Tennessee to William T. Sherman near Raleigh, North Carolina.

4/26/1865 John Wilkes Booth is killed by Federal soldiers in a barn near Bowling Green, Virginia.

5/10/1865 Confederate president Jefferson Davis is taken prisoner by Federal troops at Irwinsville, Georgia.

5/26/1865 The very last Confederate troops put down their weapons, as a rebel army west of the Mississippi River led by Kirby Smith surrenders to Union officials.

1866 The Republican Congress passes a Civil Rights Act over President Andrew Johnson's veto. The Act gives citizenship and other rights to black people.

1866 Race riots between blacks and whites erupt during the summer in Memphis, Tennessee, and New Orleans, Louisiana.

1866 Tennessee is readmitted into the Union by Congress.

1867 Congress passes the Military Reconstruction Act over President Andrew Johnson's veto.

1867 The Ku Klux Klan adopts a formal constitution and selects former Confederate general Nathan Bedford Forrest as its first leader.

1867 Former Confederate president Jefferson Davis is released from a Virginia jail after two years of imprisonment.

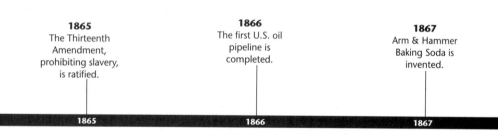

1865
The Thirteenth Amendment, prohibiting slavery, is ratified.

1866
The first U.S. oil pipeline is completed.

1867
Arm & Hammer Baking Soda is invented.

1865   1866   1867

1868   Political disagreements between Congress and President Andrew Johnson become so great that the president is impeached. He avoids being removed from office by one vote in his Senate impeachment trial.

1868   Congress passes the Fifteenth Amendment, which extends voting rights to blacks, and sends the bill along to individual states for ratification.

1868   Alabama, Arkansas, Florida, Louisiana, North Carolina, and South Carolina are readmitted into the Union by Congress.

1868   Republican Ulysses S. Grant is elected the eighteenth president of the United States.

1870   The Fifteenth Amendment, guaranteeing voting rights for blacks, is ratified by the states and becomes law.

1870   Congress passes the Enforcement Act of 1870 in an effort to protect the voting rights of all citizens—especially blacks—in the South.

1870   Georgia, Mississippi, Virginia, and Texas are readmitted into the Union by Congress.

1871   Congress passes the Ku Klux Klan Act, which outlaws conspiracies, use of disguises, and other practices of the white supremacist group.

1872   Ulysses S. Grant is reelected president of the United States.

1875   Congress passes a Civil Rights Act barring discrimination in hotels, theaters, railroads, and other public places.

1876   Republican Rutherford B. Hayes and Democrat Samuel J. Tilden run a very close race for the presiden-

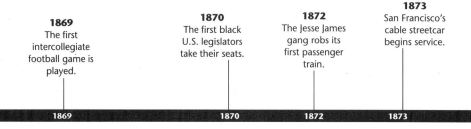

1869
The first intercollegiate football game is played.

1870
The first black U.S. legislators take their seats.

1872
The Jesse James gang robs its first passenger train.

1873
San Francisco's cable streetcar begins service.

1869   1870   1872   1873

cy of the United States. Tilden wins the popular vote, but neither candidate receives enough electoral votes for election. The two political parties eventually agree to a compromise in which Hayes becomes president in exchange for a guarantee that he remove federal troops from South Carolina, Florida, and Louisiana.

1877   President Rutherford B. Hayes removes Federal troops from the South. This withdrawal increases the vulnerability of blacks to Southern racism and marks the end of the Reconstruction period in American history.

1876
Baseball's
National League
is founded.

1877
First Bell
telephone is sold.

1876

1877

A map of the United States east of the Mississippi River shows the key battles and events of the Civil War. *(Illustration by XNR Productions: Reproduced by permission of The Gale Group.)*

Words to Know

A

Abolitionists: people who worked to end slavery

B

Black Codes: series of harsh laws passed by white legislators in Southern states during Reconstruction that discriminated against black people; the Black Codes returned black people to a condition very close to slavery

Blockade: the act of surrounding a harbor with ships in order to prevent other vessels from entering or exiting the harbor; also the act of ships or other military forces surrounding and isolating a city, region, or country

C

Civil War: conflict that took place from 1861 to 1865 between the Northern states (Union) and the Southern seceded states (Confederacy); also known in the South as the War between the States and in the North as the War of the Rebellion

Colonization: an action in which an existing country establishes a new community or state in a foreign land

Confederacy: eleven Southern states that seceded from the United States in 1860 and 1861

Conscription: forced enrollment of able-bodied men into a nation's armed forces; also known as a draft

D

Discrimination: unfair treatment of people or groups because of their race, religion, gender, or other reasons

E

Emancipation: the act of freeing people from slavery or oppression

Enlistment: the act of joining a country's armed forces

F

Federal: national or central government; also refers to the North or Union, as opposed to the South or Confederacy

Founding Fathers: political and community leaders who established the United States after the War for Independence in 1776; this term is often specifically used for the men who wrote the U.S. Constitution in 1787

G

Guerrillas: small independent bands of soldiers or armed civilians who use raids and ambushes rather than direct military attacks to harass enemy armies

I

Impeachment: formal accusation of wrongdoing made by Congress against an elected official in an attempt to remove him or her from office; the term usually includes both the bringing of charges by the House of Representatives and a trial by the Senate

Industrialization: a process by which factories and manufacturing become very important to the economy of a country or region

M

Militia: an army composed of ordinary citizens rather than professional soldiers

O

Offensive: an attack or aggressive action

P

Pardon: to forgive and release from punishment

Plantation: a large estate dedicated to farming

Q

Quakers: a religious group that strongly opposed slavery and violence of any kind

R

Rebel: Confederate; often used as a name for a Confederate soldier

Reconstruction: the period from 1865 to 1877 during which the Confederate states were readmitted into the United States

Regiment: a military unit of organized troops; regiments usually consisted of one thousand men and were divided into ten companies of one hundred men each

S

Secession: the formal withdrawal of eleven Southern states from the Union in 1860–61

Siege: surrounding and blockading of a city, town, or fortress by an army attempting to capture it

States' rights: the belief that each state has the right to decide how to handle various issues for itself without interference from the national government

T

Tariffs: additional charges or taxes placed on goods imported from other countries

Territory: a region that belongs to the United States but has not yet been made into a state or states

Treason: betrayal of one's country

U

Underground Railroad: a secret organization of free blacks and whites who helped slaves escape from their masters and gain freedom in the Northern United States and Canada

Union: Northern states that remained loyal to the United States during the Civil War

V

Veto: a power held by the U.S. president to stop a legislative bill passed by Congress from becoming a law; a bill can become law without the president's approval only if two-thirds of each chamber of Congress vote again in favor of it; such a vote is known as overriding the president's veto

People to Know

A

Robert Anderson (1805–1871): Union major who surrendered Fort Sumter to Confederates in April 1861

John Andrew (1818–1867): governor of Massachusetts, 1860–66; organized the Fifty-Fourth Massachusetts Regiment, the first black Northern unit in the Civil War

B

Pierre G. T. Beauregard (1818–1893): Confederate general who captured Fort Sumter in April 1861; also served at First Bull Run and Shiloh

John Wilkes Booth (1838–1865): American actor who assassinated President Abraham Lincoln

Braxton Bragg (1817–1876): Confederate general who led the Army of Mississippi and the Army of Tennessee; fought at Perryville, Chickamauga, and Chattanooga

James Buchanan (1791–1868): fifteenth president of the United States, 1857–61

Ambrose E. Burnside (1824–1881): Union general who commanded the Army of the Potomac at Fredericksburg; also fought at First Bull Run, Antietam, and in Ulysses S. Grant's Wilderness campaign

C

John C. Calhoun (1782–1850): South Carolina politician; vice president of the United States, 1825–32

Henry Clay (1777–1852): Kentucky politician who wrote Missouri Compromise and Compromise of 1850

D

Jefferson Davis (1808–1889): president of the Confederate States of America, 1861–65

Dorothea Dix (1802–1887): educator who fought for humane treatment of the mentally ill

Stephen Douglas (1813–1861): Illinois politician; defeated Abraham Lincoln in 1858 U.S. Senate election

Frederick Douglass (c. 1818–1895): escaped slave who became a leading abolitionist

E

Jubal Early (1816–1894): Confederate lieutenant general who led the 1864 campaign in Shenandoah Valley; also fought at First Bull Run, Second Bull Run, Antietam, Fredericksburg, Chancellorsville, Gettysburg, the Wilderness, and Spotsylvania

F

David G. Farragut (1801–1870): Union admiral who led naval victories at New Orleans and Mobile Bay

G

Ulysses S. Grant (1822–1885): Union general who commanded all Federal troops, 1864–65; led Union armies at Shiloh, Vicksburg, Chattanooga, and Petersburg; eighteenth president of the United States, 1869–77

H

Henry W. Halleck (1815–1872): general-in-chief of Union armies, July 1862–March 1864; Abraham Lincoln's chief of staff, March 1864–April 1865

Rutherford B. Hayes (1822–1893): nineteenth president of the United States, 1877–81

Thomas Wentworth Higginson (1823–1911): abolitionist who led the First South Carolina Volunteers, the first regiment of former slaves in the Union Army

John Bell Hood (1831–1879): Confederate general who commanded the Army of Tennessee at Atlanta in 1864; also fought at Second Bull Run, Antietam, Fredericksburg, Gettysburg, and Chickamauga

Joseph Hooker (1814–1879): Union major general who commanded the Army of the Potomac at Chancellorsville; also fought at Second Bull Run, Antietam, Fredericksburg, Chattanooga, and Atlanta

J

Thomas "Stonewall" Jackson (1824–1863): Confederate lieutenant general who fought at First Bull Run, Second Bull Run, Antietam, Fredericksburg, and Chancellorsville; led 1862 Shenandoah Valley campaign

Thomas Jefferson (1743–1826): primary author of America's Declaration of Independence; third president of the United States, 1801–9

Andrew Johnson (1808–1875): seventeenth president of the United States, 1865–69

Albert S. Johnston (1803–1862): Confederate general of the Army of Mississippi

Joseph E. Johnston (1807–1891): Confederate general of the Army of Tennessee who fought at First Bull Run and Atlanta

L

Robert E. Lee (1807–1870): Confederate general of the Army of Northern Virginia; fought at Second Bull Run, Antietam, Gettysburg, Fredericksburg, and Chancellorsville; defended Richmond from Ulysses S. Grant's Army of the Potomac, 1864 to April 1865

Abraham Lincoln (1809–1865): sixteenth president of the United States, 1861–65

James Longstreet (1821–1904): Confederate lieutenant general in Robert E. Lee's Army of Northern Virginia for much of the war; fought at First Bull Run, Second Bull Run, Antietam, Fredericksburg, Gettysburg, Chickamauga, Knoxville, the Wilderness, and Petersburg

M

George McClellan (1826–1885): Union general who commanded the Army of the Potomac, August 1861 to November 1862; fought in the Seven Days' campaign and at Antietam; Democratic candidate for U.S. president, 1864

George G. Meade (1815–1872): Union major general who commanded the Army of the Potomac, June 1863 to April 1865; also fought at Second Bull Run, Antietam, Fredericksburg, and Chancellorsville

N

Napoleon III (1808-1873): emperor of France, 1852-71

Florence Nightingale (1820–1910): nurse who dedicated her life to the care of the sick and those wounded in war

O

Rose O'Neal Greenhow (1817–1864): Washington socialite who was a spy for the Confederacy

P

John C. Pemberton (1814–1881): Confederate lieutenant general who commanded Vicksburg defenses during the siege of Vicksburg

John Pope (1822–1892): Union general of the Army of the Mississippi and the Army of Virginia, 1862; fought at Bull Run

R

William Rosecrans (1819–1898): Union major general of the Army of the Mississippi and the Army of the Cumberland, 1861–63; fought at Corinth, Murfreesboro, and Chickamauga

S

Winfield Scott (1786–1866): general-in-chief of U.S. Army, 1841–61; proposed so-called "Anaconda Plan" for Union in Civil War

William Seward (1801–1872): U.S. secretary of state, 1861–69

Robert Gould Shaw (1837–1863): Union colonel of the Fifty-Fourth Massachusetts Regiment, the famous all-black unit in the Civil War

Philip H. Sheridan (1831–1888): Union major general who commanded the Army of the Potomac's cavalry corps and the Army of the Shenandoah; also fought at Perryville, Murfreesboro, Chickamauga, and Chattanooga

William T. Sherman (1820–1891): Union major general who commanded the Army of the Tennessee and the Military Division of the Mississippi, October 1863 to April 1865; led the famous "March to the Sea"; also fought at First Bull Run, Shiloh, and Vicksburg

Harriet Beecher Stowe (1811–1896): abolitionist who wrote *Uncle Tom's Cabin*

T

George Henry Thomas (1816–1870): Union major general who commanded the Army of the Cumberland to victories at Chattanooga, Atlanta, and Nashville; also fought at Perryville and Chickamauga

Nat Turner (1800–1831): American slave who led violent slave rebellion in 1831

V

Elizabeth Van Lew (1818–1900): Virginian who was a spy for the Union

Queen Victoria (1819–1901): queen of Great Britain, 1837–1901

W

Eli Whitney (1765–1825): American inventor whose creations included the cotton gin

Research and Activity Ideas

The following research and activity ideas are intended to offer suggestions for complementing social studies and history curricula, to trigger additional ideas for enhancing learning, and to suggest cross-disciplinary projects for library and classroom use.

Imagine yourself as a slave on the Underground Railroad. Keep a diary of your imaginary experiences as you make your way to the North. Create a map showing your progress each day.

Divide into two groups of at least four. Assign one group to defend the South's right to secede from the Union, emphasizing the philosophy of "states' rights." The other group, meanwhile, will argue against secession from the North's point of view.

Give an oral presentation to the class in which you deliver an actual speech given by a Civil War figure. Other options include reciting a Civil War poem or singing a Civil War song.

Create a three-dimensional panoramic scene from the Civil War era using any materials that you wish. Scenes can range from a specific event like the Battle of Mobile Bay or the Richmond Bread Riots to an everyday scene of the South (slaves toiling on a plantation) or the North (workers building a railroad or a busy harbor).

Divide the class into several groups. Give each group an assignment to deliver an oral presentation on one of the Civil War's major battles. Encourage group members to explain the battle while playing the role of leading generals and politicians. Have each group conclude with a report on how people can visit the battlefield today.

Imagine how America would be different today if the Confederacy had won the Civil War. Write a report explaining what life might be like in either the North or the South for white and black people. Remember to consider how much the world has changed in terms of technology, medical knowledge, etc., when writing your paper.

Create a collage of images on a significant Civil War event such as the Battle of Gettysburg, the Emancipation Proclamation, the Union decision to use black soldiers, or Lee's surrender at Appomattox.

Divide the class into three groups, and have each group perform a skit in which a family is reunited after the war is over. In one skit, brothers who fought on opposite sides of the war see each other for the first time. In another skit, members of a Southern family gather at their Atlanta home, which has been destroyed by Sherman's troops. And in a last skit, have the group pretend that it has just learned that a family member died in one of the war's last battles.

Select one Confederate state and create a timeline of important events that took place in that state during the Reconstruction period. Include events that had an impact on all Southern states as well as events that only affected the state you selected.

Slavery and the American South

When America's Founding Fathers (the country's earliest leaders) established the United States in the late 1700s, they decided to build the new nation on principles of freedom and liberty for its people. But during America's first years of existence, the country's leaders decided not to extend those freedoms to a small but growing segment of the population. The new nation's slaves, who had been removed from Africa by force or born into captivity in the "New World," were denied the rights that their white masters enjoyed, even though they contributed a great deal to America's agricultural economy. These slaves continued to be treated as property, even as the nation's white leaders were working to build an otherwise democratic government.

Many of America's early political leaders did not like slavery, but they recognized that slaves were used extensively by farmers in the new nation's Southern states. Knowing that it would cause an uproar if slavery was outlawed, the creators of the U.S. Constitution, which was ratified (officially approved) in 1788, basically avoided dealing with the issue. Instead, they took small steps to limit slavery, hoping that the

Words to Know

Founding Fathers political and community leaders who established the United States after the War for Independence in 1776; this term is often specifically used for the men who wrote the U.S. Constitution in 1787

Industrialization a process by which factories and manufacturing become very important to the economy of a country or region

Plantation a large estate dedicated to farming

Quakers a religious group that strongly opposed slavery and violence of any kind

practice would eventually die out on its own. But rather than fading away, slavery in the American South increased dramatically. Within a few years of Eli Whitney's 1793 invention of the cotton gin, the region's economy became completely dependent on the production of cotton. Slaves became the primary work force in the production of this valuable crop, and the practice of slavery became even more ingrained in the Southern way of life.

Slavery in early America

Early European settlers brought the first African slaves to North America in the 1600s. As these colonists worked to carve a new life

out of the wilderness, they found slaves handy to have around. African slaves could be used to plant and harvest crops, clear land, build houses and shops, and take care of household chores. In addition, the owners of these slaves did not have to pay them wages or provide them with anything other than the bare necessities for survival. Finally, the black skin of slaves instantly identified them, making it impossible for them to hide among the free white population.

Throughout the remainder of the 1600s, the early colonists continued to use slaves. As time went on, the colonists passed a number of laws that ensured the continued growth of slavery. In 1671, for example, Maryland legislators passed a law stating that even if a slave was a Christian, he or she would remain the property of his or her owner. In 1700, New York passed legislation that made runaway slaves subject to the death penalty. That same year, Virginia ruled that slaves were "real estate" and passed laws that called for severe punishment for people found guilty of marrying or having sexual relations with a member of another race.

By the early 1700s, slavery was an important part of early colonial economies. This was especially true in the Southern colonies, which used slaves to produce crops like tobacco, rice, and sugar for European markets. The number of slaves increased, too, as children born to slaves were forced into the same life that their mothers and fathers endured.

As time passed, however, growing numbers of people began to feel that enslaving people of other races was morally wrong. Religious groups in the Northern colonies, such as the Quakers, who helped settle Pennsylvania, began to protest against the slave trade. Further south, white people formed a number of organizations that urged slaveholders to grant freedom to their slaves. Political leaders expressed anxiety about slavery as well, citing both moral objections and practical concerns about the soundness of slavery-based economies. Some politicians and merchants in the Northern colonies became convinced that Southern plantation (large farm) owners were building a society that was not as efficient and prosperous as it could be. These critics argued that the South should follow the North's example and invest in new businesses and industries rather than relying upon slave-based agriculture. Some people even argued that slave labor was more costly to slaveowners than a free labor force would be, since slaveholders had to pay the cost of food and shelter for their slaves. By the mid-1700s, antislavery feelings were evident in most of the American colonies.

In the 1760s and early 1770s, the issue of slavery took a back seat as England and France fought each other for control of the North American mainland east of the Mississippi River. England eventually assumed command of much of this region, only to find itself confronted with a rebellion within its own colonies. By the early 1780s, these colonies had freed themselves from English control through the War for Independence, or Revolutionary War (1775–83). With the war behind them, the leaders of these colonies turned to the monumental task of deciding exactly what sort of nation the United States was going to be. As they discussed the framework for their new country, they quickly realized that it was going to be difficult to address the issue of slavery in a way that would be acceptable to everyone.

People to Know

Thomas Jefferson (1743–1826) primary author of America's Declaration of Independence; third president of the United States, 1801–9

Nat Turner (1800–1831) American slave who led violent slave rebellion in 1831

Eli Whitney (1765–1825) American inventor whose inventions included the cotton gin

Slavery and the Constitution

In 1787, leaders from the original colonies met in Philadelphia, Pennsylvania, with the purpose of producing a Constitution that would unite all thirteen colonies into one country. (The thirteen colonies were Connecticut, Delaware, Georgia, Maryland, Massachusetts, New Hampshire, New Jersey, New York, North Carolina, Pennsylvania, Rhode Island,

Quakers Lead Opposition to Slavery

Of the various religious denominations that protested against slavery in America in the eighteenth and nineteenth centuries, the most effective group was probably the Society of Friends, also known as the Quakers. The Society of Friends is a religious body that was founded in England in the seventeenth century by a minister named George Fox (1624–1691). Unhappy with the rules and beliefs of the Church of England, which dominated religion in that country, Fox started a new religion based on pacifism, meditation, and the belief that people could find understanding and guidance directly from the Holy Spirit.

Persecuted in England for their beliefs, the Quakers immigrated to the distant corners of the world in order to practice their religion in peace. Quaker settlements were established in Asia, Africa, and in northeastern North America. During the eighteenth century, a Pennsylvania colony established by English colonialist William Penn (1644–1718) became a stronghold of Quaker life.

Members of the Society of Friends who lived in America recognized that the practice of slavery was an immoral one. Their strong belief in the equality of all people, no matter what their race or background, led Quaker leaders to organize the first formal protests against slavery on American soil. In 1688, Quakers in Germantown, Pennsylvania, publicly demonstrated against the slave trade, the first of many such Quaker protests. In 1775,

Quaker founder George Fox.

Quakers living in Philadelphia organized the world's first antislavery society.

The Quakers sustained their opposition to slavery throughout the eighteenth and nineteenth centuries, providing the abolitionist movement (which advocated that slavery be abolished) with many of its most effective leaders. Motivated by their certainty that the practice of slavery violated basic Christian values, members of the Society of Friends were consistently among the most well-spoken, persuasive, and dedicated of abolitionist voices. As Philadelphia Quaker Anthony Benezet (1713–1784) stated in 1754, "To live in ease and plenty, by the toil of those, whom violence and cruelty have put in our power, is neither consistent with Christianity nor common justice; and we have good reason to believe, draws down the displeasure of heaven."

South Carolina, and Virginia.) The delegates in attendance knew that slavery was a delicate topic that would have to be handled with care, especially since divisions between Northern and Southern states on the issue seemed to widen with each passing day. In the previous few years, a number of Northern states had formally abolished slavery within their borders, and all of the Northern states had banned future importation (bringing in from another country) of slaves. Southern reliance on slavery held steady, though, and delegates from that region warned their Northern counterparts that they would fight any effort to outlaw slavery.

In the end, the Constitution that was ratified by America's Founding Fathers did not tackle the issue of slavery head-on. Instead, the delegates agreed to compromise. For example, Southern delegates agreed to make a huge section of land that had been ceded (legally transferred) to the United States in 1783 by Great Britain completely off-limits to the slave trade. Several new states (Michigan, Wisconsin, Ohio, Indiana, Illinois, and parts of Minnesota) were eventually formed out of this region, known as the Northwest Territory. The South also agreed to a clause that would outlaw the importation of slaves from Africa (but not slavery itself) in 1808, twenty years down the road.

In return, Northern delegates agreed to allow slavery to remain in place in the South for at least twenty years before examining the issue again. In addition, representatives of the Northern states agreed that even though slaves would not be allowed to vote, each slave would be counted in the census as three-fifths of a person. (The census is the government's official calculation of the entire population.) The slavery compromise was an important victory for slaveholding states, because each state's representation in the U.S. Congress—and thus its political power—was determined by the size of its population. Other clauses of the Constitution instituted taxes on slave "property" and made it easier for slaveholders to regain custody of runaway slaves.

The U.S. Constitution was ratified in 1788. Its creators knew that the document provided for the continuation of slavery in America for at least another twenty years. This fact bothered many of the Constitution's creators, who felt that the institution of slavery cast a dark shadow over the new nation's supposed ideals of liberty and equality. Even leaders like eventual presidents Thomas Jefferson (1743–1826) and George Washington (1732–1799), who themselves owned slaves, recognized that slavery was an evil practice that should be eliminated. But they were also aware of the South's dependence on slavery, and they desperately wanted to keep the states united. Moreover, many people in both the North and the South felt that the "peculiar institution," as slavery was sometimes called, was likely to die out on its own. By the early 1790s, some white Southerners were joining their Northern brothers in speaking out against the evils of slavery. In addition, many observers predicted that as Southern states diversified their economies in the coming years (adding industries other than cotton to the mix), their reliance on slave labor would diminish. Finally, anti-slavery forces took comfort in the South's agreement to suspend importation of African slaves in 1808. They viewed this agreement as a sign that even the South saw that its dependence on slavery could not last forever.

"King Cotton"

In 1793, however, a Yankee (Northerner) named Eli Whitney (1765–1825) unveiled a new invention that took the world by storm. The invention, a simple machine called the cotton gin, revolutionized the cotton-growing industry. Before the introduction of Whitney's cotton gin, processing or cleaning of cotton crops (separating the seeds from the cotton fiber that was used to make clothing and other goods) was a tedious, time-consuming task. Mindful of cotton's production difficulties, most Southern farmers grew other crops, even though the soil and climate in the American South was ideal for cotton production. But textile mills in Europe and Northern states were making loud demands for the crop.

With the arrival of the cotton gin, which effectively separated seeds from cotton fibers, plantation owners (known as planters) could suddenly process far greater quantities of the valuable crop than ever before. All across the South, small farms and sprawling plantations alike switched to cotton production. From 1790 to 1820, production of cotton in the United States increased from 3,000 bales to 400,000 bales a year (each bale weighed about 500 pounds), with nearly all of it originating in the Deep South. By the 1830s, cotton was America's leading export product, and the value of cotton exports eventually exceeded the value of all other American exports combined. By 1860, cotton exports were worth $191 million, 57 percent of the total value of all American exports. Demand for cotton products continued to grow throughout the first half of the nineteenth century, and planters all across the South become wealthy on "King Cotton," as the crop came to be called.

The cotton gin dramatically increased the amount of money flowing into the Southern economy, but it also renewed the dying institution of slavery. Cotton producers needed laborers to plant and pick the huge quantities of cotton intended for markets in Great Britain, France, and New England, so slaves were assigned to take care of this physically demanding work. As cotton production increased, so too did Southern dependence on slave labor. From 1790 to 1810, the number of African slaves on American soil increased by 70 percent. The number of enslaved Americans continued to rise throughout the 1820s and 1830s, even after importation of foreign slaves ended in 1808. By 1860, the census counted nearly four million slaves in America, and it was clear that the institution of slavery had become completely interwoven in the fabric of Southern society.

The resurgence of slavery in the American South depressed many people, from common citizens to political leaders. They recognized that with each passing year, it would become harder and harder for the Southern states to abandon slavery and establish a free society. Reviewing the situation, Thomas Jefferson compared slavery to a dangerous wolf: "We have the wolf by the ears, and we can neither hold him, nor safely let him go. Justice is in one scale, and self-preservation in the other."

Life as a slave

Cotton delivered great wealth to Southern plantation owners, who subsequently created a comfortable society for themselves. During the first half of the nineteenth century, white Southerners developed a culture that emphasized ideals of refinement, elegance, and old-fashioned chivalry (the medieval knightly qualities of honor, courage, helping the weak, and protecting women). Even many of its poorer white citizens embraced romantic notions of the nature of Southern life in its towns and on its plantations.

Most slaves, of course, had a far different view of life in the South. The majority of slaves worked on large farms and plantations, where they were often forced to maintain a physically punishing work schedule in the fields. Slaves who lived in the towns and cities of the South were sometimes more fortunate. Those who were

Eli Whitney, the inventor of the cotton gin. *(Courtesy of the Library of Congress.)*

skilled carpenters or masons sometimes received monetary payment for their work, and they were less likely to be mistreated by their owners. "A city slave," wrote black leader Frederick Douglass (c. 1818–1895), "enjoys privileges altogether unknown to the whip-driven slave on the plantation." Nonetheless, even the most successful slave carpenter remained at the mercy of his master and the larger white society in which he lived.

Another factor in how slaves were treated was the temperament (behavior) of the master they served. Since slaves were valuable, slavehold-

Thomas Jefferson, the Slaveowner Who Wrote the Declaration of Independence

Thomas Jefferson is one of the most famous figures in American history. He was a brilliant man who served his country remarkably well in many important capacities—including an eight-year stint (1801–9) as the United States' third president. He also wrote America's Declaration of Independence, which explains the nation's democratic ideals and values and continues to be hailed as its most important document. Yet Jefferson, who wrote in the Declaration that "all men are created equal," was also a slaveholder for much of his life, despite his belief that slavery was morally wrong. This puzzling contradiction between the antislavery convictions and the slaveowning practices of one of America's greatest political leaders continues to fascinate modern-day historians.

Born and raised in Virginia, Jefferson was a wealthy plantation owner who kept a number of slaves. But even as he profited from the labor of his slaves, Jefferson recognized that enslavement of other people was immoral. By 1776, when he emerged as a revolutionary leader in America's War of Independence from England, he was so convinced of the evils of the slave trade that he included strongly worded criticisms of the practice in his first draft of the Declaration of Independence.

To Jefferson's dismay, representatives of the rebellious American colonies eliminated his antislavery remarks and changed other parts of his Declaration when they gathered in Philadelphia in 1776 for the First Continental Congress. But the democratic spirit of his historic document remained intact. When it was unanimously approved by the Congress on July 4, 1776, the Declaration of Independence immediately came to be seen as the symbolic core of the new nation's dreams and ideals.

One of the most frequently cited sections of Jefferson's Declaration of Independence states: "We hold these truths to be self-evident, that all men are created equal, that they are endowed by their Creator with certain unalienable Rights, that among these are Life, Liberty and the pursuit of Happiness." Other writings by Jefferson provide ample evidence that he believed that blacks were as entitled to these rights as were whites, even though he did not think that blacks had the same mental

ers generally made sure that they were provided with basic food, clothing, and shelter. In addition, some Southern masters were relatively kind to their slaves. They avoided separating members of slave families and tried to create environments in which their slaves could be relatively comfortable. But other masters treated their slaves like livestock. Some slaveholders whipped or beat slaves who displeased them for practically any reason. One

Thomas Jefferson. *(Courtesy of the Library of Congress.)*

abilities as whites. Despite these convictions, however, he continued to use slaves on his plantation and in factories that he owned. In addition, he sold slaves on at least two occasions, and recent deoxyribonucleic acid (DNA) testing (a sort of genetic "fingerprint" that everyone carries in their blood) indicates that he likely had a long-term sexual relationship with one of his slaves, Sally Hemings (1773–1835), which produced several children.

Historians have long debated the reasons for Jefferson's inability to abandon a practice that he knew was morally wrong. Some people claim that his financial dependence on slave labor kept him in the slaveholder camp. Others say that his desire to retain his high place in Southern society played a part in his continued ownership of slaves. In any event, the issue of slavery haunted Jefferson throughout his life, even as he helped guide America through its first years of independence. "All his adult life, Thomas Jefferson . . . tossed and turned in an agony of ambivalence [simultaneously conflicting feelings] over the dilemma of slavery and freedom," wrote biographer Willard Sterne Randall in *Thomas Jefferson: A Life.* "Repeatedly he sought to have public institutions relieve him of the burden of his conscience while he tried to avoid giving offense to his close-knit family and the slaveowning society of his beloved Virginia. He knew slavery was evil, he called it evil and spoke out against it in a series of public forums, but he would only push so far—and then he would fall back on a way of life utterly dependent on slave labor."

Georgia slaveowner, for instance, noted that he once whipped a slave "for not bringing over milk for my coffee, [forcing me] to take it without." Slaveholders also sometimes sold slaves to buyers who lived hundreds of miles away, with no regard for the agony that such actions caused to family members left behind. Slaves who tried to run away or who rebelled against their masters in any way ran the risk of being killed. As each gener-

Slaves work in a cotton field. *(Courtesy of the Library of Congress.)*

ation of black boys and girls grew to maturity in the American South, they learned that whites held complete power over their lives.

Forced to endure injustice and humiliation on a daily basis, slaves sometimes became so angry and frustrated that they resorted to violence. In 1800, for example, a slave named Gabriel Prosser (c. 1776–1800) and more than one hundred followers nearly succeeded in executing an attack on Richmond, Virginia, only to be discovered at the last minute. Prosser, his brother, and more than two dozen other slaves were hanged for their role

in the plot, even though one of the rebels pointed out that "I have nothing more to offer than what General Washington would have had to offer had he been taken by the British and put to trial. I have adventured my life in endeavouring to obtain the liberty of my countrymen, and am a willing sacrifice in their cause." Twenty-two years later, a freed slave named Denmark Vesey (c. 1767–1822), who could not bear to see the continued enslavement of other blacks, organized a violent plot against the white citizens of Charleston, South Carolina. Vesey's plan, which included burning the city and killing as many whites as possible, unraveled after a slave informed white authorities about it. Vesey and thirty-six other blacks were subsequently hanged for their involvement in the plot.

Both of these plots struck fear into the hearts of white Southerners. But the rebellion that caused the most panic in slaveholding states was an 1831 slave revolt in Virginia led by a slave named Nat Turner (1800–1831). One August night, Turner and a small band of followers murdered the family that owned them, then roamed the countryside, adding dozens of angry slaves to their group along the way. The poorly organized rebellion was crushed in less than two days, and Turner and a number of his followers were eventually executed, but the revolt frightened white communities all across the South. In the days following the "Turner Rebellion," state legislatures throughout the Southern United States passed strict new laws designed to tighten the chains of slavery around the throats of all blacks. Despite the execution of Turner and the institution of these new laws, though, whites' perennial fears of a widespread slave rebellion increased.

Two different economies

The South's growing dependence on cotton and slave labor during the first half of the nineteenth century eventually affected all aspects of Southern life. With each passing year, the production of cotton and other crops became ever more vital to the economic well-being of Southern states. As a result, a large percentage of

Slave rebellion leader Nat Turner. *(Courtesy of the Library of Congress.)*

the region's population continued to live in rural areas, and few cities of any great size developed. Some factories eventually appeared on Southern soil, and a small number of railroads, canals, and roads were in place by mid-century, but agriculture remained the cornerstone of Southern wealth.

The South's reliance on agriculture made it difficult for the region to attract whites from the North or Europe. After all, slaves took care of most of the farmwork, and the slow pace of industrialization (the development of new business) in Southern cities meant that factory jobs were scarce. As

Remembrances of Slavery

The treatment of slaves in America differed a great deal, depending on the temperament of their masters. Some slaves were provided with comfortable housing and ample food for their families, and in the years following the Civil War, some former slaves recalled their masters as kindly or considerate. But thousands of other remembrances painted a far darker picture of life as a slave. The following three accounts all show how brutal the practice of slavery could be on those who were kept in bondage:

> My master used to throw me in a buck and whip me. He would put my hands together and tie them. Then he would strip me naked. Then he would make me squat down. Then he would run a stick through behind my knees and in front of my elbows. My knee was up against my chest. My hands was tied to-

gether just in front of my shins. The stick between my arms and my knees held me in a squat. That's what they call a buck. You couldn't stand up and you couldn't get your feet out. You couldn't do nothing but just squat there and take what he put on. You couldn't move no way at all. Just try to. You just fall over on one side and have to stay there till you were turned over by him. He would whip me on one side till that was sore and full of blood and then he would whip me on the other side till that was all tore up. . . . [My mistress] took a bull whip once. The bull whip had a piece of iron in the handle of it—and she got mad. She was so mad she took the whip and hit me over the head with the butt end of it and the blood flew. It ran all down my back and dripped off my heels.—*Ella Wilson, an ex-slave interviewed in the 1930s as part of the Federal Writers' Project, from* To Be a Slave, *edited by Julius Lester, 1968.*

I knew a man who would let his slaves carry on a [religious church] meet-

a result, the size of the white population in the South did not change very much, even as the number of enslaved blacks continued to rise.

The economic situation in the North was far different. By the mid-1800s, cities all across the Northern United States were feeling the effects of the "Industrial Revolution." The Industrial Revolution was a term used to describe a period of major social and economic changes that took place around the world. During this period, amazing

inventions and new technologies enabled people to establish factories of mass production and introduce new machines and products. In contrast to the South, which was content to maintain its agriculture-based way of life, the North used these advances to build economies that relied on manufacturing, shipping, and other industries in addition to agriculture.

The North proved to be an ideal region for industrialization for several reasons. For one thing, local

ing for a while, but when they got a little happy, the overseer would come and whip them. I have known him whip a woman with 400 lashes, because she said she was happy. This was to scare religion out of them, because he thought he wouldn't be able to get anything out of them if they were religious. . . . Such things are common. There are cases that are much worse than these. There was a man in our neighborhood who belonged to a Mr. Briscoe. They treated him so bad that he ran away, and him and his wife was gone for six months, and lived out in the canebreaks. They hunted him with the hounds of Bullen, a great negro-hunter. The dogs pushed him so that he and two others ran out, and they ran them right across a bayou, right across our road, and they catched one right at the edge of the water, and hamstrung him and tore him all to pieces.—*Isaac Throgmorton, an ex-slave quoted in American Freedmen's Inquiry Commission Interviews, 1863.*

Yes, I saw some pretty hard things during slave times. At Glasgow, Missouri, I saw a woman sold away from her husband. She had a two months' old baby in her arms and was crying. A driver asked her what she was bellowing about. She said she didn't want to leave her husband. He told her to shut up, but she couldn't and he snatched her little baby from her and threw it into a pen full of hogs. That sounds like a strange story, but I saw it. . . . No wonder God sent war on this nation!. . . The slaveholders were warned time and again to let the black man go, but they hardened their hearts and would not, until finally the wrath of God was poured out upon them and the sword of the great North fell upon their first-born. Many of the slaves were kindly treated, but God alone knows what those had to endure who fell into the hands of men destitute of [totally lacking in] mercy. The curse has passed; may it return no more forever.—*L. M. Mills, an ex-slave quoted in the Philadelphia Sunday Item, July 24, 1892.*

and state governments in the Northern United States worked very hard to build an extensive transportation network of railroads, canals, and roads. These transportation options made it much easier for businesses to deliver products to their customers. In addition, many of the Northern states were blessed with an abundance of important natural resources like coal, iron, and timber. These materials were very important in the development of new industries. A growing system of laws also helped Northern businesses pros-per, providing them with legal protection in their business dealings. Finally, the North placed greater emphasis on educational issues than did the South, and its higher literacy rate made it more attractive to a range of businesses. All of these factors combined with manufacturing advances to create money-making opportunities for small businesses and giant corporations alike.

As the North became increasingly industrialized, the daily character of life in the North changed as well. The populations of many towns and cities exploded, as families that had previously supported themselves by farming rushed to grab factory jobs. Immigration to Northern states from Europe surged, too, as tens of thousands of poor people from Ireland, England, Germany, Italy, Poland, Sweden, and other nations traveled to America every year in search of a better life. Many of these immigrants headed out for America's western territories after arriving on U.S. shores. But millions of others settled in the slums of big Northern cities like New York, Boston, and Philadelphia, where they toiled in factories and shipyards. By 1860, immigration had boosted the population in America's Northern states to nearly eighteen million. By contrast, only nine million people lived in the American South, and nearly four million of those people were slaves.

The Northern Abolitionist Movement

America had always been home to people who felt that slavery was wrong and should be eliminated. These people, called abolitionists because they wanted to abolish or destroy slavery, denounced the practice as horrible and evil. Prior to the mid-nineteenth century, however, their efforts to eliminate slavery from U.S. soil failed to gather enough popular support because everyone knew how much the South depended on slaves to make its economy and society work. But in the 1830s and 1840s, organized opposition to slavery in the United States became more powerful and confrontational (meeting an issue head-on) than it had ever been before. Describing slavery as an evil and un-Christian system and a stain on the values enshrined in America's Declaration of Independence, the abolitionists finally convinced large numbers of Northerners that slavery should not continue. This development angered and frightened white Southerners, who recognized that the abolitionist movement was a serious threat to the society that they had built for themselves.

Words to Know

Abolitionists people who worked to end slavery

Colonization an action in which an existing country establishes a new community or state in a foreign land

Emancipation the act of freeing people from slavery or oppression

Quakers a religious group that strongly opposed slavery and violence of any kind

Underground Railroad a secret organization of free blacks and whites who helped slaves escape from their masters and gain freedom in the Northern United States and Canada

Early abolitionists

The very first abolitionist demonstration in America took place in 1688. A group of brave Quakers gathered in Germantown, Pennsylvania, to voice their religious objections to the slave trade. At first, few people paid much attention to the Quakers' calls for an end to slavery. During the eighteenth century, however, a growing number of people living in the American colonies looked at slavery with a more critical eye. Free blacks like Episcopal church leader Absalom Jones (1746–1818), businessman James Forten (1766–1842), and Methodist bishop Richard Allen (1760–1831) lob-

bied tirelessly for the freedom of their race, and some white people—religious leaders and politicians as well as ordinary citizens—expressed reservations about "the peculiar institution," as slavery was sometimes called. Slavery remained common across the colonies, but discomfort with the practice became more evident.

By the end of the 1700s, when America became an independent nation, slavery in the North was fading away. Even some wealthy Southern slaveholders expressed hope that slavery might pass out of existence some day. In the early 1800s, however, the South's reliance on slavery increased as white landholders turned to the labor-intensive crop of cotton for their livelihood. This development was a bitter disappointment to people opposed to slavery.

African colonization

In 1816, American abolitionists tried a different tactic to end slavery. They recognized that many whites who thought that slavery should be abolished still did not want to live with blacks, either because they saw blacks as inferior or because they thought that racial prejudice was too firmly ingrained in American society to make integration (the mixing of the two races) work. Aware that many whites opposed the idea of sharing their society with free blacks, supporters of abolition formed an organization called the American Colonization Society. This group came to include many of the nation's leading businessmen and political leaders. The Society encouraged slaveholding states to establish programs in which they would free their slaves gradually. The emancipated (freed) slaves would then be transported to Africa, where they could form their own free nation.

Boosted by financial support from the federal government and endorsements from a number of states, the Society established the nation of Liberia on the west African coast in 1822. Over the next forty years the Society transported more than six thousand blacks to its shores. Most free blacks, however, resisted the idea of returning to Africa. They had built lives for themselves and their families in the United States, and they did not want to leave and start over somewhere else. "We are natives of this country," argued Peter Williams, Jr., a leading free black abolitionist who opposed colonization. "Not a few of our fathers suffered and bled to purchase its independence [in the Revolutionary War]." Another free black named David Walker (1785–1830) stated similar feelings in an 1829 pamphlet called *An Appeal to the Coloured Citizens of the World*. "Tell us no more about colonization," Walker wrote, "for America is as much our country as it is yours."

Despite the humiliations that they and their families had endured over the years, most free blacks considered themselves Americans. Pointing to the sacrifices that their ancestors had made to help build America, these men and women said that blacks de-

served a chance to make lives for themselves on U.S. soil. As free blacks expressed their opposition to colonization, the idea eventually faded away.

The rise of the abolitionists

In the years immediately following the Missouri Compromise of 1820, which kept the United States equally balanced between slave and nonslave states, neither the North nor the South showed much interest in the subject of slavery, since it often caused anger and bitterness whenever it was discussed. In the 1830s, though, abolitionism once again became a subject of intense debate as a new generation of antislavery voices made themselves heard. But unlike earlier abolitionists, who tried to negotiate a gradual end to slavery, many of these men and women boldly called for immediate emancipation of all slaves and complete racial equality. Leading abolitionists included journalist William Lloyd Garrison (1805–1879), author Lydia Maria Child (1802–1880), business partners and

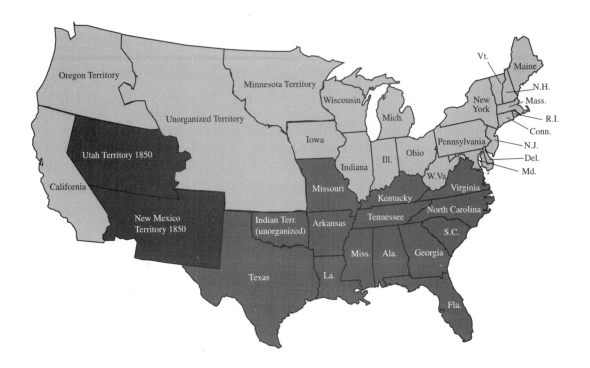

A U.S. map shows free (shown above as light shade) and slave (darker shade) states/territories following the Missouri Compromise of 1820. The Utah and New Mexico territories (darkest shade) were areas where voters determined the status of slavery. *(Illustration by XNR Productions. Reproduced by permission of The Gale Group.)*

brothers Arthur Tappan (1786–1865) and Lewis Tappan (1788–1873), writer Frederick Douglass (c. 1818–1895), writer Theodore Dwight Weld (1803–1895), and human rights leader Wendell Phillips (1811–1884).

Many of the leading abolitionists of this era were guided by their religious convictions. The 1820s and 1830s were decades in which religion took on increased importance in the lives of people all across the nation. During this time, known as the Sec-

ond Great Awakening, many religious leaders told their congregations that they could achieve salvation by building lives of morality and by speaking out against sin. Since slavery loomed as the most sinful practice in America in many people's minds, abolitionists attacked the institution with greater passion and energy than ever before.

But even though the Second Great Awakening fundamentally changed the lives of many Americans, the recharged abolitionist movement

The Shame of the American People

Born into slavery, Frederick Douglass escaped to freedom in 1838 and became one of the foremost black leaders of his era. A tireless crusader for the cause of abolitionism, he believed that the continued practice of slavery cast an ugly shadow on the ideals of liberty and justice upon which the United States had been founded. He produced many moving speeches and articles on this subject during his lifetime. His passion and convictions are prominently displayed in this excerpt from one of his lectures:

> While slavery exists, and the union of these States endures, every American citizen must bear the chagrin [embarrassment or shame] of hearing his country branded before the world, as a nation of liars and hypocrites [people who pretend to be something other than what they really are]; and behold his cherished national flag pointed at with the utmost scorn and derision. . . . Let me say again, slavery is alike the sin and the shame of the American people: It is a blot upon the American name, and the only national reproach which need make an American hang his head in shame, in the presence of monarchical governments.

Frederick Douglass. *(Courtesy of the Library of Congress.)*

met strong resistance wherever its followers tried to spread its message of freedom and equality. Predictably, resistance to this message was strongest in the American South. During the 1830s and 1840s, Southern whites came to view the Northern abolitionists as perhaps the most serious threat to their way of life that they had ever faced. Even though the majority of white households did not own any slaves, powerful Southern slaveholders had built comfortable lives for themselves. These men, who had great influence with other whites in their communities, did not want to make any changes that might threaten their wealth and position. Many poor whites wanted to keep slavery, too, because of long-standing racism and the realization that slavery's continued existence ensured that they would never occupy the lowest rung in Southern society. Finally, Southern whites hated the increase in abolitionist talk because they thought that it might spark a bloody slave rebellion.

Alarmed and angered by Northern abolitionists who charged that the very foundations of Southern culture were evil and corrupt, defenders of slavery adopted a defiant position. They claimed that Northerners would not be so eager to abolish slavery if their own regional economy depended on it. Southerners also embraced arguments that slavery actually helped to civilize African "savages," and some slaveholders even used scriptural passages from the Bible to justify enslavement of their fellow men. Northern abolitionists who attempted to spread their message in Southern states were attacked and driven out of the region. In addition, Southern states passed numerous laws designed to prevent Northern antislavery groups from discussing abolitionism on their land. In 1835, for example, Georgia passed a law imposing the death penalty on anyone who published materials that might cause slave unrest.

At the same time that the South took steps to protect itself from the speeches and literature of Northern abolitionists, the South also made it impossible for its own citizens to question the slave-dependent society in which they lived without risking their freedom or their lives. Some states passed laws designed to silence antislavery voices within their borders. In 1836, for example, Virginia passed a law that made it a felony for anyone to advocate (speak in favor of) abolition. Such laws rarely had to be enforced, however, because Southerners who expressed doubts about slav-ery learned that such statements put them in great danger from their own neighbors. By the late 1830s, whites in the American South were defending slavery and objecting to Northern interference with their way of life with one united voice.

Resistance to abolitionism in the North

Convinced that Southerners would never abandon slavery willingly, Northern abolitionists focused much of their attention on fellow Northerners. They hoped to convince the citizens of the Northern states to force the South to eliminate slavery. But even though slavery no longer existed in the North, bigotry against black people was still common throughout the region. Free blacks in the North endured all kinds of discrimination in the areas of housing, education, and legal rights. In addition, many white Northerners feared that the abolition of slavery might jeopardize their own economic well-being. Poor white laborers worried that emancipated blacks would come up from the South and take their jobs. Rich Northern merchants who conducted business in the South thought that abolition might diminish their profits. Finally, many Americans living in the North were concerned that abolitionist activities would disrupt the stability of the Union itself.

As a result, when leading abolitionists like William Lloyd Garrison and Theodore Dwight Weld first spoke out against slavery in the early and mid-1830s, violence was often directed against them by Northern laborers and businessmen. Printing presses and other equipment used by abolitionists were destroyed, and mob attacks against abolitionist gatherings became quite common. In 1835, a mob in Boston, Massachusetts, dragged Garrison through the streets and nearly lynched (hanged) him. On another occasion, antiabolitionist protestors rioted for several days in New York City during which black neighborhoods were terrorized and abolitionist churches were vandalized.

Despite the risks of speaking out, Northern abolitionists refused to back down. Important abolitionist organizations like the Female Anti-Slavery Society and the American Anti-Slavery Society (both established in 1833) gradually gathered new members. By 1840, an estimated one hundred thousand Northerners had joined hundreds of organizations devoted to the abolishment of slavery. The membership included thousands of white men, but free blacks such as John Jones and Frederick Douglass accounted for a great deal of the abolitionist movement's energy and direction. Another important source of strength for the abolitionist cause was white women. In fact, many of the women who would later become leading advocates of women's rights in America—such as Elizabeth Cady Stanton (1815–1902), Lucretia Coffin Mott (1793–1880), and sisters Sarah Grimké (1792–1873) and Angelina Emily Grimké (1805–1879)— first became politically active by working for the emancipation of slaves.

Support for abolishing slavery grows

Northern abolitionists continued to operate under the threat of violence throughout the 1830s, but by the end of that decade, the Northern view of the movement had changed considerably. One major reason for this change was the 1837 murder of an abolitionist named Elijah P. Lovejoy (1802–1837) at the hands of a proslavery mob in Illinois. A publisher of antislavery pamphlets and other materials, Lovejoy was killed trying to protect his printing press from a violent crowd of antiabolitionists. As people across the North learned of Lovejoy's murder, the abolitionist movement received a big increase in support. Indeed, former president John Quincy Adams (1767–1848) called the event "a shock as of an earthquake throughout the continent." Lovejoy became known as "the martyr abolitionist."

Lovejoy's death generated a wave of sympathy for the cause of abolitionism and spurred many Northerners to examine criticisms of slavery more closely. In addition, many whites who had opposed the abolitionists or remained undecided about supporting them started to view their cause differently. They began to see abolitionism as an issue that was dedicated to preserving civil liberties for all people, which included securing freedom for all black Americans. White Northerners noted that Southern states had placed limits on freedom of speech in order to stop the abolitionist movement, and that Lovejoy had been murdered defending his

American Slavery as It Is

Theodore Dwight Weld was one of the giants of the American abolitionist movement. A minister who had been profoundly influenced by evangelist Charles G. Finney (1792–1875), Weld organized many antislavery lectures and distributed thousands of antislavery pamphlets around the country. One of his most notable works was a book called *American Slavery as It Is*. This 1839 work, which he compiled with his wife, Angelina Grimké, and his sister-in-law, Sarah Grimké, was a collection of articles and notices from Southern newspapers that documented the inhumanity of the Southern slavery system.

The following is an excerpt from Weld's introduction to the collection. The anger and passion of his words are representative of the sentiments of the larger abolitionist movement and show why Weld came to be regarded as one of abolitionism's most powerful and eloquent voices.

> Every man knows that slavery is a curse. Whoever denies this, his lips libel [give a damaging picture of] his heart. Try him; clank the chains in his ears and tell him they are for *him*. Give him an hour to prepare his wife and children for a life of slavery. Bid him make haste and get ready their necks for the yoke, and their wrists for the coffle chains [fastened together in a line], then look at his pale lips and trembling knees, and you have *nature's* testimony against slavery.
>
> Two million seven hundred thousand persons in these states are in this condition. They were made slaves and are held such by force, and by being put in fear, and this for no crime! Reader, what have you to say of such treatment? Is it right, just, benevolent? Suppose I should seize you, rob you of your liberty,

constitutional right to free speech. They began to wonder if the issue of slavery might someday endanger their rights as well.

By the early 1840s, the Northern abolitionist movement was firmly established as a powerful force in American politics. Antislavery feelings reached heights never before seen in the Northern states. Disputes within the antislavery camp over various strategic and philosophical issues caused divisions in its ranks, but even though the movement splintered into several factions, its members never wavered from their basic goal of abolishing slavery from the shores of America.

As Northern abolitionists continued their call for immediate emancipation and racial equality, they were encouraged not only by their growing influence in the North, but also by events elsewhere in the world. They noticed that slavery was being abolished in many other countries. Throughout

Theodore Dwight Weld. *(Courtesy of the Library of Congress.)*

drive you into the field, and make you work without pay as long as you live—would that be justice and kindness, or monstrous injustice and cruelty?

Now, everybody knows that the slaveholders do these things to the slaves every day, and yet it is stoutly affirmed that they treat them well and kindly, and that their tender regard for their slaves restrains the masters from inflicting cruelties upon them. . . . It is no marvel that slaveholders are always talking of their *kind treatment* of their slaves. The only marvel is that men of sense can be gulled [tricked] by such professions. Despots [dictators] always insist that they are merciful. . . . When did not vice lay claim to those virtues which are the opposites of its habitual crimes? The guilty, according to their own showing, are always innocent, and cowards brave, and drunkards sober, and harlots chaste, and pickpockets honest to a fault.

Central and South America, former colonies of Spain and Great Britain outlawed slavery as they gained independence. In Europe, countries like France and Denmark formally abolished slavery as well. To delighted antislavery activists in the United States, these international developments made it seem as if the institution of slavery was crumbling everywhere.

Southerners watched all of these events unfold with ever-increasing anger and fear. Even when the abolitionist movement was small and weak, people in the South had been offended by its charges that their slave-based economy was evil and immoral. By the 1840s, when the abolitionists' influence in the North seemed to grow with each passing day, Southerners were completely fed up. Tired of being told what to do, they criticized the North as arrogant and dictatorial. Some people in the South also defended slavery even more vigorously, insisting that it was a good and moral system.

The Grimké Sisters

Angelina Emily Grimké (1805–1879) and Sarah Moore Grimké (1792–1873) were two of America's leading abolitionists. Born in Charleston, South Carolina, the sisters were raised in a wealthy slaveholding family. They converted to Quakerism, however, and eventually moved to the North to add their energy and talents to the cause of abolitionism. In fact, the Grimké sisters became the first American women to publicly speak out against slavery.

The Grimké sisters' decision to give lectures on the subject of abolitionism triggered heavy criticism from clergymen and other community leaders who thought that women who delivered public speeches violated standards of appropriate female conduct. Angelina and Sarah were stung by such criticisms, but they continued to deliver lectures and publish works (such as Angelina's famous *An Appeal to the Christian Women of the South*) explaining their abolitionist beliefs. A key ally in their efforts to speak out against slavery was the revivalist preacher

Angelina Grimké.

Theodore Dwight Weld, whom Angelina eventually married.

As time passed, the prejudice the Grimkés encountered—even in some abolitionist circles—convinced them to work for the cause of female equality as well. By the 1830s, they had emerged as leading spokespersons for the cause of women's rights.

As the debate over the morality of slavery swirled across America, countless families and organizations divided over the issue. Even religious denominations fell victim to this growing tension. Indeed, differences over the morality of slavery became so bitter within the national Baptist and Methodist churches that both organizations split into northern and southern branches during the mid-1840s. "The trend [throughout the United States] was unmistakable," wrote Jeffrey Rogers Hummel in

Emancipating Slaves, Enslaving Free Men. "Slavery was dissolving ideological and institutional bonds between North and South."

The Underground Railroad

One of the most valuable weapons that the abolitionist movement used in its war against slavery was the so-called "Underground Railroad." This was the name given to a secret network of free blacks and whites who helped slaves escape from their masters and gain freedom in the Northern United States and in Canada, where slavery was prohibited. The Underground Railroad system consisted of a chain of barns and homes known as "safe houses" or "depots" that ran from the South up into the North. The free blacks and whites who helped runaway slaves make it from one safe house to the next were called "conductors" or "stationmasters." The total number of runaway slaves who "rode" the Underground Railroad to freedom is unknown, but historians estimate that as many as fifty thousand blacks may have reached the free states or Canada through this method.

An early version of the Underground Railroad was constructed in the 1780s by Quakers and other church groups, but the network did not become a significant force until the 1830s. At that time, the growing abolitionist movement pumped new energy and resources into the network, and increasing numbers of runaway slaves used it to escape from the South.

Blacks living in the North were largely responsible for the success of the Underground Railroad. These activists included free blacks who had purchased their freedom from their masters and moved North, as well as former slaves like Frederick Douglass who, after successfully escaping themselves, risked their lives and freedom time after time in order to help other slaves. The most famous of the black "conductors" was Harriet Tubman (c. 1820–1913), an escaped slave who made nineteen dangerous trips back into slave territory to help more than three hundred runaways gain their freedom. White abolitionists aided the effort as well, even though they knew they would be harshly punished if their activities were discovered. For example, a Maryland minister named Charles T. Torrey, who helped hundreds of runaways escape, died in a state penitentiary after being imprisoned for his activities. Another white abolitionist named Calvin Fairbanks was imprisoned for seventeen years for his efforts on behalf of runaway slaves.

The men and women who operated the Underground Railroad were brave, but their courage was matched by that of the fugitive slaves. Many of these runaways had never traveled more than a few miles from the plantation or home in which they toiled, and they knew that they would be beaten, whipped, or perhaps even killed if they were recaptured. Yet thousands of slaves dashed for freedom every year during the mid-1800s, traveling through unfamiliar territory by night with the knowledge that

Harriet Tubman (far left) stands with a group of slaves she helped escape on the Underground Railroad. *(Courtesy of the Library of Congress.)*

angry slavecatchers might be only minutes behind them.

Most runaway slaves who escaped from the South lived in slave states that bordered the North, like Maryland, Kentucky, and Virginia. Even though it was dangerous for slaves from these states to attempt escape, they did not have to travel nearly as far as slaves from Alabama or Mississippi to reach soil where slavery was not permitted. In fact, some runaway slaves from the Deep South remained in the region since they figured that they probably would not be able to make it all the way to the North. Instead, some fled to large Southern cities like Charleston in hopes of melting into the free black population that lived there. Others hid in remote regions where few people lived. One such spot was the Florida Everglades, where fugitive slaves were aided by the Seminole Indians who made their home there. Finally, some slaves from the Deep South found refuge in Mexico, where slavery had been outlawed.

Runaway slaves became a big problem for the South from the 1830s until the Civil War began in 1861, even though slave states took several measures to stop them. Southern communities organized groups of white citizens called slave patrols that roamed the countryside. These patrols were designed to capture fugitives and intimidate slaves who might be thinking about running away. Southern representatives also insisted that the North enforce national fugitive slave laws. The primary fugitive slave law used by the South was one that had been passed in 1793. This law, known as the Fugitive Slave Law, was essentially a stronger version of a fugitive slave clause that had been included in the U.S. Constitution. It permitted slaveholders to recapture fugitive slaves living in America's free states and compelled Northern courts and legal officials to help the slaveowners in their efforts. The law also made it illegal for anyone to interfere with slaveholders attempting to regain control of their "property."

By the late 1830s, however, it was clear that many fugitive slaves using the Underground Railroad were able to evade the slave patrols and avoid slavecatchers sent North to retrieve them. The task of recapturing runaway slaves was made even more difficult for slaveholders in 1842, when the U.S. Supreme Court made a ruling that infuriated the South. In a case called *Prigg v. Pennsylvania*, the Court decided that a slaveholder could still "seize and recapture his slave [in a free state], whenever he can do it without any breach of the peace, or any illegal violence." But the Court's decision also stated that the Northern states did not have to help Southern-

A handbill from 1851 warns blacks in Boston to "keep a sharp look out" for slave catchers. *(Courtesy of the Library of Congress.)*

ers retrieve escaped slaves if they did not want to. Several state legislatures in the North promptly passed laws that ensured that slavecatchers would not receive any aid from state departments or officials.

The *Prigg v. Pennsylvania* ruling outraged Southerners because they knew that fugitive slaves who escaped to the North on their own or through the Underground Railroad would be very difficult to capture without help from Northern officials. Southern legislators immediately tried to pass a

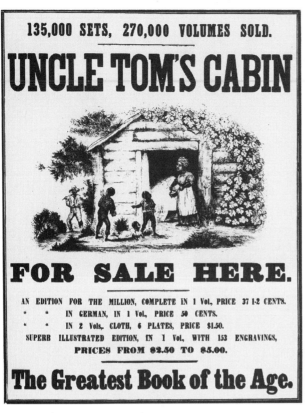

135,000 SETS, 270,000 VOLUMES SOLD.

UNCLE TOM'S CABIN

FOR SALE HERE.

AN EDITION FOR THE MILLION, COMPLETE IN 1 Vol, PRICE 37 1-2 CENTS.
"   "   IN GERMAN, IN 1 Vol, PRICE 50 CENTS.
"   "   IN 2 Vols,. CLOTH, 6 PLATES, PRICE $1.50.
SUPERB ILLUSTRATED EDITION, IN 1 Vol, WITH 153 ENGRAVINGS,
PRICES FROM $2.50 TO $5.00.

The Greatest Book of the Age.

Advertisement for Harriet Beecher Stowe's
Uncle Tom's Cabin.

tough new fugitive slave law, insisting that the Supreme Court's ruling was a violation of their property rights. Their campaign for a new law eventually resulted in the controversial Fugitive Slave Act of 1850, part of the Compromise of 1850. This law gave Southerners sweeping new powers to retrieve escaped slaves and legally bound Northerners to help in those efforts.

By 1850, however, the Underground Railroad had already done a lot of damage to the Southern slavery system. It had enabled thousands of black people to escape to Canada or the free states of the Northern United States. In addition, it provided invaluable assistance to the overall abolitionist movement. As runaway slaves made homes for themselves as free blacks, their descriptions of slavery and their inspiring stories of escape convinced countless white Northerners of the worthiness of the abolitionist cause. Given this state of affairs, passage of the 1850 Fugitive Slave Act proved to be a hollow victory for the South. Catching escaped slaves remained a difficult task even after the law was passed, and the Act further increased Northern sympathy for blacks trapped in the Southern slave system.

Uncle Tom's Cabin

During the 1830s and 1840s, the abolitionist movement distributed millions of antislavery newspapers and pamphlets in Northern cities (shipments to destinations in the South were usually intercepted by authorities and destroyed). Many of the essays and articles contained in this literature included eloquent appeals for the abolishment of slavery, helping the movement advance in the North. But the single most important piece of antislavery literature to emerge during the mid-1800s was a novel called *Uncle Tom's Cabin,* written by Harriet Beecher Stowe (1811–1896).

First published over the course of several months in 1851 in a magazine called the *National Era,* Stowe's novel appeared in book form in March 1852. *Uncle Tom's Cabin* told the story of three Southern slaves—Tom, Eva, and Eliza—living under the cruel hand of a white slaveowner named Simon Legree. It was one of the first works of American literature to depict black people as human beings with the same desires, dreams, and frailties as white people.

Stowe's dramatic story captured the imagination of thousands of readers all across the North. More than three hundred thousand copies of the book were sold in the year following its publication, and stage versions of the story attracted record crowds. But *Uncle Tom's Cabin* was far more than a bestselling novel. Its depiction of black nobility and the evils of slavery drew thousands of additional people to the abolitionist cause. "By portraying slaves as sympathetic men and women, Christians at the mercy of slaveholders who split up families and set bloodhounds on innocent mothers and children, Stowe's melo-drama gave the abolitionist message a powerful human appeal," wrote Eric Foner and Olivia Mahoney in *A House Divided: America in the Age of Lincoln.*

People in the South were very critical of Stowe's book. They complained that she exaggerated the punishments that blacks received and insisted that she did not provide her readers with a true portrait of slavery. But their accusations were drowned out by the praise that Stowe received elsewhere. *Uncle Tom's Cabin* remained an extremely popular book in the North throughout the 1850s. Most people believe that it did more to help the cause of abolitionism than any other work of American literature. In fact, when President Abraham Lincoln (1809–1865) met Stowe in the early days of the Civil War, he reportedly called her "the little lady who wrote the book that made this big war!"

1800–1858: The North and the South Seek Compromise

Throughout the first half of the nineteenth century, the Northern and Southern regions of the United States struggled to find a mutually acceptable solution to the slavery issue. Unfortunately, little common ground could be found. The cotton-oriented economy of the American South continued to rest on the shoulders of its slaves, even as Northern calls for the abolition of slavery grew louder. At the same time, the industrialization of the North continued. During the 1820s and 1830s, the different needs of the two regions' economies further strained relations between the North and the South.

The first half of the nineteenth century was also a period of great expansion for the United States. In 1803, the nation purchased the vast Louisiana Territory from France, and in the late 1840s it wrestled Texas and five hundred thousand square miles of land in western North America from Mexico. But in both of these cases, the addition of new land deepened the bitterness between the North and the South. As each new state and territory was admitted into the Union, the two sides engaged in furious arguments over whether slavery would be permitted within its borders. Urged on by the growing aboli-

Abolitionists people who worked to end slavery

Emancipation the act of freeing people from slavery or oppression

Federal national or central government; also, refers to the North or Union, as opposed to the South or Confederacy

Industrialization a process by which factories and manufacturing become very important to the economy of a country or region

Secession the formal withdrawal of eleven Southern states from the Union in 1860–61

States' rights the belief that each state has the right to decide how to handle various issues for itself without interference from the national government

Tariffs additional charges or taxes placed on goods imported from other countries

Territory a region that belongs to the United States but has not yet been made into a state or states

tionist movement, Northerners became determined to halt the spread of slavery. Southern slaveholders fiercely resisted, however, because they knew that they would be unable to stop antislavery legislation in the U.S. Congress if some of the new states were not admitted as slave states. In order to preserve the Union, the two sides agreed to a series of compromises on the issue of slavery.

Federal authority and states' rights

From the time that the original thirteen colonies declared their independence from Great Britain in 1776, Americans worked to develop an effective system of democratic government. The first comprehensive rules of government passed were the Articles of Confederation, which were ratified (legally approved) in 1781. Under the terms of this document, the individual states held most of the country's legislative power. The Articles of Confederation also provided for the creation of a central or federal government to guide the nation, but this government was given so little authority that it was unable to do much.

Within a few years, most legislators agreed that they needed to make some changes. American leaders subsequently adopted the U.S. Constitution, which provided additional powers to the federal government. But congressional leaders also made sure that the individual states retained some rights, inserting language that was designed to strike a balance between federal and state power.

Complaints about this arrangement flared up from time to time in both the northern and southern regions of the country, as Supreme Court decisions (*McCulloch v. Maryland,* 1819) and other events expanded the scope of federal authority. Southerners became particularly skeptical of federal power because they worried that the national government might someday try to outlaw slavery over the objections of individual Southern states.

Then, in the late 1820s, federal actions on two major issues made Southern lawmakers angrier than they had ever been before. First, the federal government attached high purchase prices to most of the territory out west in order to increase its revenues. Southerners had hoped that the land would be inexpensive so that they could buy land to increase their production of cotton and other crops without spending too much money.

The action that most angered Southerners, however, was the federal government's decision to impose high tariffs, or taxes, on goods from other countries. This system of tariffs was passed in 1828 at the insistence of Northern businessmen, who knew that people would continue to buy their products if European goods were made more expensive by the tariffs. Southerners reacted furiously, calling the 1828 tariff a "tariff of abominations." They said that the tariff would force Southerners to buy products from Northern merchants who, protected by the tariff on foreign goods, would be able to charge higher prices. Ignoring Southern complaints, Congress passed a second Tariff Act in 1832 that was also seen as providing benefits to the North at the expense of the South.

 People to Know

James Buchanan (1791–1868) fifteenth president of the United States, 1857–61

John C. Calhoun (1782–1850) South Carolina politician; vice-president of the United States, 1825–32

Henry Clay (1777–1852) Kentucky politician who wrote Missouri Compromise and Compromise of 1850

Stephen Douglas (1813–1861) Illinois politician; defeated Abraham Lincoln in 1858 U.S. Senate election

Thomas Jefferson (1743–1826) primary author of America's Declaration of Independence; third president of the United States, 1801–9

William Seward (1801–1872) New York politician; U.S. secretary of state, 1861–69

Led by Senator John C. Calhoun (1782–1850), a former vice president of the United States, the South Carolina legislature decided to take a stand against the new tariffs. In November 1832, state legislators passed the Ordinance of Nullification, which described the new taxes as "unconstitutional, oppressive [harsh], and unjust." The language of the bill reflected the legislature's belief that the state had the right to disregard the new federal tariff laws because it did not support them. South Carolina backed up

President Andrew Jackson was vehemently opposed to South Carolina's secession posturing. *(Courtesy of the Library of Congress.)*

this proclamation of "states' rights" by calling for the organization of a militia (an army of regular citizens) to defend the state against any federal "invasion." Suddenly, South Carolina looked as if it was on the verge of trying to secede (withdraw) from the United States.

U.S. president Andrew Jackson (1767–1845) was appalled by the passage of the South Carolina bill, and he warned state officials that he was willing to use the military to enforce federal law. "Can any one of common sense believe the absurdity that a fac-

tion of any state, or a state, has a right to secede and destroy this union and the liberty of our country with it; or nullify laws of the union?" he wrote. "Then indeed is our constitution a rope of sand. . . . The union must be preserved, and it will now be tested, by the support I get from the people. I will die for the union." But even as Jackson prepared for military action, he tried to convince Congress to address South Carolina's complaints by making changes to the tariff laws.

In early 1833, the tense situation was finally resolved. Both the federal and South Carolina governments agreed on a compromised system of reduced tariffs. But the so-called "nullification crisis" had a lasting impact in the United States. It further strained relations between the North and the South and convinced many Southerners that the concept of states' rights was their best weapon against Northern abolitionists. Finally, South Carolina's defiant stand introduced the idea of secession to a generation of Southerners. All across the South, from Richmond, Virginia, to New Orleans, Louisiana, white communities began to wonder if secession from the Union might ultimately be the only way for them to keep their way of life intact.

Missouri Compromise

Another factor that increased tensions between America's northern and southern regions was territorial expansion. In 1803, President Thomas Jefferson (1743–1826) had bought a huge parcel of land in North America from

France for $15 million. This acquisition of land, known as the Louisiana Purchase, added more than eight hundred thousand square miles to the United States. The Louisiana Purchase was a very sound investment for America, since the land would eventually make up all or part of thirteen states (Arkansas, Iowa, Missouri, Minnesota, South Dakota, North Dakota, Oklahoma, Nebraska, Louisiana, Kansas, Colorado, Montana, and Wyoming).

After completing the transaction with France, the United States divided the Louisiana Territory into several smaller territories. It was agreed that as these territories became settled, they would be able to apply for statehood and join the Union. But when the Missouri Territory applied for statehood in 1818, the issue of slavery immediately emerged as an obstacle. Missouri had petitioned Congress for statehood as a slaveholding state. This news pleased the Southerners. After all, if Missouri was admitted as a slave state, the number of slave states in the Union would be greater than the number of free (nonslave) states by a twelve-to-eleven count. This in turn would mean that the South would have more senators in the U.S. Senate than the North, since each state was represented by two senators. (State representation in the United States' other major legislative body, the House of Representatives, was determined by population size; since the population in the North was higher than in the South, the North was able to send a greater number of representatives to the House than the South.)

In the Northern United States, however, many people objected to the idea of admitting Missouri as a slave state.

At first it seemed as if North and South would never reach agreement on Missouri's status. Tempers flared as representatives of each side suggested solutions that were unacceptable to the other side. Politicians from the North argued that slavery should be banned in all new states, while Southern legislators insisted that each state should have the right to determine for itself whether to allow slavery within its borders. With each passing day, anger about the issue boiled a little higher. As the deadlock over the conditions of Missouri's admission continued, a worried Thomas Jefferson wrote that "this momentous question, like a fire bell in the night, awakened and filled me with terror. I considered it at once the knell [sign of disaster] of the Union."

Finally, a powerful senator from Kentucky named Henry Clay (1777–1852) put together a compromise plan that both sides grudgingly accepted. Under the terms of Clay's plan, Missouri would be admitted into the Union as a slave state. But at the same time, a section of the Northern state of Massachusetts known as Maine would be admitted into the Union as a free state. This arrangement would ensure a continued balance in the number of slave and nonslave states. In addition, Clay's Missouri Compromise of 1820 established a line across the midsection of American territory above which slavery would not be permitted. This line preserved most of the remaining land gained through the Louisiana Purchase from slavery. But as Northern abolitionists bitterly observed, Clay's compromise did not offer protection to present or future U.S. lands south of the line.

Few people were completely happy with the Missouri Compromise. Southern whites viewed the agreement as another indication that Northern antislavery feelings threatened to destroy their economic and social system. Northerners were distressed that the compromise allowed for the introduction of slavery into new territories. Both sides wanted to avoid a crisis, however, and most people were relieved when Clay's compromise was accepted. But even as the country congratulated itself for avoiding a showdown between the North and the South, a few people recognized that the Missouri Compromise had only delayed the clash over slavery that was brewing. Former U.S. president John Quincy Adams (1767–1848), for example, called the 1820 debate over slavery nothing less than "a title page to a great, tragic volume."

In the years immediately after the passage of the Missouri Compromise, arguments about the future of slavery in the United States subsided somewhat. In the late 1830s and 1840s, however, the Northern abolitionist movement became stronger than ever before, and arguments about the legality of slavery in America's western territories resurfaced. The

citizens of the North and the South were forced to turn their attention back to slavery once again.

Slavery and the war with Mexico

During the 1840s, American slaveholding states watched with mounting anxiety and resentment as their economy and culture came under fire from their Northern countrymen. For many Southerners, it seemed as if the debate over slavery was spiraling out of control, and that they were losing the battle. After all, opposition to slavery was growing all across the North, and the network of abolitionists known as the Underground Railroad was safely delivering hundreds of fugitive slaves to Canada and free Northern states each year.

As support for abolitionism increased in the North, the South became even more determined to defend itself and the institution of slavery. The confrontation reached a peak in the mid-1840s, when America acquired huge new parcels of western land. First, the United States annexed (added) Texas as a state in 1845, even though the region had once been a province of Mexico and was still viewed as Mexican territory by that country's rulers. The United States and Mexico quickly declared war over the disputed land. By the time a peace treaty ending the war was signed in 1848, America had not only won Texas, but had also wrestled another huge piece of western land from Mexican control. The United States would eventually divide this territory into all or part of a number of states, including California, Nevada, Utah, Arizona, Wyoming, Colorado, and New Mexico.

White Southern leaders knew that their ability to maintain slavery in their own states depended on whether slavery would be permitted in any of the new states that would be formed out of these new territories. Texas had been admitted into the Union as a slave state, but if the rest of America's new territories remained slave-free, then antislavery legislators would outnumber proslavery legislators. Abolitionists would then be able to pass antislavery legislation over the objections of the South, which would be forced to admit defeat or take the drastic step of trying to form a separate country through secession.

As Southern leaders vowed to protect slavery and the principles of states' rights in the debate over America's new lands, abolitionists signaled their determination as well. Mindful of changing Northern attitudes, some Northern politicians decided that they could no longer follow the Missouri Compromise of 1820, which had divided North America into free and slave-permitting geographical regions. A new political party called the Free Soil Party was organized in the North with the specific purpose of ensuring that new American states and territories were kept slave-free. And in 1846, U.S. representative David Wilmot (1814–1868) of Pennsylvania introduced a bill in Congress designed to prohibit slavery in any territory acquired from Mexico. This amend-ment, known as the Wilmot Proviso, was narrowly defeated by Southern legislators. But Northern abolitionists refused to give up on the bill, and they made repeated attempts to get it past furious Southern lawmakers.

As the battle over Wilmot's bill dragged on, South Carolina senator John Calhoun once again emerged as a leading spokesman for the South. He argued that since thousands of soldiers from the South had fought and died to help the United States win the western territories from Mexico, it was not fair to the South to deny it an equal say in determining the laws governing those territories. Calhoun and other South-erners also maintained that people living out West had the right to form a proslavery state government if they wanted to. Finally, they repeatedly stated their belief that any national law that restricted or outlawed slavery was unconstitutional and violated the rights of individual states to govern themselves as they saw fit.

Compromise of 1850

By 1850, the deadlock over slavery in America's western territories had become a crisis. People living in California, New Mexico, and other western lands did not want any delays in being admitted into the Union, but it appeared that there was no way for the North and the South to bridge the division between them. As their frus-tration grew, Southern policymakers started discussing the possibility of se-cession from the Union. Georgia con-gressman Robert Toombs (1810–1885),

John C. Calhoun, the South's Most Powerful Voice

John C. Calhoun was the American South's most passionate defender of slavery and states' rights for much of the first half of the nineteenth century. A native of South Carolina, he graduated from Yale College before marrying and settling down into the life of a wealthy Southern plantation owner. In 1810, Calhoun was elected to represent his home state in the U.S. House of Representatives. Over the next forty years, he served his state and country in a variety of positions. Representing South Carolina, he served six years as a congressman (1811–17) and fourteen years as a U.S. senator (1833–43, 1846–50). As a federal official, Calhoun served eight years as secretary of war (1817–25) under James Monroe (1758–1831), seven years as vice president (1825–32) under John Quincy Adams and Andrew Jackson, and one year as secretary of state (1844–45) under John Tyler (1790–1862).

In his early political career, Calhoun often expressed support for federal actions that might increase America's industrial or economic growth. During the 1820s, however, he became distrustful of the power of the federal government, which he viewed as a tool of the North. As Calhoun's fears about Northern bullying of the South increased, he stepped into the spotlight as a fierce advocate of slavery and principles of states' rights, which he believed had to be enforced to keep the South free from Northern interference. He also emerged as the leader of a group of proslavery Southerners who viewed secession as a workable alternative to continued membership in the United States.

For much of the 1830s and 1840s, Calhoun stood as one of the South's most powerful voices. After all, he had served as vice president, led the South during the Nullification Crisis of 1832–33, and engineered the admission of Texas into the Union as a slave state while secretary of state. His views, then, carried great weight with his fellow Southerners, and as the debate over slavery grew more heated, Calhoun's words were echoed by fellow legislators all across the South.

for example, said: "I do not hesitate to avow before this House and the country, and in the presence of the living God, that if, by your legislation, you seek to drive us from the territories of California and New Mexico, purchased by the common blood and treasure of the whole people . . . thereby attempting to fix a national degradation upon half the States of this Confederacy, [then] I am for disunion."

Northern leaders were very concerned about such statements.

John C. Calhoun. *(Photograph by Mathew Brady. Courtesy of the Library of Congress.)*

By the mid-1840s, Calhoun was convinced that ever-growing abolitionist sentiments in the North might well push the federal government into an attempt to force the South to emancipate (free) its slaves. He reacted to this threat with defiance, defending his unwavering conviction (belief) that slavery was a moral good and claiming that the U.S. Constitution gave each state the right to build its society as it saw fit. Calhoun urged his fellow white Southerners to stand by their convictions as well, warning that their entire society would collapse if the abolitionists triumphed. "If we flinch [on the issue of slavery] we are gone, but if we stand fast on it, we shall triumph either by compelling [forcing] the North to yield to our terms, or declaring our independence of them," he wrote in 1847.

By 1850, however, the powerful politician from South Carolina was struck down by illness. He continued to warn that Southern secession (withdrawal from the Union)—and possibly a bloody civil war—would follow any attempt by the North to outlaw slavery in America, but he became so sick that he had to rely on aides to read his senate speeches. Calhoun died in 1850, just as America began its last desperate decade of attempts to avoid war.

"There is a bad state of things here [in Congress]," wrote one Illinois legislator. "I fear this Union is in danger. . . . It is appalling to hear gentlemen, Members of Congress, sworn to support the Constitution, talk and talk earnestly for a dissolution of the Union." But antislavery feelings in the North had become so great that its representatives continued to resist laws that would allow slavery in the West. Moreover, they flatly warned the South not to make any attempt to secede. Convinced that the secession

Henry Clay, the Great Compromiser

The architect of both the Missouri Compromise and the Compromise of 1850, Henry Clay was one of the leading politicians of his era. Born in Virginia, he represented his adopted home state of Kentucky during his long political life. Working as both a U.S. senator (1806–7, 1810–11, 1831–42, 1849–52) and representative (1811–14, 1815–21, 1823–25), Clay built a reputation as a strong Union supporter and believer in federal authority.

Clay was a perennial contender for the American presidency, but although he was able to win the National Republican nomination in 1832 and the Whig Party nomination in 1844, he was never able to gather enough support to achieve victory in a general election. Despite his defeats to Andrew Jackson in 1832 and James K. Polk (1795–1849) in 1844, Clay is remembered as one of America's great statesmen. He was devoted to the continued preservation

Henry Clay. *(Courtesy of the Library of Congress.)*

of the United States, and his peacemaking efforts throughout the first half of the nineteenth century earned him the nicknames "the Great Compromiser" and "the Great Conciliator."

of the Southern states would be a crippling blow to America's growing military and economic power in the world, free-state politicians and newspapers threatened that the North would use force, if necessary, to keep the Union together.

Finally, Senator Henry Clay of Kentucky, who had authored the Missouri Compromise thirty years earlier,

stepped into the middle of the raging debate with a series of suggested compromises designed to avert a tragic war. In a stirring speech to his fellow lawmakers, Clay confirmed that the North would never allow the South to secede without a fight. He also warned that if their differences did indeed explode into war, "we may search the pages of history, and [find no war that would be] so ferocious, so bloody, so implacable [unable to be pacified], so exterminating [deadly]." Clay went on to urge "gentlemen . . . whether from the South or the North . . . to pause at the edge of the precipice, before the fearful and dangerous leap be taken into the yawning abyss below, from which none who ever take it shall return in safety."

The measures put forth by Clay required both sides to make major sacrifices. Clay's compromise called for California to be admitted into the Union as a free state and authorized the abolition of the slave trade in Washington, D.C., the nation's capital. Southern lawmakers did not like either of these measures, but Clay included other conditions that they did favor. The first of these was a $10 million payment to the slave state of Texas to give up its claim to a section of the New Mexico territory and pay off debts. The second condition was a much stronger fugitive slave law designed to help Southern slaveholders recapture runaways in the North. Finally, the last piece of Clay's compromise gave each western territory the power to decide for itself whether to allow slavery within its borders. This idea, first suggested by U.S. senator Lewis Cass (1782–1866) of Michigan, weakened the slave states' boundaries set by the Missouri Compromise back in 1820.

No one was entirely happy with Clay's solution, and Congress proved unable to pass it in its original form. In fact, some of the most influential leaders in both the North and the South denounced it. U.S. senator

William Seward (1801–1872) of the Northern state of New York, for example, rejected it because it still preserved slavery on American soil. The South's John Calhoun, meanwhile, bitterly opposed it as further evidence of Northern interference with Southern affairs. But U.S. senator Stephen A. Douglas (1813–1861) of Illinois managed to guide each piece of Clay's compromise through Congress as a separate bill.

Still, the Compromise of 1850—as Clay's compromise came to be known—probably would have never become law if not for the death of President Zachary Taylor (1784–1850). Taylor's strong antislavery feelings and fierce loyalty to the Union made him view many Southern positions unfavorably, and he would have probably vetoed the agreement because of its pro-South elements. But when he died in July 1850, Vice President Millard Fillmore (1800–1874) took his place. Fillmore was much more willing to negotiate with the slave states, and he signed the compromise into law in September 1850.

Once again, the North and the South had managed to avoid coming to blows over their differences. People all across the nation breathed a sigh of relief when the agreement was reached. Nonetheless, hard feelings remained. Politicians and ordinary citizens alike recognized that the two sides had rolled to the very brink of war, only to pull back at the last instant. Everyone wondered whether the fragile peace would last.

President Millard Fillmore (above) signed the Compromise of 1850 into law two months after the death of President Zachary Taylor. *(Courtesy of the Library of Congress.)*

Fugitive Slave Act

As it turned out, one piece of the Compromise of 1850—the Fugitive Slave Act—proved to be a disaster for the badly splintered country. At first, slaveholders in the South were quite satisfied with the law. It made the task of retrieving runaway slaves living in the North easier, and it called for severe penalties, including large fines and prison terms, for anyone who provided escaped slaves with food, shelter, or any other kind of assistance. Furthermore, it commanded all U.S. citizens "to aid and assist in the prompt and efficient execution of this law, whenever their services may be required."

But within a few months, it was clear that the Fugitive Slave Act infuriated Northern abolitionists, which ultimately hurt the Southern cause. The law had been designed so that a new class of federal officials, called commissioners, could help slaveholders capture runaways. But the law also made it possible for so-called "slavecatchers" to grab free blacks and claim that they were actually escaped slaves. Once captured, free blacks who were accused of being fugitives were given little opportunity to defend themselves. They had no right to a jury trial or to testify on their own behalf. Instead, they were brought before a commissioner, who decided whether these alleged fugitives would go free or be forced into enslavement in the South. This situation was made even worse by the fact that a commissioner received a higher salary from the government if he decided that a black brought before him was an escaped slave. As a result, many free blacks were falsely imprisoned and forcibly enslaved on cotton and sugar cane plantations in the South.

Angry Northern abolitionists vowed to fight the Compromise of 1850 at every turn. Even more importantly, however, the law turned thousands of other Northerners against slavery. "The pitiful spectacle of helpless blacks being seized in the streets and dragged off to slavery could unsettle the most prejudiced northern

The Rescue of Shadrach

After the Fugitive Slave Act of 1850 was passed, many Northern abolitionists vowed to ignore or challenge the law. One of the best-known examples of this defiance took place in Boston, Massachusetts, in February 1851, when a group of black freemen united to free a fugitive slave named Shadrach, who had been captured by federal marshals.

During his enslavement in Virginia, Shadrach had been known as Frederick Wilkins. But after escaping to Massachusetts in 1850, he adopted the name Shadrach and found work as a waiter at a coffeehouse in Boston, one of the North's centers of abolitionist activity. His slave past was discovered, however, and on February 15, 1851, he was seized by federal marshals and taken to a nearby courthouse. But within hours of his arrest, a group of black men broke into the courthouse and overpowered the marshals who were guarding Shadrach. His rescuers then hid him away and used the Underground Railroad to deliver him to Canada, where the Fugitive Slave Act could not be enforced.

Shadrach eventually settled in Montreal, Quebec, where he opened a restaurant. Back in the United States, meanwhile, his dramatic rescue triggered a storm of controversy, especially when federal prosecutors could not convince jurors to convict eight men (four black, four white) who were charged with helping Shadrach reach Canada. Clergyman Theodore Parker (1810–1860) spoke for many happy abolitionists when he wrote that "Shadrach is delivered out of his burning, fiery furnace. I think [his rescue] is the most noble deed done in Boston since the destruction of the tea [in the Boston Tea Party] in 1773." But President Millard Fillmore denounced the action, and enraged Southerners insisted that such defiance (bold resistance) of the Act could not be tolerated. "Every exertion [effort] must be made to cause the laws to be respected," stated a February 21, 1851, editorial in the *Richmond Enquirer.* "Now is the time to act with spirit; now is the time to assure the whole nation that the laws must be respected, and that 'the Union must be preserved.' A striking and decided example [of punishment has so far been lacking] to repress [restrain] the fury of the fanatics, and prevent a repetition of similar offences."

white," wrote Jeffrey Rogers Hummel. "Northern mobs, which once had directed their fury at abolitionists, now attacked slave catchers, broke into jails, and rescued fugitive slaves. . . ." The national government tried vigorously to prosecute the [Northern white] law-breakers responsible for such defiance, but northern juries refused to convict."

As Americans in the North came to see the Fugitive Slave Act as little more than government-sponsored kidnapping, their support for the abolitionist movement soared. Moving testimony from fugitive slaves who came North via the Underground Railroad further added to proabolition feelings. Then, in 1852, a novel by Harriet Beecher Stowe (1811–1896) called *Uncle Tom's Cabin* was published. *Uncle Tom's Cabin* was an enormously popular book that provided a sympathetic portrait of enslaved blacks. Written by Stowe in response to the Fugitive Slave Act, the novel became the most important work of literature in abolitionist history.

Kansas-Nebraska Act

The Fugitive Slave Act and the publication of *Uncle Tom's Cabin* combined to create unprecedented (unheard of) Northern hostility toward the South and its continued defense of slavery. Then in 1854, a new law called the Kansas-Nebraska Act made relations between the North and the South even worse. This law sparked a terrible eruption of violence between pro- and antislavery factions that ultimately took the lives of more than two hundred people.

The Kansas-Nebraska Act had been crafted by Senator Douglas of Illinois in response to the growing national call for construction of a railroad that would extend from America's East Coast to its West Coast. Douglas wanted to build this "transcontinental" railroad through the middle of the

country so that it would pass through the Chicago area. The senator, who was thinking about running for president some day, knew that if his route was chosen, he would be very popular with voters in his home state and other regions of the North. In addition, Douglas owned a lot of real estate along his proposed route, and he recognized that he could sell this land to merchants and other business owners for a great deal of money.

Douglas faced two major obstacles to his plan, however. First, his proposed route would take the railroad through a vast territory in the middle of the country that still had not formed any kind of government. Several attempts had been made to establish a territorial government in the region, but these had been blocked by Southern legislators, who knew that the territory's location would make it a nonslave state according to the terms of the Missouri Compromise of 1820. Second, the South wanted the transcontinental railroad for itself and resisted all efforts to route the railroad through the North.

As Douglas studied the situation, he recognized that there was one way that he could convince Southern legislators to give up their claim on the railroad. In return for their support of his proposed route through the North, Douglas submitted a bill that divided the disputed territory into two territories—Kansas and Nebraska—that could decide for themselves whether to permit slavery. Southern members of Congress accepted the deal, and even though many Northern lawmakers voted against Douglas's Kansas-Nebraska Act, it received enough support for passage.

Based on the concept of "popular sovereignty," which held that the citizens of each new state should be able to decide for themselves whether to allow slavery, the Kansas-Nebraska Act of 1854 was enormously popular with Southerners. It explicitly abolished the Missouri Compromise of 1820, which had drawn a line across the country and outlawed slavery in thousands of square miles of American territory. This gave the South a golden opportunity to expand the practice of slavery.

In the North, however, the new law was greeted with disgust and mounting anger. Antislavery congressmen, led by Senator Salmon P. Chase (1808–1873) of Ohio, immediately issued a document called *The Appeal of the Independent Democrats*. It denounced Douglas's bill as "a criminal betrayal of precious rights" and "part and parcel of an atrocious plot [to convert the West] into a dreary region of despotism [acting like a ruler with total power], inhabited by masters and slaves. . . . Whatever apologies may be offered for the toleration of slavery in the States, none can be offered for its extension into Territories where it does not exist." These feelings were echoed by abolitionists all across the North, and millions of the region's citizens became convinced that the South meant to spread the stain of slavery all across the West.

The fight over slavery in "Bleeding Kansas"

The passage of Douglas's Kansas-Nebraska Act triggered a wild outburst of activity. Nebraska's reputation as a solid antislavery territory spared it from becoming a battleground for abolitionist and proslavery forces, and it was allowed to move toward statehood in relative peace. It was a different story in Kansas, however.

As soon as the Kansas-Nebraska Act was passed, abolitionist and proslavery forces rushed into the Kansas territory in order to claim the land, knowing that a vote of its citizenry would determine its status. "Come on, then, gentlemen of the Slave States," said Senator Seward of New York, who held the widespread belief that the frantic race for superiority in the territory would ultimately determine slavery's future throughout all of America. "Since there is no escaping your challenge, I accept it in behalf of the cause of freedom. We will engage in competition for the virgin soil of Kansas, and God give the victory to the side which is stronger in numbers as it is in right." Southerners recognized that the fight over Kansas was an important one as well. "We are playing for a mighty stake," wrote Missouri senator David Atchison (1807–1886). "If we win we carry slavery to the Pacific Ocean [but] if we fail we lose Missouri, Arkansas, and Texas and all the territories."

The struggle to control Kansas continued on throughout 1854 and 1855. Aided by a Northern antislavery organization known as the Emigrant Aid Society, settlers who supported a free state poured into Kansas. Many of these settlers were equipped with rifles known as "Beecher's Bibles" because they had been provided by a Brooklyn, New York, church headed by abolitionist Henry Ward Beecher (1813–1887).

Proslavery forces flooded the territory in even greater numbers, however. Many of these people actually lived in the neighboring slave state of Missouri, but they were determined to see slavery's expansion into Kansas. These "border ruffians" (bullies), as they were often called, threatened and intimidated abolitionist settlers, and they cast thousands of illegal votes on behalf of proslavery political candidates. By mid-1855, a proslavery territorial legislature had established itself in Kansas on the strength of these false votes. After being formally recognized by the federal government, these antiabolitionist lawmakers promptly passed a wave of proslavery laws and expelled all abolitionists holding political office in the territory.

But antislavery groups refused to give up. Instead, they met in Lawrence, Kansas, to formally protest the earlier elections and to request admission into the Union as a free-soil state (although they also called for a law that would have prevented any blacks—free or slave—from living in the territory). By mid-1856, two separate legislatures—one fiercely proslavery, the other equally dedicated to free-soil ideals—had been established in Kansas.

As the two factions struggled for supremacy, violence swept across the territory. In May 1856, hundreds of proslavery Missourians raided the abolitionist stronghold of Lawrence, terrorizing citizens and destroying buildings. This raiding party was led by Atchison, who resigned his Senate seat to lead the battle in Kansas. A few days after the attack on Lawrence, a radical abolitionist named John Brown (1800–1859) and a number of his sons captured five proslavery settlers and executed them with broadswords in front of their families. Throughout the summer of 1856, the federal government watched helplessly as lynchings (murders by a mob without a trial), horse theft, arson, and murder became common tactics throughout "Bleeding Kansas." The territory had become a nightmarish battle zone in which no one was safe.

The violence in Kansas even spread to the nation's capitol at one point. In May 1856, abolitionist senator Charles Sumner (1811–1874) of Massachusetts launched into a speech called "The Crime Against Kansas." During his speech, Sumner bitterly criticized several proslavery senators, including the uncle of Congressman Preston Brooks (1819–1857) of South Carolina. A few days later, Brooks strode over to Sumner's desk on the Senate floor and brutally attacked him with a cane. Beaten into semi-consciousness, Sumner took nearly three years to recover from his injuries. Southerners, meanwhile, called Brooks a hero. In the weeks following the attack, the South Carolina legislator received dozens of canes in the mail from admirers, many of whom urged Brooks to "Hit [Sumner] again." Brooks's attack, for which he was fined $300, remains one of the most infamous incidents in the history of Congress.

Buchanan supports the Lecompton Constitution

In early 1858, the federal government was finally able to regain some measure of control over the Kansas territory, and the violence lessened. Both sides continued to battle in the political arena, however. As order was restored, it became clear to proslavery Kansans that they were outnumbered by abolitionists. Supporters of slavery, though, had an important ally in President James Buchanan (1791–1868), a Democrat who was sympathetic to the South. Aided by Buchanan, the territory's proslavery leaders made one final attempt to add Kansas to the Union as a slave state by presenting to Congress a proslavery state constitution called the Lecompton Constitution. ("Lecompton" comes from the fact that the constitution was signed in Lecompton, Kansas.)

Buchanan's decision to support the Lecompton Constitution infuriated Stephen Douglas, the architect of the Kansas-Nebraska Act. Douglas viewed the Lecompton Constitution as an obvious attempt to force slavery on the people of Kansas, even though the majority of its citizens did not want it. "Why force this constitution down the throats of the people of Kansas, in opposition to

In May 1856, abolitionist senator Charles Sumner of Massachusetts (above) was attacked with a cane by proslavery congressman Preston Brooks of South Carolina. *(Courtesy of the National Archives and Records Administration.)*

their wishes and in violation of our pledges?" asked Douglas. He further claimed that neither the North nor the South had the right to resort to "trickery or fraud" in the struggle over slavery. "If Kansas wants a slave-state constitution she has a right to it," said Douglas. "If she wants a free-state constitution she has a right to it. It is none of my business which way the slavery cause is decided. . . . I will stand on the great principle of popular sovereignty, which declares the right of all people to be left perfectly free to form and regulate their domestic institutions in their own way."

Led by Douglas, a coalition of Republican and Northern Democratic legislators blocked the Lecompton Constitution from being passed. Buchanan and his allies did not give up though. Instead, they attempted to bribe the people of Kansas into joining the Union as a slave state. They passed legislation that guaranteed the people of Kansas a large amount of additional federal land if they voted to accept the Lecompton Constitution in a special referendum. If Kansas voted against the controversial constitution, on the other hand, it would be unable to petition for statehood until its population reached ninety thousand. But this effort to bribe the citizens of Kansas failed, and the Lecompton Constitution was defeated decisively. In 1861, three years after the Lecompton Constitution was rejected, Kansas was finally admitted into the United States as a free state.

Legislation triggers political upheaval

Kansas endured several years of fear and hatred in the years after Douglas's Kansas-Nebraska Act became law, but the Act's impact also was felt far beyond the Kansas and Nebraska borders. The entire nation was deeply involved with political change and uncertainty in the months and years following its passage. The law triggered the disintegration of the nation-

al Whig political party, which finally divided into Northern and Southern factions over the slavery issue. The Southern Whigs, also known as "Cotton Whigs," subsequently joined the proslavery Democratic Party, while members of the Northern Whigs and the Free-Soil Party combined to form the antislavery Republican Party in the North.

This political turmoil was reflected in the national elections of 1856. When the Whig Party fell apart, the Democratic Party stood as the only political party in America with significant influence in both the North and the South. As the only national party still in existence, the Democrats were able to nudge their presidential candidate, James Buchanan, into the White House. But the 1856 election results showed that the proslavery leanings that made the party so powerful in the South were eroding its popularity in the North. In addition, the 1858 fight over the Lecompton Constitution further bruised the Democrats, sparking bitter divisions among party leaders like Buchanan and Douglas.

The Republicans took full advantage of the growing fragmentation in the Democratic Party. Gathering support throughout the North with their message of abolitionism and economic opportunity in the West, Republicans replaced Democrats in many Northern states by the late 1850s. But Republican officeholders remained practically nonexistent in the South during this time. Indeed, the Democrats had assumed a stranglehold on positions of power throughout the South on the strength of their increasingly proslavery attitudes. As observers looked over the new political landscape, they saw that the North and the South were pitted against one another once again.

1857–1861: The South Prepares to Secede

The 1850s were violent and tension-filled years in the United States, as arguments about slavery and states' rights exploded all over the country. Despite all the efforts of many lawmakers, the hostility between the North and the South seemed to increase with each passing month. A number of events in the early and mid-1850s contributed to this deterioration in relations between the two sides, from the publication of Harriet Beecher Stowe's *Uncle Tom's Cabin* to the bloody battle for control of Kansas. But the blows that finally broke the Union in two took place in the final years of that decade, as the North and the South finally saw that their vastly different views of slavery would never be resolved to everyone's satisfaction. "There were serious differences between the sections," wrote Bruce Catton in *The Civil War*, "[but] all of them except slavery could have been settled through the democratic process. Slavery poisoned the whole situation. It was the issue that could not be compromised, the issue that made men so angry they did not want to compromise."

Words to Know

Abolitionists people who worked to end slavery

Emancipation the act of freeing people from slavery or oppression

Federal national or central government; also, refers to the North or Union, as opposed to the South or Confederacy

Popular sovereignty the belief that each state has the right to decide how to handle various issues for itself without interference from the national government; this is also known as the "states' rights" philosophy

Secession the formal withdrawal of eleven Southern states from the Union in 1860–61

States' rights the belief that each state has the right to decide how to handle various issues for itself without interference from the national government

Tariffs additional charges or taxes placed on goods imported from other countries

Territory a region that belongs to the United States but has not yet been made into a state or states

Dred Scott's bid for freedom

One of the most important legal decisions in American history took place in 1857, when the U.S. Supreme Court had to decide whether a slave named Dred Scott (c. 1795–1858) should be granted his freedom. The Court's ruling against Scott further increased the hostility and distrust between America's Northern and Southern regions, in part because it suggested that slavery could be legally instituted anywhere in the country.

Dred Scott was a Missouri slave who had been the property of an Army surgeon named John Emerson. In 1846 Emerson died, and ownership of Scott was passed along to the surgeon's widow. Scott subsequently attempted to purchase freedom for himself and his wife, Henrietta, but Emerson's widow refused to set them free. Scott then filed a lawsuit against the widow, claiming that he should be given his freedom because he had spent large periods of time with Emerson in areas of the country where slavery was banned.

Scott's lawsuit traveled through the American court system for the next eleven years. By the time his case reached the U.S. Supreme Court in 1857, the slave had actually been purchased by a man named John F. A. Sanford. Scott's case thus became known as *Dred Scott v. Sandford* in the courts (official Supreme Court records misspelled Sanford's last name).

On March 6, 1857, Chief Justice Roger B. Taney (1777–1864) announced the court's decision on Scott's lawsuit. Led by five justices who were Southerners, a majority of the nine-person court ruled against Scott. They declared that no black man could ever become a U.S. citizen, even if he was a free person. Since only citizens were allowed to sue in federal court, the Court decided that Scott had no legal right to file his lawsuit in the first place.

Taney also said that the federal government did not have the right to outlaw slavery in any U.S. territories. He claimed that laws banning slavery were unconstitutional (went against the principles outlined in the U.S. Constitution) because they deprived slaveholders of property. He also stated that slaveholders could legally transport their slaves anywhere in the country since slaves were considered property.

Antislavery organizations in the North saw the verdict as a horrible one that opened the door to slavery throughout the United States. Public criticism of the Supreme Court reached heights that had never been seen before. Northern newspapers denounced the decision as a "wicked and false judgement" and claimed that "if people obey this decision, they disobey God." Many Northerners also saw the Court's decision as proof of a "great slave conspiracy" designed to spread the institution of slavery into free states as well as the disputed Western territories. After all, the ruling made it theoretically possible for slaveholders to move permanently into a free state without ever releasing their slaves from captivity. Many people worried that the Court's decision meant that each Northern state might be powerless to prevent slavery from being practiced within its borders.

Southerners, on the other hand, were overjoyed by the Supreme

People to Know

John Brown (1800–1859) American abolitionist who led raid on Harpers Ferry

James Buchanan (1791–1868) fifteenth president of the United States, 1857–61

Stephen Douglas (1813–1861) American politician; defeated Abraham Lincoln in 1858 Senate election

Abraham Lincoln (1809–1865) sixteenth president of the United States, 1861–65

Dred Scott (c. 1795–1858) American slave who became famous for *Dred Scott* Supreme Court decision

Court's decision. For years, outsiders from the North had been demanding major changes in the Southern economy and social system. But with the *Dred Scott* decision, whites in the South thought that they finally had a way to halt the flood of criticism that had been directed at them ever since the passage of the Missouri Compromise of 1820. As one newspaper in the South happily noted, "The Southern opinion upon the subject of Southern slavery . . . is now the supreme law of the land."

Ultimately, though, the *Dred Scott* case ended up hurting the South in a couple of major ways. First, the abolitionist movement attracted thousands of new supporters as people became convinced that the Supreme

Chief Justice Roger Taney, who was part of the majority of the U.S. Supreme Court that ruled against Dred Scott in the *Dred Scott v. Sandford* case.

Court's ruling paved the way for future legalization of slavery across the nation. Second, the *Dred Scott* decision served to further divide the Northern and Southern wings of the Democratic Party. Even as proslavery Democrats in the South celebrated their triumph in the federal courts, more observant members of the party in both the North and the South began to recognize that the slavery issue was threatening to tear the party in two. And if that happened, the antislavery Republicans might be able to take control of the White House in the next presidential elections.

Finally, the *Dred Scott* decision put the proslavery South in an awkward position. For years, Southerners had insisted that the slavery question in each territory and state should be decided only by the people who lived in that territory or state. This concept of states' rights, sometimes called "popular sovereignty," was based on the idea that the people of each state or territory should not be bound by federal laws concerning slavery. But when Taney stated that federal law actually protected the rights of slaveholders, the theory of popular sovereignty became a threat to the South. In the wake of *Dred Scott v. Sandford*, slaveholders worried that abolitionists in antislavery states or territories might use the notion of popular sovereignty to challenge the Supreme Court ruling.

As reaction to the 1857 *Dred Scott* verdict swept through American cities, towns, and countrysides like a wildfire, Scott himself, whose lawsuit had sparked the whole controversy, quietly faded out of public view. He and his wife were released from slavery soon after the Court's ruling, but his emancipation was short-lived. Scott died in 1858, after enjoying only a few months of freedom.

North-South tensions grow

By 1858, the sectional rivalry in America had become incredibly bitter and hateful. But although both the South and the North were exhausted by their constant battles over slavery, many Southerners felt that the momentum was finally shifting their way. After all, the Supreme Court had supported their stand on slavery with its *Dred Scott* decision. In addition, an 1857 financial panic that slammed the industrialized North passed over the agricultural South, doing little damage to its cotton-based economy. Murmurs in support of secession (the South leaving the Union) still rippled through Southern legislatures and plantation houses, but most Southerners were willing to wait and see if the North might finally give up on its stubborn pursuit of emancipation for blacks.

In the North, on the other hand, the free states were struggling on several fronts. The so-called "Panic of 1857" caused a severe business depression throughout the North. This in turn led Northern political leaders to call for higher tariffs (government-imposed payments) on imported goods and a homestead act that would encourage development of the western territories. But these efforts to re-energize Northern businesses were not popular in the South, and they were stopped by Southern lawmakers and President James Buchanan (1791–1868), a Pennsylvania Democrat who was friendly to the South.

Adding to these economic worries, the South's ongoing defense of slavery in America continued to anger Northerners. The Supreme Court's decision in *Dred Scott v. Sandford* had thrown the entire region into an uproar, and as the 1858 elections approached, the subject that had frustrated Americans for so many years emerged as a major campaign issue in the Northern states. In fact, the subject of slavery in America became the central issue in one of the most famous political contests in U.S. history: the 1858 Illinois senatorial campaign between incumbent (currently in office) Democrat Stephen A. Douglas (1813–1861) and a tall, largely unknown lawyer named Abraham Lincoln (1809–1865).

Lincoln challenges Douglas

Douglas was a powerful politician who had long dreamed of becoming president of the United States. Sometimes he was called the "Little Giant" in recognition of his small size and his big influence in the Senate. Douglas was a leading supporter of the idea of popular sovereignty, which stated that each western territory had the right to decide about slavery for itself. This position had made him very popular in the South and in his home state of Illinois, which had a large population of white Southerners who had emigrated (moved away) from slave states. But in his 1858 reelection campaign, Senator Douglas ran into an opponent who took full advantage of Northern antislavery sentiment and the dispute over the Supreme Court's 1857 Dred Scott decision.

Douglas's challenger was Republican Abraham Lincoln, who quickly caught the attention of Illinois citizens with a campaign that called for a strong federal government, preservation of the Union, and policies that would limit slavery to the South and prevent it from spreading into America's western territories. Lincoln believed that the United States could not continue to exist as a country if its Northern and Southern halves maintained their current differences on slavery. "A house divided against itself cannot stand," Lincoln said. "I believe that this government cannot endure, permanently half slave and half free. I do not expect the Union to be dissolved—I do not expect the house to fall—but I do expect it will cease to be divided. It will become all one thing, or all the other."

But while Lincoln was certain that the nation's treatment of slavery had to change, he also recognized that the issue was a very difficult one for the United States to handle. Lincoln strongly believed that slavery was an immoral institution. But he also thought that blacks were inferior to whites, and that the U.S. Constitution provided some legal protection to slaveholders. His conflicted feelings on the subject—as well as his fierce desire to keep America united—convinced him to adopt a moderate position on slavery. He strongly opposed Southern calls for the unchecked expansion of slavery into the American West, for instance. But unlike some other Northern leaders, Lincoln also opposed calls for the immediate abolishment of slavery in the American South. Instead, Lincoln concentrated on stopping slavery from spreading elsewhere in the country. He believed that if slavery was limited to the South, it would eventually die out as a result of changing economic and social trends.

The Lincoln-Douglas debates

As the 1858 Senate contest between Douglas and Lincoln progressed, it quickly drew the attention of people all around Illinois and the nation. This spotlight fell on the two men for several reasons. Both men were energetic campaigners who roamed all across the state to win people to their side. Moreover, most observers agreed that the race was a close one, and that either man might win. But the Douglas-Lincoln contest became most famous because it included a series of heated public debates that caught the imagination of people all across America. Each one of the seven face-to-face debates was held in a different Illinois town, but all of them focused almost entirely on the issue of slavery. "Until then candidates for northern office had usually avoided discussing slavery," wrote Jeffrey Rogers Hummel, author of *Emancipating Slaves, Enslaving Free Men*. "During the Lincoln-Douglas contest, it was *the* issue. No one talked much about anything else."

As the campaign progressed, Douglas repeatedly defended his belief in the concept of popular sovereignty, even though many people thought that the Supreme Court's ruling in the 1857 Dred Scott decision meant that no legal steps could be taken to halt the spread of slavery. In a debate in Freeport, Illinois, the senator ex-

Stephen Douglas, "The Little Giant"

Stephen Arnold Douglas was one of the most notable American statesmen of the nineteenth century. Born in Brandon, Vermont, he became a powerful legislator in Illinois in the early 1840s. Douglas was small in size, but he was armed with a sharp mind, great ambition, and a heartfelt belief that squabbles over slavery could not be allowed to stand in the way of America's westward expansion. First as a Democratic congressman (1843–47), and then as a U.S. senator (1847–61), Douglas insisted that each state should be able to decide whether to allow slavery for itself, without interference from the federal government or other states.

During the 1850s, Douglas became one of America's leading defenders of this concept, known as popular sovereignty (sometimes also called squatter sovereignty). In fact, he incorporated its basic framework into the Compromise of 1850 and the Kansas-Nebraska Act of 1854, both of which were intended to ease the growing tensions between the North and the South. But despite Douglas's best efforts, neither of these compromise measures lasted for very long.

Douglas is also famous for his 1858 debates with Abraham Lincoln, who challenged him for his Illinois Senate seat. Douglas barely managed to escape with a victory, but their fierce verbal battles over the

Illinois senator Stephen A. Douglas. *(Courtesy of the Library of Congress.)*

issue of slavery vaulted Lincoln into national prominence. In 1860, Douglas and two other candidates were defeated by Lincoln in the U.S. presidential election. But when the Civil War began, Douglas issued a strongly worded statement of support for Lincoln and the Union. "There can be no neutrals in this war, only patriots—or traitors," he declared. Douglas then launched a speaking tour in the western states to generate support for Lincoln's efforts to restore the Union. But in June 1861, he died quite suddenly, possibly from cirrhosis of the liver.

plained that American territories that did not want to have slavery could simply refuse to pass any laws that were required for slavery to exist. Lincoln ridiculed this argument, which came to be known as the Freeport Doctrine, and emphasized his own belief that the continued practice of slavery in the United States ignored American ideals of liberty and freedom. He also charged that if men like Douglas continued to lead the country, slavery would spread all across the American West and North.

Douglas, though, continued to claim that individual states' rights should be considered above all other factors. "[Lincoln] says that he looks forward to a time when slavery shall be abolished everywhere," Douglas said in one debate. "I look forward to a time when each state shall be allowed to do as it pleases. . . . I care more for the great principle of self-government, the right of the people to rule, than I do for all the Negros in Christendom." Douglas also appealed to the racist feelings that dominated many white Illinois communities. He repeatedly accused Lincoln of being a dangerous extremist who thought that blacks were just as good as whites, and many of Douglas's speeches capitalized on common white fears that freed black men might take their jobs and women. Lincoln sometimes responded to these remarks with statements that made it clear that he was not supporting total equality between the races. "I have no purpose to introduce political and social equality between the white and black races," Lincoln stated in one de-

bate. "I am not, nor ever have been in favor of making voters of the negroes, or jurors, or qualifying them to hold office, or having them to marry with white people." Despite these beliefs, however, Lincoln never wavered from his conviction that all black people deserved release from enslavement.

Both Lincoln and Douglas sometimes resorted to name-calling and misleading statements in their campaigns. But the Lincoln-Douglas debates ultimately revealed two men who were both concerned about the preservation of the Union. They just had different beliefs about the course that should be taken to keep the North and the South together. Douglas sincerely believed that the Union could be preserved only if the federal government let each state decide how to handle slavery by itself. Lincoln, on the other hand, was equally convinced that slavery was poisoning the country and that it had to be stopped and eventually wiped out.

In the end, Douglas barely defeated Lincoln to retain his Senate seat. But their contest—and especially their debates, which riveted the nation—would have a lasting impact on their political fortunes. Douglas, for example, had been a long-time ally of the South because of his support for states' rights. But his opposition to the Lecompton Constitution (proslavery leaders' attempt to add Kansas to the Union as a slave state) and his support for the so-called Freeport Doctrine dramatically reduced his popularity in the slaveholding states in the late

1850s. This change would come back to haunt him during the 1860 elections, when he ran for the Democratic presidential nomination.

Lincoln's performance during the 1858 campaign, meanwhile, had transformed him into one of the rising stars in the Republican Party. Even though he lost to Douglas, his campaign vaulted him onto the national political scene. As the months passed by, he began to be mentioned as a possible Republican candidate for the upcoming 1860 presidential elections.

John Brown leads the raid at Harpers Ferry

In 1859, relations between the North and the South continued to deteriorate. Resentment of the North reached an all-time high in white communities throughout the South. Weary of Northern criticism of their morals, Southern whites also worried that antislavery feelings in the North were growing so strong that the federal government might soon force the South to abolish slavery against its will. In the North, meanwhile, anger at the South's continued defense of slavery and its occasional threats to secede was widespread. As people all around the country struggled to control their anger and frustration, it did not seem as if relations between America's Northern and Southern sections could get any more strained. But in October 1859, the activities of a radical abolitionist named John Brown (1800–1859) managed to worsen an already hostile and distrustful environment.

John Brown was a deeply religious man who viewed slavery as an evil institution that should be immediately abolished. A white Northerner, he allied himself with the abolitionists during the 1830s and 1840s. Brown's willingness to use violence in the antislavery cause, however, did not become evident until the mid-1850s, when he joined the abolitionist settlers who were trying to establish Kansas as a free state. Four days after proslavery raiders attacked the abolitionist town of Lawrence, Brown and four of his sons slaughtered five proslavery settlers in revenge, even though they had not been involved in the raid.

By the late 1850s, Brown had decided that Southern whites would never willingly abolish slavery. Convinced that the only way to end slavery was through force, he made plans to start a violent slave rebellion all across the South. Aided by a group of Northern abolitionists that came to be known as the Secret Six, Brown decided to attack a federal armory in Harpers Ferry, Virginia (now part of West Virginia). He believed that he could use the weapons stored in the armory to outfit nearby slaves, and convinced himself that once the uprising started, slaves all across the South would join the rebellion.

The first part of Brown's scheme unfolded according to plan. Leading a band of twenty-two men— black and white—the radical abolitionist successfully captured the Harpers Ferry armory on the night of

Abolitionist John Brown. *(Courtesy of the Library of Congress.)*

October 16, 1859. But as the evening wore on, it became clear that Brown's plan was flawed. Slaves in the area were unsure about what was going on, and they elected not to join Brown. In addition, white citizens of Harpers Ferry managed to surround the raiding party's position, and by the next day, Brown and his men were trapped.

Brown refused to surrender. But on October 18, a company of marines commanded by Lieutenant Colonel Robert E. Lee (1807–1870) captured the abolitionist and his crew after a brief but bloody battle. Brown and the remnants of his band were led away, leaving behind several dead civilians, including the mayor of Harpers Ferry, and ten dead abolitionists. Brown and seven of his men were subsequently convicted of murder, treason, and inciting a slave insurrection, and they were all executed. But Brown remained defiant during and after his trial. "This Court acknowledges, as I suppose, the validity of the law of God," he proclaimed after being sentenced to hang. "I believe that to have interfered as I have done, as I have always freely admitted I have done in behalf of His despised poor, is no wrong, but right. Now, if it is deemed necessary that I should forfeit my life for the furtherance of the ends of justice, and mingle my blood further . . . with the blood of millions in this slave country whose rights are disregarded by wicked, cruel, and unjust enactments, I say let it be done."

Brown's death further divides America

Brown's actions at Harpers Ferry—and his execution a few weeks later—had a major impact on communities all across America. In the North, reaction was mixed. Many people criticized Brown's violent methods, and most Northern lawmakers agreed with Senator William Seward (1801–1872) of New York, who called the abolitionist's execution "necessary and just." But many other Northerners saw Brown as a heroic figure who was willing to die for his beliefs. A number of

Northern communities tolled church bells on the day of his hanging as a way of saluting his efforts. Many abolitionists throughout the North praised him for his bravery and his hatred of slavery. Writer Henry David Thoreau (1817–1862), for instance, spoke for many Northerners when he called Brown "a crucified hero" and an "angel of light."

In the South, on the other hand, Brown's raid cause a wild ripple of fear and hysteria throughout white communities. Even though Brown had been unable to rally a single slave to his side, whites still remembered the bloody slave rebellion of 1831 led by Nat Turner (1800–1831). Many of them became convinced that antislavery forces in the North were willing to sacrifice the lives of thousands of Southern whites in their zeal to end slavery. The reaction to Brown's execution in some parts of the North further increased Southern anger and fear. To many whites in Alabama, Mississippi, South Carolina, and other slave states, the Northern threat to their way of life had never seemed more real or immediate.

The 1860 presidential campaign

The 1860 campaign for the presidency of the United States was waged under a dark cloud of anxiety and fear. Some Southern politicians and newspaper editors warned that the region was prepared to secede from the Union if an antislavery politician was elected president.

The Electoral College

The United States elects its president and vice president through an institution known as the electoral college. The electoral college consists of a small group of representatives from each state legislature, called "electors," who gather in their respective states to cast ballots in elections for the presidency and vice presidency of the United States. These elections take place every four years. Historically, the electoral college meets one month after the public vote for the president and the vice president. When the electoral college meets, each state elector casts his or her ballot for the candidate who received the most popular votes in that state. Electors are not legally required to vote for the candidate who received the most popular votes in the state, but they are honor bound to do so. After the electoral college results are tallied, the person who receives a majority of available electoral votes around the country is declared president, and his or her running mate assumes the position of vice president. The offices of the president and the vice president are the only elective federal positions that are not filled by a direct vote of the American people.

The rules of the electoral college call for each state to be represented by a number of electors that is equal to the total of its U.S. senators and representatives in Congress. All states are represented by two senators, but states with large populations are given greater representation in the U.S. House of Representatives than are states with smaller populations. As a result, they also receive a greater number of electoral votes in presidential elections.

As of 1999, there are a total of 538 members in the electoral college. This means that presidential and vice presidential candidates can only be elected if they win a majority (270 or more) of those 538 votes. In modern elections, heavily popu-

Northern reaction to this threat was mixed. Some people thought that threats of secession were just words designed to scare Northern leaders into abandoning abolitionist positions. Others recognized that the South's threats needed to be taken seriously, but continued to maintain their belief that slavery had to be stopped. It was in this environment that America's major political parties selected their candidates for the 1860 election.

The Republican Party knew that it would not get any votes in the South because of its reputation as a party devoted to a strong central government and antislavery positions. But the Republican leaders believed that their candidate might still win the election if he could make a good

lated states like California, New York, Florida, and Texas have had a far greater number of votes in the electoral college than sparsely populated states like Wyoming, North Dakota, and Delaware. The only other territory held by the United States that has any electoral votes is the District of Columbia, which was given three electoral votes by a 1964 law.

The electoral college system has been in place in America ever since it became a country, but many people have criticized it over the years. The primary complaint that has been raised about the system is that it makes it possible for a candidate to become president without winning a majority of popular votes. In fact, on three different occasions in American history—1824, 1876, and 1888—the electoral college has selected a candidate who received fewer popular votes than another candidate. In other words, the candidate that was supported by the most voters did not win the election.

In 1876, Rutherford B. Hayes (1822–1893) received fewer popular votes than Samuel J. Tilden (1814–1886), but won the election by an electoral vote of 185 to 184. In 1888, Benjamin Harrison (1833–1901) defeated incumbent president Grover Cleveland (1837–1908) in electoral votes, 233-168, even though Cleveland had received more popular votes. And in 1824, although Andrew Jackson (1767–1845) received more popular *and* electoral votes than John Quincy Adams (1767–1848), he had not earned a majority of electoral votes, as two other candidates won a total of 78 votes. In a special vote in the U.S. House of Representatives, Adams eventually gained enough support to defeat Jackson. Despite such results, however, periodic attempts to change or abolish the electoral college have always failed.

showing in the more populous North. (Since more people lived in the North than in the South, the Northern states also had more votes in the electoral college, the institution that determines who the nation's next president will be). With these factors in mind, the Republicans chose Abraham Lincoln as their candidate. They believed that Lincoln's moderate reputation and the party's pro-business and anti-slavery positions would attract a wide range of voters in the North.

The Democratic Party, meanwhile, had a terrible time deciding who its nominee would be. In April 1860, when the party's leaders gathered to reach agreement on its presidential candidate and its major campaign issues, the Democrats stood as the only political party in America with a na-

John Breckinridge. *(Courtesy of the National Archives and Records Administration.)*

tional base of support. It remained powerful in the North—although the Republicans were gaining in popularity—and it dominated politics in the South because of the proslavery positions of Southern Democrats.

But as the Democratic convention got underway, it became clear that the divide between the party's Northern and Southern wings had become a serious one. As soon as the convention opened, a radical faction of proslavery Southerners insisted that the party support the passage of a "slave code" that would legally protect slavery in all the western territories.

When Northern Democrats refused to go along with this demand because of its certain unpopularity in their home states, a large group of radical proslavery Southerners—sometimes known as "Fire-Eaters"—walked out of the convention in protest. Two months later, a second Democratic convention was held, but it, too, ended in failure, as the two sides bickered over the slave code idea.

In the end, the Northern and Southern wings of the Democratic Party could not agree on the slavery issue, and they ended up nominating two different candidates for president. The Northern wing nominated Stephen Douglas, the Illinois senator who had defeated Lincoln in the 1858 Senate elections. Douglas was a strong candidate in the North, but he was no longer popular in the South because of his opposition to the Lecompton Constitution and his support of popular sovereignty, which Southern leaders now opposed. Dissatisfied with Douglas, the Southern wing of the Democratic Party decided to nominate Vice President John C. Breckinridge (1821–1875), a proslavery Kentuckian. This decision to nominate a second candidate shattered the party in two and dramatically increased Lincoln's chances of victory.

Finally, a fourth candidate for the office of the presidency emerged in May 1860, when a group of politicians from the former Whig Party formed the Constitutional Union Party. This group said that it was dedicated to upholding the U.S. Constitution. But the party refused to take a clear stand on slavery and other issues, and its presidential candidate, John Bell (1797–1869) of Tennessee, looked unlikely to gather much support in the North or the Deep South.

Lincoln wins the election

In the weeks leading up to the November election, anxiety about the outcome was evident all over the country. All of the competing parties waged nasty campaigns, heaping abuse on other candidates and warning of terrible consequences if their candidate did not win the election. The most serious of these warnings was voiced in America's Southern states. All across the South, people grumbled that if Lincoln was elected, then they would have no choice but to secede.

Lincoln knew how unpopular he was in the South, so he did not even bother campaigning there. Instead, he concentrated on beating Douglas in the North, where most of the nation's voting population—and most of America's electoral votes—were located. He knew that if he was victorious in the North, he would have enough electoral votes to secure the presidency, no matter what happened in the South.

Despite widespread warnings of secession from the South, Lincoln was indeed victorious. He received only 40 percent of the popular vote (the actual number of citizens who cast ballots) in the United States, and his name was not even included on

Republican candidate Abraham Lincoln was elected president in 1860. *(Reproduced by permission of Corbis-Bettmann.)*

the ballot in ten Southern states. But he carried the entire North, capturing 54 percent of the region's popular vote and all of its electoral votes. Most of the South went with Breckinridge, but he was shut out in the North. Three other Southern states sided with Bell, but he too was unable to collect any support in the Northern states. Douglas, who only two years earlier had defeated Lincoln in their famous Illinois Senate race, ended up with 1.3 million popular votes, second only to Lincoln's total of 1.8 million votes. He was the only candidate who received

"Brother Jonathan's Lament for Sister Caroline"

When South Carolina announced its intention to secede from the United States, American lawyer and poet Oliver Wendell Holmes (1809–1894) reacted with sadness rather than anger. Holmes strongly supported the Union, and he thought that South Carolina's decision was a rash one that would bring pain and suffering to North and South alike. But rather than heap abuse or scorn on the state, he instead composed a poem that reflected his deep regret about South Carolina's decision, as well as the hope of many American citizens that the state—"Caroline," the Union's "stormy-browed sister"—might some day return to the Union in peace:

> She has gone,—she has left us in passion and pride,—
>
> Our stormy-browed sister, so long at our side!
>
> She has torn her own star from our firmament's glow,
>
> And turned on her brother the face of a foe!
>
> O Caroline, Caroline, child of the sun,

> We can never forget that our hearts have been one,—
>
> Our foreheads both sprinkled in Liberty's name,
>
> From the fountain of blood with the finger of flame!
>
> You were always too ready to fire at a touch;
>
> But we said, "She is hasty,—she does not mean much."
>
> We have scowled, when you uttered some turbulent threat;
>
> But Friendship still whispered, "Forgive and forget!"
>
> Has our love all died out? Have its altars grown cold?
>
> Has the curse come at last which the fathers foretold?
>
> Then Nature must reach us the strength of the chain
>
> That her petulant children would sever in vain.
>
> They may fight till the buzzards are gorged with their spoil,
>
> Till the harvest grows black as it rots in the soil,
>
> Till the wolves and the catamounts troop from their caves,

significant support in all parts of the country. But the "Little Giant" only won two states outright (Missouri and New Jersey), as his continued support of popular sovereignty made him an unsatisfactory choice to radicals on both sides of the slavery issue. A majority of Northern voters had decided that his views were too friendly to slaveholders. At the same time, most Southern voters had reached the conclusion that Douglas would not fight to extend slavery into America's western territories.

Oliver Wendell Holmes. *(Courtesy of the Library of Congress.)*

And the shark tracks the pirate, the lord of the waves.

In vain is the strife! When its fury is past,

Their fortunes must flow in one channel at last,

As the torrents that rush from the mountains of snow

Roll mingled in peace through the valleys below.

Our Union is river, lake, ocean and sky:

Man breaks not the medal, when God cuts the die!

Though darkened with sulphur, though cloven with steel,

The blue arch will brighten, the waters will heal!

O Caroline, Caroline, child of the sun,

There are battles with Fate that can never be won!

The star-flowering banner must never be furled,

For its blossoms of light are the hope of the world!

Go, then, our rash sister! afar and aloof,

Run wild in the sunshine away from our roof;

But when your heart aches and your feet have grown sore,

Remember the pathway that leads to our door!

South Carolina secedes, other Southern states follow

On November 6, 1860, Lincoln was formally recognized as the winner of the election, and the American South erupted in anger and despair. Many white Southerners believed that Lincoln's election meant that a final Northern push to abolish slavery throughout the United States was just around the corner. Countless furious speeches and editorials reflected the Southern certainty that the

"Yankees," as the Northerners were sometimes called, would soon begin the process of reshaping Southern society without regard for the feelings of its white citizenry. The *New Orleans Daily Crescent,* for example, charged that the Republican Party's primary goal was to establish "absolute tyranny over the slaveholding States," and bring about "subjugation [the conquering] of the South and the complete ruin of her social, political, and industrial institutions."

As soon as Lincoln's victory was announced, calls for secession from the Union could be heard all across the South. South Carolina was the first slaveholding state to act. Its state legislature called a special meeting to consider secession, and on December 20, 1860, state lawmakers unanimously approved (by a vote of 169 to 0) a declaration that South Carolina was no longer a member of the United States. Within the next six weeks, Mississippi, Florida, Alabama, Georgia, and Louisiana followed South Carolina's lead and announced their secession from the Union.

Not all whites living in these states were certain that secession was the best course of action. Some Southern whites wanted to remain in the Union despite the years of strain between America's Northern and Southern regions. Others pointed out that although a Republican had been elected president, Democrats continued to hold majorities in both the U.S. Senate and House of Representatives. But as Louisiana senator Judah P. Benjamin (1811–1884) admitted, Lincoln's election had triggered a tidal wave of secessionist sentiment that seemed to sweep all other arguments out of its path. "It is a revolution . . . of the most intense character," said Benjamin, "and it can no more be checked by human effort, for the time, than a prairie fire by a gardener's watering hose."

1861: Creation
of the Confederacy

In the first weeks of 1861, six Southern states began the process of establishing their own government, even as Northerners debated whether to let them leave the Union in peace or use force to stop them. On February 23, two weeks before Abraham Lincoln (1809–1865) was inaugurated as the sixteenth president of the United States, Texas became the seventh state to leave the Union. After taking office, President Lincoln reacted cautiously to these events. He felt very strongly that the states that had seceded (left the Union) had no right to do so, and he was determined to keep the Union together. But he also did not want to upset the large number of states in the mid-South—sometimes called the border states—that had yet to decide whether to join the Confederacy.

On April 12, 1861, however, South Carolina troops attacked Fort Sumter, a U.S. outpost located in the harbor of Charleston, South Carolina. A day later, the Federal troops stationed at Fort Sumter were forced to surrender, and Lincoln prepared for war. He promptly proclaimed that the seceding states were in "a state of insurrection" and vowed to drag the states of the newly born Confederacy back into the Union. Lin-

Words to Know

Confederacy eleven Southern states that seceded from the United States in 1860 and 1861

Federal national or central government; also refers to the North or Union, as opposed to the South or Confederacy

Rebel Confederate; often used as a name for Confederate soldiers

Secession the formal withdrawal of eleven Southern states from the Union in 1860–61

States' rights the belief that each state has the right to decide how to handle various issues for itself without interference from the national government

Union Northern states that remained loyal to the United States during the Civil War

coln's call to arms was warmly received in the North, but it also convinced four important states—Virginia, North Carolina, Tennessee, and Arkansas—to leave the United States and join the Confederate States of America.

The Crittenden Compromise

In the days and weeks immediately following the secession of South Carolina and six other Southern states, the people living in America's Northern states reacted with a mixture of anger, confusion, and surprise. De-

spite all the pre-election warnings that the South had delivered, many Northerners never really believed that their Southern neighbors might actually decide to leave the Union.

When it became apparent that the slave states of the Deep South were willing to make good on their threat, however, several lawmakers scrambled to bring them back into the fold. Political leaders in Virginia organized a peace convention in which representatives from twenty-one states tried—but failed—to come up with a compromise that would satisfy both sides. President James Buchanan (1791–1868) also made some half-hearted attempts to repair the damage that had been done. But Buchanan, a Democrat, blamed Lincoln and the Republicans for the crisis. After all, the Republicans had been the ones taking a hard line against slavery. The Southern states only planned to secede because they felt that Lincoln could not possibly represent their interests as president. In the end, the outgoing president seemed willing to leave the messy situation to Lincoln, who was scheduled to take over the presidency after his inauguration on March 4, 1861.

The most serious proposal to restore the Union was crafted by a Kentucky lawmaker named John Crittenden (1787–1863). A senator from one of several mid-South states that had not yet decided whether to stay with the Union or secede, Crittenden called for a series of compromises on a wide range of issues. The major elements of his proposal, however, were two proposed constitutional amendments (revisions). One amendment would protect slavery in all of the states where it already existed, and the other one would provide for the extension of slavery all the way to the Pacific Ocean in American territory located south of the old Missouri Compromise line.

The Crittenden Compromise was studied by both sides, but in the end it was rejected. The states that had already seceded were tired of compromising and arguing, and their leaders showed little interest in resuming their tense relationship with the North. Lincoln, meanwhile, was willing to consider an amendment protecting slavery where it currently existed. But he and his fellow Republicans flatly rejected the proposal that would have allowed the South to expand slavery into new areas. "We have just carried an election," Lincoln wrote, "on principles fairly stated to the people. Now we are told in advance that the government shall be broken up unless we surrender to those we have beaten, before we take the offices. . . . If we surrender, it is the end of us and the end of the government."

Formation of the Confederate States of America

By early 1861, the North was engaged in a bitter debate with itself over the secessionist activities taking place in the South. Some people argued that the United States should allow South Carolina and the other secessionist states to establish their own country without any interference. This sentiment was voiced in towns

People to Know

Robert Anderson (1805–1871) Union major who surrendered Fort Sumter to Confederates in April 1861

Pierre G. T. Beauregard (1818–1893) Confederate general who captured Fort Sumter in April 1861; also served at First Bull Run and Shiloh

James Buchanan (1791–1868) fifteenth president of the United States, 1857–61

Jefferson Davis (1808–1889) president of the Confederate States of America, 1861–65

Abraham Lincoln (1809–1865) sixteenth president of the United States, 1861–65

William Seward (1801–1872) U.S. secretary of state, 1861–69

and cities all across the North by citizens and political leaders who were weary of dealing with their stubborn Southern neighbors. This feeling was also strong in some abolitionist circles, since the departure of the secessionist states meant that slavery might be more easily stamped out in other parts of the United States. But other Northern communities called for the Federal government to maintain the Union by force if necessary. These people ranged from farmers, who wanted to make sure that they could continue to transport goods down the

Kentucky senator John Crittenden's proposed series of compromises regarding slavery was rejected by both the Union and Confederacy. *(Courtesy of the Library of Congress.)*

Mississippi River, to Northern manufacturers and merchants, who worried about the impact of Southern independence on their business dealings. The most important factor in the North's opposition to Southern secession, however, was the widespread feeling that Southern selfishness was threatening to destroy a growing nation just when it was on the verge of becoming a world power.

In the South, meanwhile, the states that had seceded went about the business of forming a new government. In February 1861, delegates from each of the six states gathered in Montgomery, Alabama, to draw up a constitution for their new nation, called the Confederate States of America. As it turned out, the Confederate Constitution was very similar to the U.S. Constitution in most respects. But the document created in Montgomery was different in two major ways. First, it gave individual states greater freedom to run their own affairs while also putting significant restraints on the power of the central government. Second, the Confederate Constitution explicitly protected the rights of slaveowners and confirmed slavery's importance to the states of the Confederacy. After the Constitution was approved, newly elected Confederate vice president Alexander H. Stephens (1812–1883) of Georgia rejoiced, saying that "the new constitution has put at rest, forever, all the agitating questions relating to our peculiar institution—African slavery as it exists among us. . . . [Our new government's] foundations are laid . . . upon the great truth, that the negro is not equal to the white man; that slavery—subordination to the superior race—is his natural and moral condition. This, our new government, is the first, in the history of the world, based upon this great physical, philosophical, and moral truth."

The Confederacy selects its first president

On February 9, 1861, delegates of the Confederate States of America elected Jefferson Davis (1808–1889), a wealthy slaveholding senator from Mississippi, to be its first president. Davis had served as the United States' secretary of war in the mid-1850s under President Franklin Pierce (1804–1869). Dedicated to the principle of states' rights and respected throughout the South, Davis was seen as a solid choice for the presidency, even though he had expressed reservations about secession in the past.

Immediately after his February 18, 1861, inauguration, Davis began the process of putting together his administration and organizing a military. Forming a new nation involved a multitude of other tasks, from introducing new legal and government systems to developing new commerce and banking systems that were independent from the North. Davis and other Confederate officials spent a great deal of time and energy on these issues. But although this process of nation-building was complex and time-consuming, it was helped along by a number of different factors.

One major development was the defection of another state to the Confederate side. On February 23, 1861, the vast state of Texas formally seceded from the United States over the strong objections of its governor, Mexican War hero Sam Houston (1793–1863). The addition of Texas to the Confederacy encouraged the white populations of the other secessionist states, some of whom continued to harbor quiet doubts about the course that they had taken.

Confederate vice president Alexander H. Stephens. *(Courtesy of the Library of Congress.)*

Another factor that helped the Confederacy develop quickly was the undeniable excitement that many Southerners felt upon beginning this new chapter in their lives. Schools, churches, and taverns throughout the Deep South echoed with songs and speeches touting the many fine qualities of the Confederate states, and pride in the region's history and traditions became even stronger than it had already been. All throughout the Confederacy, the move to secede from the Union was compared to the American Revolution of a century earlier, when independent-minded people re-

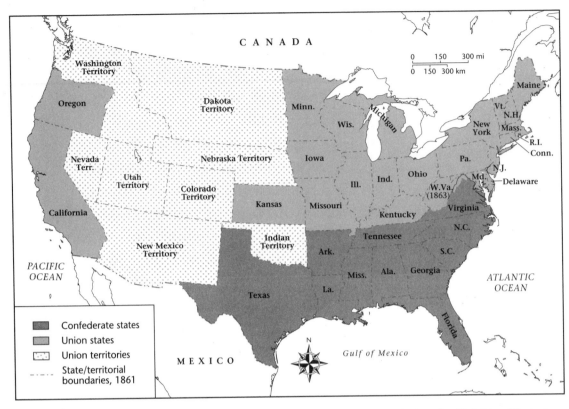

A breakdown of the Union and Confederate states/territories during the Civil War. *(Illustration by XNR Productions. Reproduced by permission of The Gale Group.)*

belled against the tyrannical orders of a distant ruler.

Lincoln signals determination to preserve the Union

President Lincoln and other Northern political leaders watched events unfold in the South with considerable concern. After all, the Confederate states had gone about the process of creating a recognizable nation for themselves in energetic fashion, and Federal authority in those states was diminishing quickly. Post offices, courts, military posts, customs offices, financial institutions, and other Federal offices were taken over by state troops loyal to the Confederacy in villages and cities across the Deep South. With each passing day, Confederate leaders worked to erase all signs of their previous membership in the Union. By the time Lincoln took office in March 1861, the only four military institutions located on secessionist soil that were still under Union control were three forts along the Florida coastline and a lone fort, called Fort Sumter, located in Charleston Bay in South Carolina.

Despite these developments, however, Lincoln adopted a reasonable tone in his March 4 inaugural address. He made it clear that he was determined to preserve the Union, stating that "the Union is unbroken, and to the extent of my ability I shall take care, as the Constitution itself expressly enjoins upon me, that the laws of the Union be faithfully executed in all of the states." But he also declared that he had no wish to go to war against his countrymen. "There needs to be no bloodshed or violence, and there shall be none unless it be forced upon the national authority," he proclaimed. "In your hands, my dissatisfied fellow-countrymen, and not in mine, is the momentous issue of civil war. The Government will not assail [attack] you. You can have no conflict without being yourselves the aggressors." Lincoln then concluded his address with an appeal for reconciliation, saying that "we must not be enemies. Though passion may have strained it must not break our bonds of affection. The mystic chords of memory, stretching from every battlefield and patriot grave to every living heart and hearthstone all over this broad land, will yet swell the chorus of the Union, when again touched, as surely they will be, by the better angels of our nature."

Lincoln's speech reflected his belief that there was still a chance to preserve the Union without resorting to warfare, provided that he did not offend the eight other slaveholding states in the Mid- and Upper South that remained undecided about whether to stay in the Union or join the Confeder-

April 12, 1861: South Carolina troops launch an artillery assault on the Union garrison at Fort Sumter, beginning the Civil War.

Fort Sumter, near Charleston, South Carolina. *(Illustration by XNR Productions. Reproduced by permission of The Gale Group.)*

acy. He also knew that some people in the Confederate states remained doubtful of the wisdom of secession, and he thought that the rebels might eventually return to the Union of their own free will. As a result, he did his best to avoid violent confrontation with the rebel states throughout his first month in office in hopes of keeping Virginia, Maryland, North Carolina, and other Mid-South states from bolting from the already tattered Union.

On April 12, 1861, though, Lincoln's hopes of restoring the Union

Major Robert Anderson. *(Photograph by George Cook. Courtesy of the Library of Congress.)*

the command of Major Robert Anderson (1805–1871). A five-sided brick building that stood guard over the port of the largest city in South Carolina, it remained in Union hands throughout the first few months of 1861, even as the Confederacy took control of most other Federal military outposts and offices in the Deep South.

The continued occupation of Fort Sumter by Union troops quickly developed into a major point of disagreement between North and South. In the aftermath of secession, the people of South Carolina and the rest of the Confederacy regarded the Union garrison at Fort Sumter as a foreign military presence that should not be permitted to operate in their territory, especially since it was located right in the middle of one of the Confederacy's most important harbors. With each passing week, the sight of the American flag flying over the fort further infuriated the people in Charleston and other Confederate communities.

Confederate representatives made a number of efforts to convince the Union to hand over the fort to South Carolina troops peacefully during the first few months of 1861, but all of these attempts failed. First, Confederate officials tried to convince President Buchanan to give up the fort before he left office in March. Buchanan had withdrawn Federal troops from other locations in the Confederacy because of his strong desire to finish his term before war erupted. But Buchanan refused to abandon Fort Sumter, which had come to be regarded throughout the

without bloodshed were shattered. It was on that night that South Carolina troops launched an artillery assault on the Union garrison at Fort Sumter, and the awful civil war that had threatened to envelop the United States for years and years finally began.

The controversy over Fort Sumter

Located at the entrance to Charleston Harbor in South Carolina, Fort Sumter was manned by approximately sixty-eight U.S. soldiers under

North as a symbol of Union strength and pride. "If I withdraw [Major] Anderson from Sumter, I can travel home to Wheatland [after leaving office] by the light of my own burning effigies," said Buchanan, referring to his home in Lancaster, Pennsylvania.

The South had no better luck with Lincoln after he took office, despite the secret activities of William Seward (1801–1872), Lincoln's secretary of state. Seward was a talented and distinguished politician who ranked as one of the most powerful figures in the Republican Party. But despite Lincoln's decision to select him for the important position of secretary of state, Seward remained bitter about the party's decision to nominate Lincoln instead of himself as its presidential candidate in the 1860 elections. In fact, Seward did not hold a high opinion of the new president, and he believed that he would be able to shape Lincoln's policies to his own liking from his position as secretary of state.

Seward thought that if the United States avoided angering the Confederate states, they would eventually return to the Union. He thus believed that U.S. forces should vacate Fort Sumter and leave it to the citizens of South Carolina. Acting on this conviction—and on his belief that he could manipulate Lincoln—Seward offered secret assurances to the Confederacy that the Union would soon abandon Fort Sumter. But as the days passed by, it became clear that Seward had underestimated the will of his new president.

Lincoln attempts to send supplies

Almost as soon as he took office, Lincoln found out that the situation in Fort Sumter was even more serious than he had previously believed. A day after delivering his inaugural address, he was informed that Major Anderson and his men had only enough food and supplies to remain at the fort until about April 15. If the Union proved unable to resupply Anderson before then, he and his men would have to surrender the fort or face starvation. Moreover, Lincoln was told that on March 3, South Carolina military troops under the command of General Pierre Gustave Toutant Beauregard (1818–1893) had taken up positions all around the harbor, their cannons poised to fire upon Fort Sumter at any time.

After consulting with his cabinet to review his options, Lincoln decided that he would attempt to resupply Anderson's troops at Fort Sumter. He knew that any attempt to send food and other provisions to the fort was risky. The Union had attempted to transport supplies and reinforcements to the fort two months earlier via a ship called the *Star of the West,* only to be turned away by a hail of artillery fire from South Carolina cannons. Despite that earlier clash, though, Lincoln was unwilling to abandon the fort. He knew that if Federal control of Fort Sumter was relinquished, Northern morale would suffer, and Southern confidence in the Confederacy's ability to break away

President James Buchanan

James Buchanan was president of the United States from 1857 until 1861, when Abraham Lincoln took his place. Born in Pennsylvania, Buchanan established a thriving law practice before turning to politics. He spent ten years (1821–31) as a member of Pennsylvania's U.S. House delegation, then moved over to the Senate, where he represented his home state from 1834 to 1845. A Democrat, he left the Senate in 1845 to serve as secretary of state for President James K. Polk (1795–1849). During his four-year stint in that position, Buchanan helped prosecute the Mexican War (1846–48), which ultimately gave the United States huge expanses of new territory in the West.

After serving as minister to Great Britain in the administration of President Franklin Pierce from 1853 to 1856, Buchanan won the 1856 presidential election as the nominee of the Democratic Party. Soon after assuming office, however, he found that the slavery issue made it al-most impossible for his administration to get anything done. Indeed, he was assuming leadership of the country at a time when Northern and Southern positions on slavery and states' rights were hardening. As these two sides battled in the legislature and the nation's newspapers, the Buchanan administration's fumbling attempts to resolve these issues did little to bridge the widening gap between America's Northern and Southern regions.

Buchanan's personal views of slavery were mixed. On the one hand, he thought that slavery was morally wrong. But he also believed that the South's claims that slavery was not unconstitutional were correct, and that the region would never accept the abolishment of slavery. This conviction, combined with his knowledge that the Democratic Party owed much of its national power to support in the South, made Buchanan fairly sympathetic to Southern demands.

from the Union permanently would increase.

On March 29, 1861, Lincoln ordered the U.S. military to send ships bearing food and supplies to the surrounded outpost, but he declined to send reinforcements to help Anderson defend the fort. He believed that any attempt to increase Federal troop strength at Sumter might be interpreted as an aggressive action by the Confederate military and the remaining slave states in the Union, and that such a step would increase the likelihood of a violent clash between Anderson's troops and the forces under Beauregard's command.

James Buchanan. *(Courtesy of the Library of Congress.)*

After Lincoln won the November 1860 presidential election and Southern threats of secession exploded, Buchanan was faced with the task of holding the nation together until the Republican formally took office in March 1861. Buchanan refused to support one side or the other dur-

ing this period, for while Buchanan did not believe that states had the right to secede from the Union, he also did not believe that the Federal government had the right to force them to stay. During his last months of power, Buchanan adopted a cautious position designed to ensure that he would not preside over the beginning of a civil war.

In March 1861, Abraham Lincoln was sworn in as America's sixteenth president, and Buchanan left the White House, relieved that he had managed to get out before hostilities exploded between the nation's two angry sections. Within a few weeks of his departure, Buchanan's worst fears were realized, as a battle for control of Fort Sumter in South Carolina ignited the Civil War. For years, Buchanan, who died in 1868, was often viewed as a key reason why the Civil War occurred. In recent years, however, historians have judged Buchanan's policies more kindly.

Determined to avoid a bloody clash if possible, Lincoln notified South Carolina governor Francis Pickens (1805–1869) on April 8 of his plan to send ships carrying food and other supplies to Fort Sumter. Two days later, a small fleet of Union ships headed by Captain Gustavus Fox (1821–1883) set out

for the fort from New York to deliver the provisions.

Upon learning of the Union plan to resupply Fort Sumter, Confederate president Jefferson Davis called his cabinet together to discuss their options. The letter that Pickens had received from Lincoln made it clear

Abraham Lincoln. *(Painting by Douglas Volk. Courtesy of the Library of Congress.)*

fort will inaugurate a civil war greater than any the world has yet seen," warned Confederate secretary of state Robert Toombs (1810–1885). "You will wantonly strike a hornet's nest which extends from mountains to ocean, and legions now quiet will swarm out and sting us to death." But Davis and many other leaders believed that the Confederacy needed to take a strong stand. On April 10, Beauregard was ordered to take the fort by force if he could not convince Anderson to surrender willingly.

Southern forces attack Fort Sumter

Over the next few days, Beauregard tried to convince Anderson to surrender. But Anderson, who had been one of Beauregard's instructors at the U.S. Military Academy at West Point in New York, refused to give in. The Confederate assault on Fort Sumter was launched early in the morning of April 12, 1861. All day long, Confederate guns under Beauregard's command rained fire on the fort held by the rebel commander's former teacher. As the onslaught continued, pockets of flame and smoke erupted around the outpost, a sight that delighted the many Charleston citizens watching the battle unfold from their rooftops. Anderson and his men put up a brave defense in hopes of holding their foes off until help arrived, but rough seas and indecision slowed Fox's fleet, and they were never able to lend a hand. Finally, after enduring more than thirty-four hours of cannonfire, the Union troops

that Seward's secret assurances of an impending federal departure from the outpost could no longer be believed. Davis and his cabinet were thus left with two choices: permit Fox's fleet to carry out its mission to Fort Sumter, which would allow Anderson's troops to man the outpost for several more months; or attack the garrison before the supplies could be delivered and risk triggering an all-out war with the Union.

Some Confederate leaders cautioned against launching any attack on Fort Sumter. "The firing on that

The Confederate flag flies following the South's victory over the North at Fort Sumter on April 4, 1861. *(Courtesy of the National Archives and Records Administration.)*

ran out of ammunition. No longer able to defend the fort, Anderson was forced to surrender on April 13. The defeat saddened Anderson, although he took comfort in the knowledge that none of his men had been killed in the assault.

One day later, Anderson and his troops assembled to evacuate the fort as Fox's fleet watched helplessly from just outside the harbor. Beauregard had agreed to let the Union soldiers give the tattered American flag that they had defended a 100-gun salute before lowering it and leaving

the fort. Midway through the salute, however, one of the cannons exploded. Private Daniel Hough died in the explosion, and Private Edward Galloway died a few days later from injuries suffered in the accident. Hough and Galloway thus became the first casualties in a war that would ultimately claim more than 620,000 American lives.

Undecided states join the Confederacy

The battle for Fort Sumter marked the beginning of the Ameri-

Perspectives on the Battle for Fort Sumter

As the following newspaper accounts show, reaction to the assault on Major Robert Anderson's troops at Fort Sumter in Charleston, South Carolina, was far different in the North than it was in the South:

The perspective of the North, as editorialized in the *New York Times,* April 15, 1861—

> The reverberations from Charleston Harbor have brought about what months of logic would have been impotent to effect—the rapid condensation of public sentiment in the Free States. The North is now [united]. . . . In entering upon this struggle [against the South], the great community of Free States does so, prepared to bring to bear on the vindication [justification] of its national honor inexhaustible material resources. . . . As to

> moral force, it panoplies [armors] the Republic as with a wall of fire. She enters the contest with that triple arming which justice gives to a cause. The moral conscience of the world is on her side. . . . The [Lincoln] Administration is not brought face to face with a *Revolution.* This is not the attitude. It has to deal with a plot, a conspiracy. There will be no 'fraternal blood' shed, unless it be the blood of men who are willfully and persistently in the position of traitors. . . . That Treason should be claimed as a right—that anarchy [complete absence of government] should rule—it is this which thrills with indignant amazement. How profound has been the humiliation, how hot the indignation, are shown in the tumultuous surgings of passion that are now baptising with one common sentiment of constitutional unity and patriotic devotion every loyal American heart.

can Civil War. The Confederate attack on Union forces convinced Lincoln and his cabinet—which had previously been deeply divided over how to deal with the secessionist states—that such aggression could not go unpunished, and that the Confederate states could only be brought back into the Union through the use of force. Lincoln subsequently announced to the nation that "combinations too powerful to be suppressed" by peaceful efforts now controlled the Deep South, and he called on the remaining states of the Union to provide the Federal government with seventy-five thou-

sand soldiers in order to stop the secessionist rebellion.

Lincoln's April 15 announcement was immensely popular in the free states of the North. News of the Confederate attack on Fort Sumter had enraged Northerners, and thousands of volunteers eagerly rushed to join the Federal army. Reaction to Lincoln's call to arms was far different in the slave states that sat between the North and the states of the Confederacy, however. Although they had been unwilling to secede over the issue of slavery, these so-called "bor-

The view from the South, as described in *Charleston Mercury,* April 13, 1861—

The bombardment of Fort Sumter, so long and anxiously expected, has at length become a fact. . . . [At dawn] the circle of batteries with which the grim fortress of Fort Sumter is beleaguered opened fire. The outline of this great volcanic crater was illuminated with a line of twinkling lights; the clustering shells illuminated the sky above it; the [cannon] balls clattered thick as hail upon its sides; our citizens . . . rushed again to the points of observation; and so, at the break of day, amidst the bursting of bombs, and the roaring of ordnance [artillery], and before thousands of spectators, whose homes, and liberties, and lives were at stake, was enacted this first great scene in the opening drama of what . . . will be a most momentous military act. It may be a drama of but a single act. The madness which inspires it may depart with this single paroxysm [sudden outburst]. It is certain that the people of the North have rankling at their hearts no sense of wrong to be avenged; and exhibiting to those who expect power to reconstruct the shattered Union, its utter inadequacy to accomplish a single step in that direction, the Administration of the old Government may abandon at once and forever its vain and visionary hope of forcible control over the Confederate States. But it may not be so; they may persist still longer in assertions of their power, and if so, they will arouse an independent spirit in the South, which will exact a merciless and fearful retribution [payback].

der" states quickly decided to stand with their Southern neighbors once it became clear that war was imminent. On April 17, the state of Virginia announced that it was leaving the United States to join the Confederacy, and Arkansas, Tennessee, and North Carolina joined the Confederate cause a few weeks later (although much of eastern Tennessee remained loyal to the Union throughout the war). The Confederacy promptly made arrangements to transfer its capital from Montgomery, Alabama, to Richmond, Virginia, thus creating a situation in which the Union and Confederate capitals sat only one hundred miles from one another.

The defections of these states were a severe blow to Lincoln, who had hoped that they would ultimately fight to keep the Union intact. Conversely, the addition of these four states greatly strengthened the Confederacy. Each possessed large populations of white men who could be added to the still-forming Confederate Army. Southern strategists recognized that factories located in these states could be used to manufacture ammunition, clothing, and other supplies for its military. Finally, military leaders on both sides recognized that Virginia's decision to stand under the Confederate flag posed a great threat to the Union because the state was located right next to Washington, D.C., the Union's capital.

The Union fights to keep other border states

After losing Virginia, Arkansas, Tennessee, and North Carolina to the Confederacy, Lincoln turned his attention to four border slave states—Delaware, Maryland, Kentucky, and Missouri—that had not yet announced their support for North or South. Lincoln was certain that Delaware would remain loyal to the Union, but he knew that Confederate sympathies were strong in the other three states.

Determined to prevent any other states from joining the Confederacy, Lincoln took drastic measures in both Maryland and Missouri. Keeping Maryland in Union hands was particularly important because it was situated north of Washington, D.C. This meant that if the state joined the Confederacy, then the U.S. capital would be cut off from the rest of the Union and would almost certainly fall to the Confederate Army. With these considerations in mind, Lincoln acted swiftly.

Lincoln silences Maryland secessionists

First, Lincoln decided to clamp down on secessionist activities in Baltimore, a big city that had become a center of Confederate support. The extent of Baltimore's sympathy to the Confederate cause had become clear on April 19, when the 6th Massachusetts militia—a Union regiment under the command of Benjamin Butler (1818–1893) that was traveling to Washington, D.C.—came under attack in the city from a secessionist mob. By the time the clash ended, dozens of injured people and dead bodies littered the city's streets.

The Union eventually gained control of Baltimore and the rest of Maryland, but Lincoln was forced to establish martial law to do so. Martial law is a situation in which military forces take over the responsibility of administering and enforcing laws in a city or region from civilian lawmakers. Moreover, the president suspended a piece of the Constitution known as the writ of *habeas corpus* in Maryland in order to quiet anti-Union voices. The writ of habeas corpus was designed to protect Americans from being arrested and held in custody on unreasonable charges or without being charged with a crime. But Lincoln had decided that it would be very difficult to control Maryland if the state's secessionist movement was not neutralized.

Ignoring protests from a wide range of people, including U.S. Supreme Court chief justice Roger Taney (1777–1864), Lincoln took advantage of his suspension of habeas corpus to silence secessionists all around the state. Over the course of several weeks, Federal officials arrested the mayor and police chief of Baltimore, thirty-one state legislators, and a number of newspaper publishers and editors, and threw them all in jail. With his leading opponents out of the way, Lincoln then made sure that Maryland would remain in the Union camp. In the fall of 1861, Federal forces manipulated state elections so that pro-Union legislators assumed firm control.

The Union struggle to keep Missouri and Kentucky

In Missouri, Federal military units managed to establish some measure of control over most of the state through the use of martial law. But despite the sometimes ruthless measures employed by Union authorities to maintain control over the state, violent raids by Confederate supporters tormented Missouri throughout the war, and large numbers of Missouri natives served in the Confederate Army during the conflict.

In Kentucky—the birth state of both Abraham Lincoln and Jefferson Davis—the struggle for control of the state basically ended in a draw. After four months of official neutrality (showing no support for either side) in the conflict, separate Union and Confederate state governments were organized. Given this political deadlock, it is not surprising that both the rebel (Confederate) and Federal armies eventually included large numbers of Kentuckians.

The struggle in Kentucky seemed to symbolize the larger division that had taken place all across the United States. With each passing day, Kentuckians watched as long-time neighbors and friends marched off in opposite directions, perhaps to face one another again on some future battlefield. Even the grandsons of Henry Clay (1777–1852), the Kentucky senator who had crafted both the Missouri Compromise and the Compromise of 1850 in an effort to ward off civil war, were not immune to this sad phenomenon. As the American Civil War dragged on, three of Clay's grandsons would fight on behalf of the Union, while four others would march under the Confederate flag.

Europe's View of the War

As the military leaders of the North and the South pre-pared their armies for the coming war, the politicians of the Union and the Confederacy were also very busy. During the spring of 1861, President Abraham Lincoln (1809–1865) and Northern senators and representatives worked to provide the Union Army with all of the resources it would need for the upcoming conflict. Meanwhile, Confederate president Jefferson Davis (1808–1889) and other Southern leaders scrambled to establish a whole new government while also preparing their people for war. But the men who led the Union and Confederate governments also spent a great deal of time trying to figure out what the European reaction to a civil war might be.

Both sides knew that if a powerful country like England or France decided that the Confederacy's claim of independence was legitimate, the South's position would be greatly strengthened. Davis and other Southerners realized that English or French support for the Confederacy might force the Union to let the Southern states go or risk a disastrous trade war with Europe. A trade war is a situation in which two coun-

Words to Know

Blockade the act of surrounding a harbor with ships in order to prevent other vessels from entering or exiting the harbor; also the act of ships or other military forces surrounding and isolating a city, region, or country

Confederacy eleven Southern states that seceded from the United States in 1860 and 1861

Emancipation the act of freeing people from slavery or oppression

Federal national or central government; also refers to the North or Union, as opposed to the South or Confederacy

Union Northern states that remained loyal to the United States during the Civil War

diers to fight on the South's behalf. With these possibilities in mind, Southern diplomats launched a major effort to secure European allies, while representatives of the Union tried to convince England, France, and other nations to stay out of the dispute.

European concerns about the rebellion

England and France were, along with the United States, the most powerful countries in the world during the mid-nineteenth century. As a result, other countries watched with great interest to see if either of the two nations would help the Southern states in their bid to secede from the United States. But while the leaders of those two European powers did not always agree with the actions or policies of the United States, they were in no hurry to see the country torn in two by civil war.

At the time of the American Civil War, both France and England were ruled by monarchies, a system of government in which a single person holds complete power over everyone else in the country. Napoleon III (1808–1873) was the ruler of France, and Queen Victoria (1819–1901) sat on the throne in England. Both monarchies, supported by a small number of rich and powerful families and individuals, saw the South's decision to secede from the Union as a form of revolt against established governmental rule. This view of the conflict did not help the South, because the leaders of both France and Eng-

tries or regions use measures like price increases or trade laws to punish the other side for its position on one issue or another. Trade wars often have a negative economic impact on the citizens of both countries, so most governments try to avoid them at all costs.

Some Southern leaders also believed that formal recognition from France or England might even help them on the field of battle. They speculated that if England or France decided that their claim of independence was legitimate, the governments of one or both nations might send solland were always worried that such rebellions might erupt in their own nations and threaten their own systems of government. Some officials in France and England even feared that their own citizens would follow the South's example if its efforts to make a new government were successful.

Another factor that made it much more difficult for the South to obtain support from France or England was its reliance on slavery. The institution of slavery had been outlawed in England and all of its colonies in 1833, and France had taken the same action in 1844. Most people in Europe realized that the practice was a terrible and savage one that should be abolished wherever it existed. French and English leaders knew that any efforts to help the South would spark a great deal of anger and unrest in their own countries if citizens believed that such aid served to advance the practice of slavery.

The South hopes for support

Despite these considerations, however, the leaders of the Confederacy believed that other factors might convince France or England to support them. For example, in the months leading up to and immediately following the start of the war, President Lincoln and other Federal leaders continued to insist that they entered the war solely to restore the Union, not to eliminate slavery. Some Southern and European diplomats argued that since the North itself claimed that the war was not about slavery, any assistance provided to the Con-

People to Know

Jefferson Davis (1808-1889) president of the Confederate States of America, 1861-65

Abraham Lincoln (1809-1865) sixteenth president of the United States, 1861-65

Napoleon III (1808-1873) emperor of France, 1852-71

Queen Victoria (1819-1901) queen of Great Britain, 1837-1901

federacy by England or France would not necessarily be regarded as a defense of slavery.

Another factor that favored the South was Europe's interest in seeing the United States divide itself in two. Both England and France were used to getting their way in world affairs, but the leaders of both nations worried that the United States was becoming too powerful. For example, Napoleon III wanted to establish a French presence in Mexico, but he held back because of concerns about how the Americans might react. The French ruler knew that it would be easier for his country to assume power in Mexico, America's southern neighbor, if the military force of the United States was divided in two.

In addition, many members of the English and French aristocracy (privileged noblemen who wielded

French ruler Napoleon III.

clothing and other materials. The climate in those countries made it impossible for them to grow large quantities of cotton themselves. Southern legislators reasoned that if European mills began to experience severe shortages of cotton and other goods that they were used to getting from the South, French or British leaders might ask the North to call off the war and negotiate a treaty that would recognize the Confederacy. With this in mind, Southern leaders stopped shipments of cotton to Europe in hopes of pressuring England and France into supporting their bid for independence. But the strategy ended up backfiring, with severe consequences for the South.

South uses cotton as a weapon

On April 12, 1861, Confederate troops opened fire on the Union garrison at Fort Sumter in South Carolina, an action that marked the beginning of the American Civil War. Around this same time, the South suspended shipments of cotton to Europe in hopes of convincing Queen Victoria or Napoleon III to announce their support for the Confederacy.

But England, France, and most other countries believed that since the North enjoyed big advantages in weaponry and army size over the South, the war would be over in a few short months, with the Union victorious. Their political leaders did not want to anger Lincoln and other Northern leaders, so they decided to

great power and influence over their neighbors) recognized that the culture of the South was similar to their own, with a relatively small number of people serving as the region's primary decision makers. Moreover, the wealthy plantation owners in the American South cultivated an image of style and old-fashioned elegance that appealed to the ruling classes in England and France, who instinctively identified with the Southerners' desire to protect their way of life.

Finally, the leaders of the South knew that both England and France bought huge quantities of cotton from their plantations to make

Confederate Commerce Raiders

The Union's military superiority helped it maintain control over much of America's waters during the Civil War. President Abraham Lincoln was able to establish a largely effective blockade of the Confederate coastline with the Union's naval forces, and the North, using its greater manufacturing capacity, dramatically widened its advantage in fleet size during the war.

The South did not surrender the seas without a fight, however. By mid-1862, Confederate ships known as commerce raiders were prowling the North Atlantic in search of Union merchant vessels traveling along the Northern coastline or trading with Europe. These raiders seized millions of dollars in Union goods, and they destroyed or captured hundreds of vessels (the Confederate raider *Alabama* alone burned fifty-five American ships valued at more than $4.5 million). These rebel cruisers did not "alter the outcome of the war," wrote James M. McPherson in *Battle Cry of Freedom,* but "they diverted numerous Union navy ships from the blockade, drove insurance rates for American vessels to astronomical heights, forced these vessels to remain in port or convert to foreign registry [the raiders concentrated their attacks on ships flying the American flag], and helped topple the American

merchant-marine from its once-dominant position, which it never regained."

The best-known Confederate raiders were the *Florida* and the *Alabama.* Both of these vessels had been built in English shipyards and sold to the rebels (Confederates) by shipbuilders who managed to find loopholes in Great Britain's declaration of noninvolvement in the American conflict. The *Florida* destroyed thirty-eight American ships before the Union Navy captured it in October 1864. The *Alabama* was even more deadly to Northern ship commerce. The rebel cruiser, under the command of Captain Raphael Semmes (1809–1877), raided 294 ships, capturing or destroying 64 of them, before the U.S.S. *Kearsarge* sank it in a battle off the coast of France in June 1864.

After the Civil War was over, the United States demanded payment from Great Britain for the destructive activities of the British-built Confederate cruisers. At first, England refused to acknowledge the American claims. In 1872, though, an international court in Geneva, Switzerland, ordered England to pay the United States $15.5 million for damage caused by the *Alabama,* the *Florida,* and a third British-built raider called the *Shenandoah.*

stay on the sidelines. On May 13, 1861, Queen Victoria announced British neutrality (showing favoritism to neither side), although she noted that the Confederacy was free to purchase arms from England and other neutral nations. Napoleon III made a similar announcement of French neuto continue its strategy of withholding cotton from European markets.

This decision proved disastrous for the South for two major reasons. First, Confederate leaders had seriously overestimated demand for cotton in Europe. Cotton crops in the years immediately prior to the Civil War had been very good. These big harvests had enabled France, England, and other nations to store large surpluses (stockpiles) of cotton. Even after the South stopped sending cotton, the British and French did not experience shortages of cotton for more than a year. Second, the South could have traded cotton to Europe in exchange for the bullets, guns, artillery, medicine, and other materials that the Confederate Army so desperately needed. Instead, the Confederacy's decision to hoard its cotton deprived its army of a golden opportunity to improve its firepower.

John Slidell was one of two Confederate diplomats involved in the "Trent Affair." *(Courtesy of the Library of Congress.)*

trality on June 13. By taking positions of neutrality, both countries were telling the warring sides in America that they refused to take part in the conflict on behalf of either side. The announcements disappointed Jefferson Davis and other leaders of the Confederacy, but the South thought that France and England might change their positions if the cotton shortage became severe enough. After all, more than 150,000 millworkers in England alone would be left unemployed if the country ran out of cotton. As a result, the Confederate government decided

The South eventually realized that its decision to hold on to its cotton was a serious strategic error. In 1862, it belatedly attempted to resume its exports of the "white gold," as cotton was sometimes called, to Europe. By that time, however, the North had established an effective naval blockade around all of the South's major harbors. Union warships took up positions at all Southern ports, cutting off any boats that tried to pass through. Occasionally, Confederate or privately owned British ships known as blockade runners were able to slip past the Union ships, but this trickle of supplies did not come close to meeting the South's many needs. Even the most optimistic Southern politician had to admit that the new Confederate government had committed an enormous blunder. By holding on to its cotton during the first months of the war, when the Union blockade was still forming, the South actually made the blockade effective until the Union Navy was able to enforce it.

The "Trent Affair"

France and Britain maintained their neutral positions throughout the summer of 1861. But in October 1861, an incident on the high seas threatened to spark outright war between the Union and the British Crown. On October 11, a Confederate ship carrying two Southern diplomats, John Slidell (1793–1871) and James Murray Mason (1798–1871), slipped out of Charleston, South Carolina, on a very important mission. Slidell and Mason had been selected to go to France and England in order to ask personally for official recognition of the Confederacy.

Mindful of the Union naval blockade that intercepted vessels bound for Europe, the ship carrying the two diplomats instead raced for Cuba, an island country off the southern coast of Florida that lay outside the area of the blockade. Once they arrived at their destination, Slidell and Mason quickly jumped on the *Trent*, a British steamer scheduled to leave for England. Since the *Trent* was leaving from Cuba rather than a Southern harbor, the two Confederate representatives thought that they

James Murray Mason and one other Confederate official left for England from Cuba in what became known as the "Trent Affair." *(Photography by Mathew Brady. Courtesy of the Library of Congress.)*

would be able to make it to Europe without any trouble.

But shortly after taking off, the *Trent* was intercepted by the U.S.S. *San Jacinto*, a Union ship commanded by Captain Charles Wilkes (1798–1877) that had stopped in Cuba on its way back from a tour of duty along the African coast. While in Cuba, Wilkes had heard about the mission of the two Confederate diplomats, and he was determined to stop them. As soon as he caught up with the *Trent*, he ordered

Union captain Charles Wilkes was hailed a hero in the North and a villain in the South after his role in the "Trent Affair." *(Courtesy of the Library of Congress.)*

the *San Jacinto* to fire two cannon shots across the British steamer's bow as a warning to halt. The commander of the *Trent* recognized that if he did not stop his boat, the *San Jacinto*'s next volley of cannonballs might sink his vessel on purpose. The *Trent* stopped dead in the water, and Wilkes arrested Mason and Slidell over the angry objections of the *Trent*'s British captain.

A day later, Wilkes arrived in Boston with his two Confederate captives. The commander of the *San Jacin-* to received a hero's welcome from the people of the North, and the U.S. Congress formally thanked him for his "brave, adroit, and patriotic conduct in the arrest of the traitors." Over in England, however, Queen Victoria and her subjects were outraged by the incident. They could not believe that Wilkes had stopped a British ship and forcibly removed two passengers from its decks. British officials accurately charged that Wilkes' actions were a flagrant violation of international law. Lord Palmerston (1784–1865), England's foreign minister, warned that Britain would attack the United States if the two diplomats were not released. Furious editorials by English newspapers, meanwhile, called Wilkes a criminal and branded the United States as a country of cowards and bullies. The *Times of London,* for example, commented that "by Capt. Wilkes let the Yankee breed be judged. Swagger and ferocity, built on a foundation of vulgarity and cowardice, these are the characteristics, and these are the prominent marks by which his countrymen, generally speaking, are known all over the world."

Initially, both the United States and Britain refused to back down. But when England decided to send eleven thousand troops to Canada and place its naval fleet on battle alert, Lincoln realized that things were getting out of hand. Commenting that he was only prepared to fight "one war at a time," he told Secretary of State William Seward (1801–1872) and Charles Francis Adams (1807–1886), the Union's minister to Great Britain,

Keeping Great Britain on the Sidelines

Historians credit the diplomatic skills of Charles Francis Adams, America's minister to Great Britain from 1861 to 1868, as being a key factor in the Union's successful efforts to keep England neutral during the Civil War. Adams was raised in one of America's most distinguished political families. In fact, his grandfather, John Adams (1735–1826), had been America's second president, and his father, John Quincy Adams (1767–1848), had served as the nation's sixth president. Charles Francis Adams never managed to reach the White House himself, but he did carve out a significant reputation for himself during the mid-1800s as a distinguished statesman and leader in the efforts to keep slavery from expanding into America's western territories.

As a dedicated opponent of slavery, Adams was happy when Abraham Lincoln won the 1860 presidential election. One day after the Republican's victory, Adams wrote in his diary, "The great revolution has taken place. . . . The country has once and for all thrown off the domination of the Slaveholders." A short time later, Lincoln asked him to join his administration as ambassador to Great Britain, and Adams accepted.

Once the Civil War started and Confederate officials began to lobby England for help and recognition, Adams's job

Charles Francis Adams, the U.S. minister to Great Britain during most of the 1860s, helped keep Europe neutral during the Civil War. *(Courtesy of the Library of Congress.)*

became difficult. As he admitted in December 1862, "the great body of the aristocracy and the commercial classes [in Great Britain] are anxious to see the United States go to pieces." But Adams proved to be a very good choice. His quiet and reserved manner appealed to English diplomats like John Russell, Great Britain's ambassador to the United States, and his carefully crafted communications with British officials were vital in convincing them to stay on the sidelines for the duration of the war.

Queen Victoria of England. *(Courtesy of the Library of Congress.)*

Europe considers Confederate successes

Mason and Slidell were unable to convince Queen Victoria or Napoleon III to support the Confederacy publicly. But by the fall of 1862, a string of Confederate victories on the battlefield forced England to reconsider its assumption that the Union would be able to put down the Confederate rebellion. After all, by that time the South had not only turned back the Union's bid to capture the Confederate capital of Richmond, Virginia, but had also mounted offensives that threatened to overrun key Northern cities, including the Union capital of Washington, D.C. Moreover, the Confederacy had managed to acquire a number of British-built warships despite England's official position of neutrality, and these "commerce raiders," as they were called, had launched a number of successful and highly publicized attacks on Northern vessels on the open sea.

As British officials watched these surprising developments unfold, they began to talk openly about recognizing the Confederacy's claims of independence. British foreign secretary John Russell (1792–1878), for example, wrote in mid-September that "whether the Federal army is destroyed or not, it is clear that it is driven back to Washington, and has made no progress in subduing the insurgent [rebellious] States. . . . I agree . . . that the time is come for offering mediation to the United States Government, with a view to the recognition of the independence of the Confederates."

to smooth things over. Over the next few weeks, Adams and Seward skillfully defused the tense situation, and on January 1, 1862, Mason and Slidell were released to the British with an apology.

But in the final days of September 1862, two major events convinced England and France to keep quiet. First, Union forces stopped the advance of General Robert E. Lee (1807–1870) into Union territory at the bloody Battle of Antietam. Then, a few days later, President Lincoln issued his famous Emancipation Proclamation, in which he announced that all slaves held in rebelling Southern states would be free as of January 1, 1863. At the time that Lincoln made this announcement, the United States did not have the power to enforce this new law in the South, causing Confederate lawmakers to ridicule the president's action. But the Emancipation Proclamation was an important step because it gave the people of the North a new reason to continue the fight against the South. Lincoln's decision to cast the Union as a force dedicated to ideals of human freedom unified the people of the North, who subsequently showed a renewed willingness to support the war effort.

The Emancipation Proclamation also had a profound effect on Europe's view of the war. After Lincoln's announcement, people around the world began to see the conflict as one that revolved around slavery. Suddenly, the Union was viewed as a government dedicated to destroying the monstrous practice of slavery, while the Confederacy found itself cast in the role of slavery's villainous defender. As this new view of the war took hold, the leaders of England and France realized that their peoples would be very angry if any official recognition was given to the Confederate government. As a result, Queen Victoria and Napoleon III stayed out of the war. "The open recognition, the active aid, the material and financial support which the South needed so greatly was never forthcoming," wrote Bruce Catton in *The Civil War*. "North and South were left to fight it out between themselves."

1861: The War Begins

7

As both the Union and the Confederacy began to build their armies for the coming conflict, a strange mood of excitement rippled across the divided nation. People in the North and the South had been struggling against each other for so long that it seemed like a great relief when it became clear that the clash between the two sides was going to be settled once and for all. In addition, many Americans of the nineteenth century held a romantic and glamorous idea of war. Young men all across the divided nation saw the coming conflict as a chance to fight for a heroic cause.

This enthusiasm for the approaching war also could be traced to the confidence that both sides felt about their ability to win. Southerners believed that the North would field an army of weaklings with no real appetite for fighting. Northerners, meanwhile, viewed Southern soldiers as disorganized and undisciplined troops who would be easily overwhelmed by superior Union firepower. Only after the war began in earnest and the casualties began to mount did either side fully begin to appreciate their opponents' dedication to their cause.

Words to Know

Civil War conflict that took place from 1861 to 1865 between the Northern states (Union) and the Southern seceded states (Confederacy); also known in the South as War between the States and in the North as War of the Rebellion

Confederacy eleven Southern states that seceded from the United States in 1860 and 1861

Enlistment the act of joining a country's armed forces

Federal national or central government; also refers to the North or Union, as opposed to the South or Confederacy

Guerrillas small bands of soldiers or armed civilians who use raids and ambushes rather than direct attacks to harass enemy armies

Militia an army composed of ordinary citizens rather than professional soldiers

Rebel Confederate; often used as a name for Confederate soldiers

Regiment a military unit of organized troops; regiments usually consisted of one thousand men and were divided into ten companies of one hundred men each

Secession formal withdrawal of eleven Southern states from the Union in 1860–61

Union Northern states that remained loyal to the United States during the Civil War

Celebrations of the impending war

In the days and weeks following the Confederate seizure of Fort Sumter and the Union and Confederate calls to arms, citizens of both the North and South celebrated the coming war with amazing energy and enthusiasm. Towns and cities across the Union and Confederacy erupted in flag-waving celebrations and rallies. These gatherings further inflamed each side's passionate belief that their cause was a just one. One observer in the North wrote that "the whole population, men, women, and children, seem to be in the streets with Union favors and flags." Another Northerner commented that "I look with awe on the national movement here in New York and all through the Free States. After our late discords, it seems supernatural." Similar scenes unfolded across the South. A citizen of Richmond, Virginia, for example, wrote that the entire city "seemed to be perfectly frantic with delight. I never in all my life witnessed such excitement."

This frenzy of flag-waving, parties, and patriotic speeches made it easy for both sides to recruit soldiers. Thousands of young men in both the North and the South volunteered to become soldiers in the weeks after the war began. Most people did not expect the war to last very long, so some volunteers worried that it would be over before they got a chance to join the action. The large number of early volunteers completely overwhelmed both the Union and Confederate governments. Neither side had enough weapons, ammunition, food, or clothing to supply all their prospective recruits, and they had not yet set up programs to train them. "One of the greatest perplexities [complications] of the government," President Abraham Lincoln (1809–1865) admitted, "is to avoid receiving troops faster than it can provide for them." Gradually, though, both armies learned to adjust to the heavy flow of soldiers pouring in from big towns and small farming villages alike.

In both the North and the South, countless communities watched regiments of volunteer soldiers depart for war with a mixture of excitement and anxiety. As the soldiers left home, they were almost always sent off by cheering crowds of adoring friends and neighbors. "The war is making us all tenderly sentimental," admitted Southern diarist Mary Boykin Chesnut (1823–1886) in June 1861. "[So far the war is] all parade, fife, and fine feathers."

The North builds its army

In the spring of 1861, when the Civil War finally began, the Union did not have a significant military advantage over the Confederate states. The North controlled the country's regular army, but this force consisted of no more than 16,000 men. Most of these soldiers were stationed at frontier posts scattered all across the far western territories. The Union also controlled the Federal Navy, but this branch of the military was very small

People to Know

Pierre G. T. Beauregard (1818–1893) Confederate general who captured Fort Sumter in April 1861; also served at First Bull Run and Shiloh

Jefferson Davis (1808–1889) president of the Confederate States of America, 1861–65

Thomas "Stonewall" Jackson (1824–1863) Confederate lieutenant general who fought at First Bull Run, Second Bull Run, Antietam, Fredericksburg, and Chancellorsville; led 1862 Shenandoah Valley campaign

Joseph E. Johnston (1807–1891) Confederate general of the Army of Tennessee who fought at First Bull Run and Atlanta

Robert E. Lee (1807–1870) Confederate general of the Army of Northern Virginia; fought at Second Bull Run, Antietam, Gettysburg, Fredericksburg, and Chancellorsville; defended Richmond from Ulysses S. Grant's Army of the Potomac, 1864 to April 1865

Abraham Lincoln (1809–1865) sixteenth president of the United States, 1861–65

George McClellan (1826–1885) Union general who commanded the Army of the Potomac, August 1861 to November 1862; fought in Seven Days campaign and at Antietam; Democratic candidate for presidency, 1864

Winfield Scott (1786–1866) general-in-chief of U.S. Army, 1841–61; proposed so-called "Anaconda Plan" for Union in Civil War

Neighborhood Regiments

As the Civil War got underway, both the North and the South accepted as many volunteers as they could and began forming them into groups called regiments. Regiments usually consisted of one thousand men and were divided into ten companies of one hundred men each.

Most regiments were made up of recruits who came from the same state, and sometimes even the same city or county. Members of the same family often served in one regiment, as did members of certain ethnic groups, such as Germans and Italians. As a result, many soldiers felt strong loyalty toward their regiments. "Localities and ethnic groups retained a strong sense of identity with 'their' regiments," according to James M. McPherson in *Battle Cry of Freedom: The Civil War Era.* "This helped to boost morale on both the home and fighting fronts, but it could mean sudden calamity for family or neighborhood if a regiment suffered 50 percent or more casualties in a single battle, as many did."

A musical regiment. *(Courtesy of the National Archives and Records Administration.)*

as well. In early 1861 the navy owned only about ninety warships, and a majority of these vessels were falling apart or patrolling waters thousands of miles away.

As President Abraham Lincoln looked over his small military force, he knew that he would have to strengthen the Union's might dramatically in order to triumph over the Confederacy. He thus ordered a big increase in shipbuilding in the North. He also told Gideon Welles (1802–1878), his secretary of the navy, to purchase or lease merchant ships to be used in the coming war. This determined effort to boost the North's naval power paid off. By the end of 1861, more than 260 warships were patrolling the Atlantic Ocean and the Gulf of Mexico, and 100 more were under construction. The North's tremendous advantage in manufacturing capability eventually enabled it to establish firm control over the Southern coastline.

Lincoln also recognized that he would need to increase the size of the Union's small army through the enlistment of volunteer soldiers. His first appeal for volunteers—when he called for seventy-five thousand soldiers after the attack on Fort Sumter—asked for only ninety days of service. But within a few weeks, the Lincoln administration realized that the Union might need soldiers for longer than three months. Later calls for volunteers usually asked for three-year commitments, though a few states offered two-year terms.

The Union's efforts to increase the size of its army were spectacularly successful. The Federal army added thousands of soldiers from existing state militia units, and it incorporated thousands of other volunteers into its ranks as well. Each state acted as its own little war department, recruiting new volunteer regiments and appointing officers to lead them, before turning control over to the Federal government. The Union had a sizable advantage in its population of white men of military age. This advantage became evident during the final months of 1861. By early 1862, more than seven hundred thousand men had joined the Union Army, most of them for two- or three-year terms.

As it turned out, however, the Union Army's rapid growth made it very difficult for the North to provide adequate supplies to all its soldiers. The Northern states had a far greater capacity than their counterparts in the South to manufacture ammunition, ri-fles, boots, clothing, and other provisions for their soldiers. But in the early months of the war, supplies intended for Union regiments often did not reach their destination. Instead, the process of supplying Union soldiers became riddled with problems. For example, some Northern businesses charged excessively high prices or produced inferior goods. Complaints of War Department corruption and mismanagement became so great that Secretary of War Simon Cameron (1799–1889) submitted his resignation in January 1862. He was replaced by Edwin Stanton (1814–1869). Fortunately for the Union, many Northern governors and mayors made special efforts to provide food, clothing, and weapons for their soldiers until the Federal army could get itself organized.

The South struggles to provide for its soldiers

The military situation in the South was somewhat different. The Confederates did not really have a navy, since the North retained most Federal ships and personnel. And unlike the Union, which had a vast network of shipyards and factories that could be used to produce new ships and naval weaponry, the South had an extremely limited ability to manufacture warships. It had few qualified shipbuilders, few factories capable of producing the necessary parts, and little in the way of shipbuilding materials. Given these handicaps, the Confederacy never had a chance to create a navy capable of challenging the Federal navy. As the war dragged on, this inferiority on the high seas would emerge as a key factor in the South's eventual defeat.

The Confederate Army was in far better shape though, at least in terms of manpower. As each state had seceded, it had taken steps to make sure that its militia—which in some cases had faded away over the years because of disuse—was revived and made ready for battle. As a result of this preparation, the South already had a sixty-thousand–man army in place by the time Lincoln issued his April 15 call for seventy-five thousand volunteers. Many of these sixty thousand soldiers in the South were outfitted by their cities or states. Other Confederate soldiers brought their own personal horses and weapons with them when they joined their units.

But as the weeks passed and the Confederate government worked to further increase the size of its military, the South found itself confronted with a shortage of basic supplies for its soldiers. This shortage, which would become severe over the course of the Civil War, also could be traced to the South's farming-based economy. While the North developed a diverse blend of farming, shipping, manufacturing, mining, and lumbering industries during the first half of the nineteenth century, the South had stuck to its agricultural roots.

The South's decision to cling to its slave-based farming existence meant that it never developed the manufacturing capacity that would prove so vital in the North's final victory. The Confederacy lagged far be-hind the Union in its ability to produce everything from bullets to boots to railroad cars. In 1860, for example, Northern states produced 90 percent of the nation's boots and shoes. That same year, Northern factories account-ed for 93 percent of the nation's pig iron, 94 percent of its cloth, and 97 percent of its guns and rifles. More-over, the North was better equipped to distribute supplies, transport food, and move soldiers than the South be-cause it had a far more advanced sys-tem of railroads, shipping canals, and roadways in place.

The South's weakness in the areas of manufacturing and distribu-tion thus hampered its war prepara-tions from the beginning. These prob-lems became even worse after May 1861, when the Confederate Congress authorized the enlistment of four hundred thousand additional volun-teers for three-year terms. Nonethe-less, young Southern white men en-listed in the forming Confederate Army by the thousands, eager to de-fend the South from the bullying "Yankees" of the North.

North and South scramble for military leadership

At the same time that the two sides rushed to build their armies, they also scrambled to find military leaders to command those inexperienced troops. In the South, President Jeffer-son Davis (1808–1889)—himself a vet-eran of the Mexican War of the 1840s—and the Confederate War De-partment filled most command posi-

The 96th Pennsylvania Infantry Regiment during drill; the soliders' camp is in the background. *(Courtesy of the National Archives and Records Administration.)*

tions with people who had some military training. Some of these officers were Southern graduates of West Point (a prestigious military training school in New York) who had resigned from the regular army after secession (of 266 Southern-born West Point graduates who fought in the Civil War, only 39 served the Union). Others were cadets and graduates from such Southern military colleges as the Virginia Military Institute in Lexington and The Citadel in Charleston, South Carolina.

In the North, however, selection of commanding officers depended to a much greater degree on politi-

cal factors. Military units in both the North and the South selected many of their company and regimental officers through votes taken by the troops themselves. Southern units usually elected officers with previous war experience or military training. Northern troops, on the other hand, often elected men as officers simply because they were community leaders in the towns from which the company or regiment hailed.

Political concerns influenced the North's selection of officers for major commands, too. Some Northern governors filled the officer ranks of state regiments with their friends. In addition, many Northern politicians influenced Lincoln to have themselves or friends named as generals for the forming Federal army. The president often did so, because he thought that ignoring some of these requests might erode political support for his decision to pursue the war. Prominent Northern leaders like Benjamin F. Butler (1818–1893), Daniel E. Sickles (1825–1914), John McClernand (1812–1900), and Carl Schurz (1829–1906) thus received generalships despite their lack of military experience.

Confederate president Jefferson Davis also passed out generalships for political reasons, but he did so less frequently than did Lincoln. "For a variety of reasons, the South had a keener appreciation of military professionalism than the North did," Herman Hattaway wrote in *Shades of Blue and Gray*. "Early in the Civil War the South did a better job than the North in identifying its more able officers and getting them sooner into high levels of command. More to the point is that the South—from the outset—was much more welcoming to its military professionals and capitalized upon their talents."

Amateur officers and West Pointers

The performance of the so-called amateur officers of the Civil War—civilians who were made captains or generals despite a lack of military training or experience—varied tremendously. Some of these officers were completely incompetent, and their companies or regiments suffered

accordingly. The shortcomings of many of these officers were discovered fairly quickly though. Both the Union and the Confederacy eventually created military review boards to examine officers and remove those who were unable to do their jobs. After these boards were created, hundreds of officers were discharged or resigned voluntarily rather than face examination. The practice of electing officers on the basis of political considerations also faded away over time. It was replaced by systems that rewarded military experience and battlefield accomplishments.

Many civilian officers proved unable to handle their military duties, especially in the North. But a considerable number of them recognized the extraordinary responsibilities of their new positions. These men studied hard to gain a mastery of military strategy and an understanding of their many other duties. In fact, a number of officers pulled from civilian life performed admirably during the Civil War for both sides. In some cases they even outperformed graduates of West Point, The Citadel, and other military schools.

Still, students and graduates of West Point and the Southern military schools comprised the backbone of both sides' armies. For many of these men, the decision to fight for the North or the South was a difficult one, influenced by sometimes conflicting loyalties to family, state, and the Federal army. West Pointers who had become officers in the Federal army were

Lee's Decision to Join the South

During the spring of 1861, members of the Lincoln administration tried very hard to convince Robert E. Lee to join the Union side. After all, he had built an outstanding military reputation in the Mexican War (1846–48). That battlefield experience, along with his performance as a cavalry officer and superintendent of West Point Military Academy, made him one of the most highly prized officers in the entire army. U.S. general-in-chief Winfield Scott had such a high opinion of Lee that he urged President Abraham Lincoln to appoint him field commander of the Army of the Potomac. But after receiving the offer, Lee regretfully turned it down and announced his intention to join the Confederate Army.

Lee's decision to join the Confederate cause was a very difficult one for him. He had always opposed slavery. In fact, he once called it "a moral and political evil." In addition, he did not like the idea of seceding from the Union. But when his home state of Virginia joined the Confederacy, Lee felt that he had no choice but to stand with his fellow Virginians. "I cannot raise my hand against my birthplace, my home, my children," he explained.

Confederate general Robert E. Lee. *(Photograph by Mathew Brady. Courtesy of the National Archives and Records Administration.)*

Lee subsequently resigned from the U.S. Army and joined the forming Confederate military. But he did so with a heavy heart. "I should like, above all things, that our difficulties might be peaceably arranged," he wrote to a girl from the North who had asked for a picture of him. "Whatever may be the result of the contest [between North and South], I foresee that the country will have to pass through a terrible ordeal."

courted by both sides. For example, West Pointer Robert E. Lee (1807–1870)—who eventually assumed command of the entire Confederate Army—was offered field command of the Union Army in April 1861. But he reluctantly declined the offer, choosing instead to fight for his native Virginia on the side of the South.

As West Point cadets and graduates serving in the Federal military left to take their places in the Union and Confederate armies, a strange situation took shape. The opposing armies would be led by men who in many cases had served together under the same flag only weeks earlier. In fact, many of the veterans who took command positions with the North and the South assumed their duties with the grim knowledge that they would likely face former comrades—men with whom they had become friends during the Mexican War or during stints at frontier outposts—on some future field of battle.

The Northern strategy

By the early summer of 1861, tens of thousands of Union troops had gathered outside Washington, D.C., in preparation for the coming war. This army, which came to be known as the Army of the Potomac, was the Union's largest and most important. It was charged with defending the nation's capital from any Confederate offensive, and it was the biggest weapon in the Union's arsenal. But as the Federal army worked to outfit its troops and organize its chain of command, impatient Northerners began to wonder if the campaign to crush the Southern rebels would ever get underway. Ordinary citizens and newspaper editorial writers alike urged the Union Army to march southward as soon as possible. These people were convinced that the North's superiority in manpower, supplies, and military experience would result in a quick and decisive victory over the Confederacy. The influential *New York Tribune,* headed by Horace Greeley (1811–1872), emerged as a particularly vocal advocate of swift military action. It repeatedly urged the Union leadership to capture the Confederate capital of Richmond before July 20, when the Confederate Congress had scheduled its next session.

Some Northern leaders, however, expressed reluctance about conducting a full-scale invasion of the South. The reasons for this reluctance varied. Some Union leaders were concerned about the quality of the troops that the North was fielding. Others maintained that the Union could still win back the loyalty of the Southern people if it proceeded carefully with a limited offensive plan. Finally, some leaders, such as General-in-Chief Winfield Scott (1786–1866), believed that an immediate invasion was a strategically flawed idea.

Scott was the commander of all Union forces at the onset of the Civil War. He did not share the opinion of other Unionists who thought that the Southern rebellion would collapse after one or two Union victories. He thought that the war might last for quite a while. He also believed that a full-scale invasion—even if successful—would produce "fifteen devastated [slave states] not to be brought into harmony with their conquerors, but to be held for generations, by heavy garrisons."

Instead of an invasion plan, Scott devised a strategy in which the North would concentrate its efforts on blockading Southern ports and controlling the Mississippi Valley and the mighty river that ran through it. The general believed that such a plan would slowly squeeze the life out of the Confederacy by cutting off its main means of supplying itself with provisions. Once the South was rendered helpless, argued Scott, the Union could then invade and smash what was left of the Confederate Army into pieces.

Scott believed that his strategy was a sound one, but he worried that impatience in the North would make it unacceptable. "Our patriotic and loyal Union friends . . . will urge instant and vigorous action, regardless, I fear, of the consequences," he said. Scott was correct. As news of his plan leaked out, Northern newspapers and community leaders ridiculed it as unnecessarily cautious and slow. They called Scott's strategy the Anaconda Plan, after the large snake that kills its victims by slowly squeezing them to death. These critics remained convinced that one big Union victory in battle would bring a swift end to the secessionist rebellion. Lincoln quickly recognized that the Northern uproar for action would soon have to be addressed.

Ultimately, some of Scott's Anaconda Plan was implemented by the Union. The Union Navy established a blockade of Southern ports that eventually became extremely effective. In addition, his proposal to seize control of the Mississippi Valley became a key part of Union strategy by 1862. But the calls for invasion could not be ignored, and even those who recognized that the war had the poten-tial to be a long one realized that any Union victory would ultimately have to be grabbed on the field of battle. During the summer of 1861, Lincoln and his military advisors studied various plans to invade the South. These plans hinged on using the Union's superior troop sizes and materials to defeat the rebellious secessionists.

The Southern strategy

At the same time that the North was consumed with debate about various invasion plans, Jefferson Davis and the leaders of the Confederate military prepared to defend themselves from the coming assault. Southern leaders recognized that although the Union Army enjoyed significant advantages in men and materials, the Confederacy had some factors that weighed in its favor as well. In fact, many Southern political and military leaders believed that the North would never be able to accomplish its goal of restoring the Union.

One of the chief reasons for Southern confidence in an ultimate Confederate victory was the sheer size of their territory. At 750,000 square miles, the secessionist states occupied a region that was larger than all of western Europe. They knew that the Union would have to devote a huge amount of its troop strength and supplies just to maintain control of any significant segment of territory that it conquered.

Southern strategists believed that Confederate soldiers had a psychological advantage over their Northern counterparts as well. Whereas Northerners would be fighting on unfamiliar terrain for the abstract notion of preserving the Union, Southerners would be defending their beloved land, homes, and families from Northern aggression. Moreover, most Southerners were certain that they could outfight their Northern opponents. After all, Southerners were raised in a primarily rural culture that placed a high value on such skills as hunting and horsemanship. They viewed the gathering Union Army as a collection of meek store clerks and inexperienced city dwellers.

Ironically, the Southern soldiers' confidence in their superiority to the Northern soldiers made it difficult for Jefferson Davis to adopt the sort of strategy that he wanted. Davis recognized that the Confederacy would continue to exist if the people of the North lost their desire to fight. The Confederate States of America did not have to *win* the war against the North; they simply had to avoid *losing* the war. Davis and some other Confederate leaders thus favored a defensive strategy. They planned to use strategic retreats, counterattacks, and raids rather than all-out assaults in an effort to exhaust and demoralize the Northern invaders. If the war dragged on long enough, Southern tacticians (war strategists) believed that disillusioned Northerners might decide that the war was not worth it and leave the Confederacy alone.

The temperament of the Southern people, however, made it difficult for Davis to fight an exclu-

sively defensive war. Taking their cue from popular sentiment, Southern newspapers cried out for an advance into the North, certain that Confederate soldiers could whip far larger numbers of Yankees. "The idea of waiting for blows, instead of inflicting them, is altogether unsuited to the genius of our people," exclaimed one newspaper editorial. This confidence, coupled with several significant Confederate victories, eventually spurred the South to undertake a number of major offensives into Union territory.

Lincoln makes a new state out of western Virginia

The first meaningful fighting of the Civil War took place in July 1861 in western Virginia, a region that remained sympathetic to the Union despite Virginia's decision to secede. This mountainous area's culture and economy were more closely linked to the neighboring free states of Ohio and Pennsylvania than to the slave economy of Virginia's more heavily populated eastern counties. In addition, western Virginia's white citizens, who owned few slaves, had long been resentful of eastern Virginia's influence over the state's government and economy. "Western Virginia has suffered more from . . . her eastern brethren than ever the Cotton States all put together have suffered from the North," claimed one regional newspaper during the winter of 1860–61.

By June 1861, Union loyalists in western Virginia were calling for the establishment of a new state—initially called "Kanawha"—that would separate from Virginia and join the Union. These loyalists then elected pro-Union senators and administrators to represent them in Washington, D.C., and at home. But the effort to establish a new state out of western Virginia did not really pick up any momentum until Union generals George McClellan (1826–1885) and William S. Rosecrans (1819–1898) led a mid-July assault against a small Confederate force stationed deep in the region's hills and valleys. The successful offensive chased most Confederate troops out of western Virginia, and cleared the way for Unionists in the region to move ahead with their plans for establishing their own state.

Confederate forces led by General Robert E. Lee attempted to regain control of the region, but Union troops forced them back. Afterward, the white citizens of western Virginia held an October 24 referendum to vote on leaving Virginia and forming a new Union state. The voters approved the measure over the objections of pro-Confederate communities within the region. The vote established western Virginia as a pro-Union region from that point forward, although rebel guerrillas harassed Federal troops stationed in the area throughout the war.

On June 20, 1863—two years after the region passed its referendum—West Virginia joined the Union. Interestingly, West Virginia joined the Union as a slave state (less than five percent of its population were slaves). But West Virginia's politi-cal leaders recognized that Lincoln and other Republicans would never welcome the region as a new state unless it expressed its intention to eventually do away with slavery. As a result, West Virginia's constitution called for the freeing of all slaves born after July 4, 1863, and the freeing of all other slaves on their twenty-fifth birthdays.

The Union Army moves south

Northerners were tremendously encouraged by the early Union victories in western Virginia. Northern newspapers characterized the clashes as major battles. Calls for a major advance into Confederate territory thus grew even louder among impatient Northern newspaper publishers and political leaders, and Lincoln called his staff together to discuss his options.

The Lincoln administration ultimately decided to launch a major attack on a large Confederate encampment at Manassas (pronounced muh-NA-suss) Junction, Virginia. Located less than thirty miles from Washington, D.C., this rebel force was seen as a significant threat to the Federal capital. In addition, the Confederate troops gathered at Manassas blocked the Union's path to the rebel capital of Richmond, now viewed as the very heart of the Confederacy.

Some of Lincoln's counselors warned against launching a major offensive so quickly. General Scott, in particular, believed that the Union troops needed several more months of

Joseph Johnston, the Confederate general of the Army of the Tennessee. *(Courtesy of the Library of Congress.)*

training before they would be ready for combat. But Lincoln did not accept this argument, pointing out that Confederate troops also were inexperienced. Instead, Lincoln approved the plan. He thought that a victory at Manassas would satisfy Northern calls for action, ultimately leading to the capture of Richmond and an early end to the war.

On July 16, 1861, thirty-five thousand Federal troops under the command of Brigadier General Irvin McDowell (1818–1885) set out from Washington, D.C., to join forces in Virginia with a fifteen thousand–man army led by Major General Robert Patterson (1792–1881). (The aged Patterson was a distinguished veteran, having fought in the War of 1812). Awaiting the Union forces were two Confederate armies. One of these armies was an eleven thousand–troop force commanded by General Joseph E. Johnston (1807–1891). This army was camped at Harpers Ferry, Virginia (now in West Virginia), in the nearby Shenandoah Valley. The other rebel army, led by Brigadier General Pierre G. T. Beauregard (1818–1893), who had captured Fort Sumter earlier in the year, consisted of twenty thousand men stationed around Bull Run, a river that ran past Manassas.

The Union offensive called for Patterson's troops to keep Johnston's rebel forces busy. McDowell would then use his advantage in troop size to push Beauregard out of Manassas. But a Confederate spy network headed by Rose O'Neal Greenhow (c. 1815–1864) kept Beauregard and Johnston informed of the Union plan, and they devised a strategy to defeat McDowell.

The First Battle of Bull Run

"There is nothing in American military history quite like the story of Bull Run," wrote Bruce Catton in *The Civil War*. "It was the momentous fight of the amateurs, the battle where everything went wrong, the great day of awakening for the whole nation, North and South together. It marked the end of the ninety-day militia, and it also ended the rosy time in which men

Soldiers inspect the ruins of a house following the First Battle of Bull Run. *(Photograph by George N. Barnard. Courtesy of the Library of Congress.)*

could dream that the war would be short, glorious, and bloodless. After Bull Run the nation got down to business."

The First Battle of Bull Run (also sometimes known as the First Battle of Manassas) began on the morning of July 21, 1861, when the Union's McDowell launched his assault on Beauregard's Confederate outfit at Manassas. Initially, McDowell's troops seemed to have the upper hand, even though misunderstood orders and undisciplined troops bogged down the Northern attack. But Beauregard's troops were equally disorga-

nized, and the Southern hero of Fort Sumter watched in dismay as his planned counterattack crumbled in confusion.

As the clash continued, the scene on the smoky battlefield became progressively more confused. One major reason for this confusion was the bewildering array of uniforms that each side wore. Some Union troops were outfitted in blue uniforms, but others wore gray or other colors. Similarly, a number of the Confederate units wore gray, but others were garbed in blue. This situation made it very difficult for soldiers to determine the identity of other soldiers. On a number of occasions, soldiers fired on friendly troops by mistake or withheld fire on enemy troops in the mistaken belief that they were allies. (Such mistakes eventually convinced the Union to outfit all of its soldiers in blue and the Confederacy to use gray as its uniform color.)

McDowell pressed his numerical advantage over Beauregard through much of the afternoon. At one point, Union troops nearly broke the Confederate defenses at a place called Henry House Hill. But during an extended period of fierce fighting, a brigade commander from Virginia named Thomas J. Jackson (1824–1863) led a successful effort to hold the position. Jackson's determined stand at Henry House Hill earned him the nickname "Stonewall." Jackson went on to become one of the Confederacy's most legendary figures.

McDowell continued to push on against the outnumbered Confederate enemy. Before he could grind out a victory, however, the Confederate defenses were boosted by the arrival of thousands of Johnston's troops via the Manassas Gap Railroad line. McDowell did not know it, but Johnston had completely outmaneuvered Patterson over the previous three days. Using Confederate calvary personnel led by Colonel Jeb Stuart (1833–1864), Johnston fooled his Union counterpart into thinking that rebel troops were about to launch an attack on the Union position. Patterson promptly withdrew his troops to prepare his defense. Instead of attacking, however, Johnston snuck away and loaded his men on railroad cars to go help Beauregard at Manassas. The addition of Johnston's troops saved the day for Beauregard's forces. Their combined firepower forced McDowell to break off his attack, and a Confederate counterattack sent the Union Army stumbling in retreat.

The South spoils the North's grand picnic

At first the Union retreat was conducted in somewhat orderly fashion, despite the soldiers' lack of experience. But midway through the retreat, Northern soldiers, wagon trains, and artillery units ran into a panicky swarm of Washington civilians who had gathered on the hills east of Bull Run to watch the battle. Supremely confident that McDowell's Union forces would crush the rebel army, these spectators held a massive picnic as the battle roared in the distance. But when the Union forces began their retreat, hundreds of suddenly frightened Washingtonians rushed to return home, clogging the main road with carriages and wagons. The scene quickly dissolved into chaos, as civilians and soldiers alike dashed for the safety of the capital, discarding picnic baskets and rifles along the way.

Southern confidence and Northern anger

The Confederate victory at Bull Run thrilled people throughout the

How the Armies Decided on Their Uniform Colors

During the first months of the war, the Union and Confederate armies sometimes had a very difficult time identifying battlefield military units. This confusion stemmed from the fact that army units on both sides initially wore uniforms with a wide range of colors.

When the North and the South first formed their armies, they combined state militia units that were already in existence. Many of these state militia units wore uniforms featuring colors that were not used by other militias. In the South, for instance, Confederate military officers discovered that some soldiers wore yellow uniforms, while others wore blue or green or red clothing. Northern officers had the same problem. Some of their regiments showed up for duty wearing gray, blue, or red shirts and pants, while others arrived in extremely colorful uniforms patterned after those used by French soldiers stationed in Africa. These uniforms—which included red pants, blue belts, and lacy shirts—were also used by some Confederate regiments. This similarity in uniforms made it even more difficult for soldiers to determine whether another soldier on the battlefield was a friend or an enemy.

At first, both sides tried to get along with the different uniforms. But both armies changed their minds after it became clear that the different uniform colors were causing widespread confusion on the battlefield. On some occasions, soldiers accidentally shot members of their own army. Other times, they mistakenly identified enemy soldiers as friends, only to come under deadly attack.

By the fall of 1861, both sides realized that they needed to decide on a single uniform color for their troops. The Confederacy selected gray as its official uniform color, and the Union made blue its official uniform color. By the summer of 1862, nearly all soldiers on both sides of the war were garbed in their army's colors.

South, although the battlefield losses endured by the rebels (almost two thousand killed or wounded) muted the celebration somewhat. One congressman called the First Battle of Bull Run "one of the decisive battles of the world" and argued that it "has secured our independence." Southern newspapers mocked the Union Army and confidently predicted that the North would quickly abandon its attempts to restore the shattered United States.

In the North, meanwhile, the defeat shocked the population out of its belief that the rebellion could be snuffed out quickly. Confidence was replaced by anger and shame at the whipping that the Union had endured in the war's first major battle. The U.S.

Confederate fortifications at the Battle of Manassas. *(Photograph by George N. Barnard. Courtesy of the Library of Congress.)*

Congress promptly approved Lincoln's call for five hundred thousand volunteers to serve three-year military terms, and thousands of white men rushed to serve. The disaster at Manassas also resulted in the removal of McDowell as commander of the Army of the Potomac. He was replaced by General McClellan, the star of the Union campaign in western Virginia. A few months later—on November 1, 1861—McClellan was promoted to commander of all Union troops, taking over for the elderly Winfield Scott. Finally, the defeat convinced Lincoln to take a more active role in the Union's military planning and strategy.

1862: Near Victory for the Confederacy

The second year of the Civil War started quietly, as the North concentrated on training and organizing its inexperienced troops and the South elected to conserve its strength for the coming spring. Once the winter of 1861–62 was over, though, the divided nation erupted in violence from Virginia to the banks of the Mississippi River.

At first, it appeared that the war was turning the Union's way. Northern troops tallied a number of significant victories in the western states during the spring of 1862, including the captures of Nashville and New Orleans. But within a few months, the war's momentum changed dramatically. In fact, Confederate general Robert E. Lee (1807–1870) brought the rebels to the brink of total victory. Only a desperate Union stand at Antietam in Maryland saved the North from losing all hope of regaining the secessionist states.

The calm before the storm

Both the Federal and the Confederate armies used the winter of 1861–62 to organize, outfit, and train their troops. The North was particularly in need of this break. Its confidence

Words to Know

Abolitionists people who worked to end slavery

Blockade the act of surrounding a harbor with ships in order to prevent other vessels from entering or exiting the harbor; the word blockade is also sometimes used when ships or other military forces surround and isolate a city, region, or country

Civil War conflict that took place from 1861 to 1865 between the Northern states (Union) and the Southern seceded states (Confederacy); also known in the South as the War between the States and in the North as the War of the Rebellion

Confederacy eleven Southern states that seceded from the United States in 1860 and 1861

Conscription forced enrollment of able-bodied men into a nation's armed forces; also known as a draft

Emancipation the act of freeing people from slavery or oppression

Enlistment the act of joining a country's armed forces

Federal national or central government; also refers to the North or Union, as opposed to the South or Confederacy

Offensive an attack or aggressive action

Rebel Confederate; often used as a name for a Confederate soldier

Regiment a military unit of organized troops; regiments usually consisted of one thousand men and were divided into ten companies of one hundred men each

Union Northern states that remained loyal to the United States during the Civil War

---

had been shaken by the disastrous defeat at Bull Run, and it now realized that the superior size of its army would not mean anything unless its troops were adequately organized and trained.

General George McClellan (1826–1885) proved to be an excellent leader in this regard. Supremely self-confident and a superb administrator, he instituted training drills and upgraded all aspects of operation of the Army of the Potomac, from supply distribution systems to camp layout.

As general-in-chief over all Union forces, McClellan also worked to improve communications between himself and those Federal armies that he did not personally command, such as the Union forces operating in the western states of Kentucky and Tennessee. (During the Civil War, references to battles and other events in "the West" generally referred to the region of America lying between the Appalachian Mountains to the east and the Mississippi River on the west.) McClellan's tireless work during the fall

People to Know

Pierre G. T. Beauregard (1818–1893) Confederate general who captured Fort Sumter in April 1861; also served at First Bull Run and Shiloh

Ambrose E. Burnside (1824–1881) Union general who commanded the Army of the Potomac at Fredericksburg; also fought at First Bull Run, Antietam, and in Ulysses S. Grant's Wilderness campaign

Jefferson Davis (1808–1889) president of the Confederate States of America, 1861–65

David G. Farragut (1801–1870) Union admiral who led naval victories at New Orleans and Mobile Bay

Ulysses S. Grant (1822–1885) Union general who commanded all Federal troops, 1864–65; led Union armies at Shiloh, Vicksburg, Chattanooga, and Petersburg; eighteenth president of the United States, 1869–77

Henry W. Halleck (1815–1872) general-in-chief of Union armies, July 1862–March 1864; Abraham Lincoln's chief of staff, March 1864–April 1865

Thomas "Stonewall" Jackson (1824–1863) Confederate lieutenant general who fought at First Bull Run, Second Bull Run, Antietam, Fredericksburg, and Chancellorsville; led 1862 Shenandoah Valley campaign

Albert S. Johnston (1803–1862) Confederate general of the Army of Mississippi

Joseph E. Johnston (1807–1891) Confederate general of the Army of Tennessee who fought at First Bull Run and Atlanta

Robert E. Lee (1807–1870) Confederate general of the Army of Northern Virginia; fought at Second Bull Run, Antietam, Gettysburg, Fredericksburg, and Chancellorsville; defended Richmond from Ulysses S. Grant's Army of the Potomac, 1864 to April 1865

Abraham Lincoln (1809–1865) sixteenth president of the United States, 1861–65

George McClellan (1826–1885) Union general who commanded the Army of the Potomac, August 1861 to November 1862; fought in the Seven Days campaign and at Antietam; Democratic candidate for presidency, 1864

John Pope (1822–1892) Union general of the Army of the Mississippi and the Army of Virginia, 1862; fought at Bull Run

of 1861 and the winter of 1861–62 had a dramatic impact on the Army of the Potomac. Troop discipline and ability improved greatly, and many Union soldiers became deeply devoted to their young commander.

The South, meanwhile, spent the winter of 1861–62 preparing their defenses for the Union offensive that they knew was coming. Confederate leaders worked hard to find food, clothing, and weapons for their soldiers. They also spread out additional regiments wherever they thought that the South was most vulnerable (open to attack).

Grant leads Union victories in the West

The first major battles of 1862 took place in the West, where Union troops led by Major General Henry W. Halleck (1815–1872) and Brigadier General Don Carlos Buell (1819–1898) faced Confederate forces commanded by General Albert S. Johnston (1803–1862). In February 1862, both sides concentrated their attention on western Kentucky. There, two major rivers offered access deep into Confederate territory. These rivers—the Cumberland and the Tennessee—were protected by two Confederate forts, but Halleck was determined to seize control of the waterways. As Buell engaged some of Johnston's Confederate troops in central Kentucky, Halleck ordered one of his commanders, a little-known soldier named Ulysses S. Grant (1822–1885), to launch an assault on the two rebel forts.

Leading fifteen thousand infantrymen and a fleet of ironclad gunboats under the direction of Commodore A. H. Foote (1806–1863), Grant quickly overwhelmed Fort Henry, the Confederate fortress that guarded the Tennessee River. After capturing Fort Henry on February 6, Grant turned his attention to Fort Donelson, the rebel stronghold that stood watch over the Cumberland River. Grant launched his initial assault on February 12, but conquering Fort Donelson proved to be a difficult task. Protected by a garrison (armed force) of fifteen thousand soldiers equipped with cannons, the Confederate fort put up a hardy fight. By February 16, though, it was clear that the fort was doomed to fall, and Grant demanded an "unconditional and immediate surrender." The beaten Confederate garrison complied, surrendering control of the fort to the Federal troops.

Grant's exploits at Fort Henry and Fort Donelson made him a hero in the North, and he was quickly promoted to the position of major general. The conquest of the two forts also gave the Union control over two major Southern rivers. Halleck wasted little time in taking advantage of this situation. His Union forces immediately made their way down the Cumberland, and on February 24 they captured Nashville, the Confederate state capital of Tennessee.

The Battle of Shiloh

Grant's dramatic victories and the capture of Nashville stunned the

South. Halleck continued to press his advantage, instructing Grant to pursue Johnston's battered rebel troops. Johnston was forced to retreat all the way to the northern Mississippi town of Corinth. Once he arrived there, however, he combined his army with Confederate troops under the command of Pierre G. T. Beauregard (1818–1893). The addition of Beauregard's men gave Johnston a total of approximately forty-four thousand rebel soldiers under his command. Grant, meanwhile, stopped his advance about twenty miles north of Corinth, near a small country church called Shiloh in Tennessee.

Grant's army of forty-five thousand troops stopped at Shiloh to wait for an additional twenty-five thousand soldiers that Buell was bringing from Nashville. When he had all seventy thousand Union soldiers at his disposal, Grant intended to crush Johnston's army once and for all. But as Grant waited for his reinforcements to arrive, he made a serious strategic error. Confident that Johnston's exhausted army would not dare to attack him, Grant never bothered to prepare for such a possibility.

Johnston, meanwhile, decided that the only way he might beat Grant was if he launched a surprise attack before Buell arrived with his additional Union troops. On April 3, Johnston's Confederate troops marched out of Corinth in the direction of Grant's camp. Three days later, on the morning of April 6, a wave of gray-clad Confederate troops charged out of the woods surrounding Shiloh just as Grant's soldiers were settling down to enjoy their morning coffee. The surprise attack delivered brutal punishment to the unprepared Yankee troops, who fell by the hundreds. But Grant rallied his men. In the furious battle that followed, Johnston was killed. When Beauregard learned of Johnston's death, he immediately assumed command of the Southern troops.

Both armies withdrew from the field of battle at nightfall to rest for the next day. During the night, though, Grant received much-needed assistance in the way of troops from Buell's army. Grant ordered a full-scale Union attack the following morning, and the bloody battle resumed. Beauregard's Confederate troops fought valiantly. But as the day wore on, Grant's advantage in firepower and troop size became increasingly clear. Beauregard finally called for a retreat in order to avoid defeat, and the battered remains of the rebel force limped back to Corinth. Grant made little effort to pursue his foe, for his troops were similarly bruised and exhausted.

When news of the Battle of Shiloh reached the rest of the country, all visions of the war as a glorious and glamorous conflict were shattered. Approximately thirteen thousand Federal soldiers had been killed or wounded in the battle, while the South had lost another ten thousand men. This horrendous toll cast the war in a grim new light and made everyone wonder just how bad the war might yet become.

The *Monitor* and the *Virginia*

The most famous naval battle of the Civil War took place in March 1862, when the U.S.S. *Monitor* fought the C.S.S. *Virginia* to a draw. The *Virginia* was the pride of the Confederate Navy. The vessel had formerly been a Union ship known as the *Merrimac,* but the South had captured it and made major changes in its design. The Confederate Navy added sheets of iron armor to its sides and added iron to its bow (front) so that it could punch big holes in the Union's wooden ships.

On March 8, 1862, the *Virginia* went into battle for the first time. The Confederate government wanted to break the Union's naval blockade surrounding the harbor at Hampton Roads, Virginia. Confederate officials hoped that the *Virginia* could wreck the blockade—a gathering of warships designed to prevent other vessels from entering or leaving a harbor—by destroying the Union ships in the area. At first, it looked like the rebel plan might

work. The *Virginia* sank one Union warship by ramming it, then crippled another one with cannon fire. At the same time, the Union ships were unable to do any damage to the *Virginia* because their shells just bounced off the vessel's iron armor. To happy Confederate sailors, it seemed as if the *Virginia* might be able to whip the whole Union Navy.

News of the *Virginia*'s performance deeply alarmed Secretary of War Edwin Stanton and other members of the Lincoln administration. Luckily for the Union, however, its navy had recently built a ship that could challenge the *Virginia*. By the evening of March 8, a Union ship called the *Monitor* was steaming toward Hampton Roads to fight the *Virginia.* The *Monitor* was equipped with iron armor, too, and its top featured two big guns that could revolve in any direction.

The two ships joined in combat on the morning of March 9. The vessels ham-

Preparation for the attack on New Orleans

The military situation in the West became even more desperate for the South in mid-April, as Federal forces targeted the city of New Orleans for conquest. Located in southern Louisiana near where the Mississippi River flows into the Gulf of Mexico,

New Orleans was a very important Confederate city. It was the largest city in the South, and its port was used by many Confederate ships looking to obtain supplies from Europe.

By the spring of 1862, the Union had used its navy to take control of many Southern ports along the Atlantic coast. As the South's ability to

The deck and the turret of the U.S.S. *Monitor*. *(Photograph by James F. Gibson. Courtesy of the Library of Congress.)*

mered away at each other for two solid hours, using big guns and ramming maneuvers in a desperate battle for survival. Neither ship could sink the other, though, and the two vessels finally turned away from each other in exhaustion.

Over the next few months, the two ironclads remained in the same area, but never fought each other again. The *Virginia* took up a position outside of the James River in Virginia, where it helped protect other rebel ships from Union attacks. In May 1862, however, Union forces captured the ship's home harbor in Norfolk, Virginia. The crew of the *Virginia* then blew up the ship rather than allow it to be seized by the North. The *Monitor,* meanwhile, sank in a storm off Cape Hatteras in North Carolina on New Year's Eve, 1862.

Neither ship had a long life. But their clash in March 1862 convinced naval experts around the world that the era of the wooden warship was over. It also persuaded the North to use its vast factories and shipyards in the production of additional ironclad ships. As these vessels were put into service, the Union was able to further strengthen its control of the seas.

use these ports was reduced, New Orleans' strategic importance became even greater. Northern military leaders knew that if they could capture the city, the Confederacy's ability to trade with Europe for badly needed weapons and supplies would be limited to occasional "blockade runners"—ships that tried to sneak past the Union blockade.

After studying New Orleans' defenses, Union naval leaders decided to appoint Admiral David G. Farragut (1801–1870) as commander of the attack. A veteran of the U.S. Navy who had sailed the open seas since he was nine years old, Farragut was a tough and crafty officer. He knew that taking New Orleans would be difficult. It was guarded by a flotilla (small fleet) of ships and two big Confederate fortresses, Fort Jackson and Fort St. Philip. But Farragut received command of a giant fleet of warships that included nineteen schooners armed with mortar cannons.

Farragut devises a bold plan

Farragut's fleet sailed into the Gulf of Mexico and reached New Orleans' defenses in mid-April. The Union commander promptly ordered a heavy bombardment of the two Confederate forts. The Union fleet and the Confederate forts fired shells back and forth at one another for the next several days in an attempt to pound the other into submission. After a week or so, Farragut decided that his mortar attack was not working. He then devised a daring plan to sail past the forts under cover of darkness and proceed on to New Orleans.

Farragut launched his plan early in the morning of April 24, even though many of his officers advised him not to try it. As his fleet moved up the river, it was met by a tremendous hail of shellfire from the forts. The Confederate flotilla attacked as well, firing its cannons and sending flaming rafts down the river to smash into Farragut's ships. Farragut's warships dodged most of the rafts, however, and launched a furious counterattack on the Confederate defenses. At its most intense, the battle lit up the Mississippi sky in what historian James M. McPherson called "the greatest fireworks display in American history."

Farragut's bold strategy succeeded. His fleet destroyed the smaller Confederate flotilla and pushed past the forts, losing only four ships in the process. He sailed on to New Orleans, which was taken without a fight. Fifteen thousand Union troops under the command of Benjamin Butler (1818–1893) immediately took complete control of the city. The soldiers of Fort St. Philip and Fort Jackson, meanwhile, realized that the Union conquest of New Orleans meant that the North controlled the entire lower Mississippi River. With no means of obtaining food and other supplies, both forts quickly surrendered.

Farragut's victory shocked and depressed Confederate president Jefferson Davis (1808–1889) and other Confederate leaders. They knew that the capture of New Orleans—coupled with a series of Union victories in Arkansas, Missouri, and Tennessee in the weeks immediately following the Battle of Shiloh—placed the North in a commanding position in the West.

The Confederacy passes the Conscription Act

Events in the eastern United States unfolded more slowly. In Richmond, President Davis spent the first months of 1862 battling with the Confederate Congress over the best way to increase the size of the Confederate Army. At the outset of the war, the South had enlisted its troops for one-year terms. This meant that by the spring of 1862, when the South

President Abraham Lincoln meets with George B. McClellan in the Union general's tent.
(Photograph by Alexander Gardner. Courtesy of the Library of Congress.)

needed additional troops, many of its existing soldiers would soon be ready to leave the military. Davis and some Confederate lawmakers wanted to pass a conscription act to address this looming problem. This act would require Southern white males between the ages of eighteen and thirty-five to enlist in the Confederate military for three-year terms.

This proposal angered many other Southerners, though. Some people objected to it because it allowed rich whites to hire substitutes to serve in their place. They also protested a later rule that allowed white men who owned twenty or more slaves to take an exemption from the military draft (not be forced to join). These provisions made many people think that poor folks would end up shouldering most of the burden for the war. Other Southerners, meanwhile, criticized the proposed law because it made it seem as if Davis was building a powerful national government that did not pay enough attention to the rights of individual Southern states. Since the South had long insisted that it had seceded from the United States over the issue of states' rights, this argument carried weight with many Southern lawmakers and citizens.

Supporters of the Conscription Act dismissed these complaints. Davis pointed out that the Confederate Constitution gave the national government significant powers "to provide for the common defence" of their new nation. His allies declared that failure to pass the Conscription Act would doom the Confederacy. "Cease this child's play," warned Texas senator Louis Wigfall (1816–1874). "The enemy are in some portions of almost every state in the Confederacy. . . . We need a large army. How [else] are you going to get it?" Faced with this grim reality, the Confederate Congress passed the bill. Davis signed the act into law on April 16, thus instituting the first military draft in American history. Boosted by the act, the total number of men in the Confederate Army increased from 325,000 at the beginning of 1862 to 450,000 at the end of the year.

Lincoln grows impatient with McClellan

In Washington, meanwhile, President Abraham Lincoln (1809–1865) waded through political difficulties of his own during the early months of 1862. In December 1861, U.S. senators nervous about Union defeats at First Bull Run and Ball's Bluff (located a mere thirty miles from the U.S. capital) had established a Joint Committee on the Conduct of the War in order to review military strategies and leadership. By the spring of

1862, Lincoln could tell that this Republican-dominated committee posed a threat to his leadership. Its members continually tried to interfere with his control of the military and his efforts to set administration policy in a number of areas. Lincoln never allowed this committee to seize control of the Union war effort, but handling its membership challenged the president's powers of diplomacy and persuasion over the next few years.

Lincoln's relationship with his top general turned sour during the first months of 1862 as well. General McClellan insisted that he was eager to move against the South, but he kept his Army of the Potomac in Washington. One reason for McClellan's inaction was an attack of typhoid fever that sent him to bed for a few weeks in December 1861. Another reason was his tendency to overestimate the strength of his opponents. He routinely misjudged the numbers of Confederate troops to an amazing degree, in part because his military intelligence department often misinterpreted the information it received on enemy movements.

The existence of the Joint Committee on the Conduct of the War also may have slowed McClellan. By the spring of 1862, the committee had become a severe critic of a number of the Union's military leaders. McClellan knew that he would take a lot of abuse if his offensive was unsuccessful. As a result, he continued to train his troops and explore various strategies, ignoring the growing number of radical Republicans who said that McClellan might actually be a Confederate sympathizer.

As time passed, however, President Lincoln became more impatient with McClellan's inactivity. In January 1862, the two men clashed on a number of occasions. By January 27, Lincoln had become so fed up that he released General War Order No. 1, which called for a Union offensive into Virginia by February 22. But the Army of the Potomac still remained in Washington. On March 11, Lincoln punished McClellan for his inaction by stripping him of his title as general-in-chief over all Union forces.

McClellan begins his advance on Richmond

McClellan retained his command over the Army of the Potomac, however, and in mid-March he finally moved forward. Instead of moving from Washington, D.C., through northern Virginia, however, McClellan intended to transport his army down the Chesapeake Bay via boat to the eastern tip of a Virginia peninsula situated between the York and James rivers. From there, he planned to advance up the peninsula to the Confederate capital of Richmond, sixty-five miles to the northwest.

The Union's desire to capture Richmond reflected the belief—held by both the North and the South—that Virginia was the most strategically important region in the entire conflict. After all, the Confederate capital of Richmond was located within its bor-

ders. In addition, the state sat next to Washington, the Federal capital. Each side knew that it would be almost impossible for it to win the war if its capital was captured by the other side. At the same time, both the North and the South recognized that they might be able to win the war quickly if they could somehow take control of the other side's capital. Given these factors, both sides deployed (spread out according to a plan) a large number of their troops in Virginia. Citizens across the divided nation followed developments in the region with great interest.

McClellan's plan was designed to capture Richmond and deal the Confederacy a crushing blow. Nonetheless, Lincoln and his advisors worried that the general's strategy would leave Washington vulnerable to an attack from Confederate forces in northern Virginia. Lincoln gave his approval only after making sure that forty thousand soldiers of the Army of the Potomac would remain behind to protect the capital. This reorganization of troops left McClellan with approximately ninety-five thousand men, far fewer than he had wanted to take with him.

McClellan successfully transported his troops to the coastline of the Virginia peninsula in late March. Once McClellan began his advance up the peninsula, however, his plan quickly unraveled. Confederate Major General John B. Magruder (1810–1871) fooled McClellan into believing that a major rebel force was entrenched at Yorktown, a short distance up the peninsula. The Union force could have over-

John Pope became commander of the Federal Army of Virginia in June 1862.
(Photograph by Mathew B. Brady. Courtesy of the Library of Congress.)

hesitation gave Confederate commander Joseph E. Johnston (1807–1891) plenty of time to prepare his Army of Northern Virginia for the defense of Richmond.

Stonewall Jackson's Shenandoah campaign

The Confederate defense of Richmond was aided in great measure by the exploits of Thomas "Stonewall" Jackson (1824–1863), one of the Confederate heroes at the First Battle of Bull Run. In mid-March 1862, Jackson entered western Virginia's Shenandoah Valley with an army of about eight thousand men. Over the next three months, he roamed across the region in a dazzling campaign that thoroughly baffled his Federal Army counterparts. On several occasions, Jackson's Confederate troops won big victories over Union armies of much greater size. At other times, he and his troops seemed to melt into the valleys and woodlands of the Shenandoah region, repeatedly eluding (escaping from) Union armies in the area.

Even before mid-May, when Jackson's army received eight thousand reinforcements, the Lincoln administration had grown fearful that he might attempt an attack on Washington. This perceived threat was what convinced Lincoln to station forty thousand of McClellan's troops at the U.S. capital, rather than allow them to take part in McClellan's Peninsula Campaign. Lincoln also ordered additional Union troops into the Shenandoah Valley to neutralize Jackson. But Jackson moved

whelmed Magruder with one big push, but McClellan proceeded cautiously. Magruder's actions kept the Union Army stalled for a month. McClellan's

his outnumbered troops masterfully. He continued to dodge Federal attempts to corner his army, often inflicting punishment on Union forces in the process.

Jackson and his army remained in the Shenandoah Valley until mid-June. The legendary general then slipped away to aid in Johnston's defense of Richmond. He left behind approximately sixty thousand frustrated Union troops who—were it not for Jackson's campaign of deception—might have been part of McClellan's Peninsula Campaign.

Lee stops McClellan's advance

McClellan finally pushed past Yorktown in early May. From there he resumed his march on Richmond, but his army continued to move slowly. In fact, Lincoln became so impatient with McClellan's progress that on May 25 he issued an order directing him to either launch his attack or return to Washington.

On May 31, the long-awaited clash between the two gathering armies finally erupted at Fair Oaks, only six miles from the outskirts of Richmond. The two-day battle ended in a virtual draw, but it also resulted in a change in Confederate military leadership. Joseph Johnston suffered a serious wound during the battle, so Jefferson Davis replaced him with Robert E. Lee.

Lee immediately proved that he was up to the job. On June 25, he led a force of seventy thousand rebel troops (including Stonewall Jackson's army) against McClellan's units. Over the following week, the two sides engaged in a

Henry Halleck became general-in-chief of the Union Army in 1862. *(Photograph by J. A. Scholten. Courtesy of the Library of Congress.)*

series of fierce battles across the Virginia peninsula. These clashes, which came to be known as the Seven Days Battles, stopped McClellan in his tracks. Confederate losses were grave—twenty thousand rebel soldiers were killed or wounded in the Seven Days Battles—but North and South alike viewed the final result as a loss for the Union. Led by Lee, the Confederacy had successfully protected Richmond from a major Union offensive. In the days following the Seven Days Battles, the entire South erupted in praise for Lee, the newest hero of the Confederacy. "He has established his reputation forever," gushed the *Richmond Whig*, "and has entitled himself to the lasting gratitude of his country."

Lincoln makes changes in the Union military leadership

McClellan's shaky performance during the Peninsula Campaign convinced many Union leaders—including President Lincoln—that the cocky young general behaved far too cautiously to be an effective field commander. Lincoln thus became determined to change the leadership of the Union Army. On June 26, President Lincoln named John Pope (1822–1892) to command a new army—the Federal Army of Virginia—created out of the various armies that had been chasing Stonewall Jackson around the Shenandoah Valley. Pope had been involved in a number of the Union's successes along the Mississippi earlier in the year, and the Lincoln administration hoped that he could help the North turn things around in the East.

Three weeks after sending Pope to northern Virginia to assume command of his new army, Lincoln and Secretary of War Edwin Stanton (1814–1869) made another major change. They appointed Henry W. Halleck as the Union Army's general-in-chief. This position had remained vacant since Lincoln had stripped McClellan of the title in March.

Halleck arrived in Washington at what he described as "a time of great peril" for the Union. After all, both Pope and McClellan were miles away from the capital and far apart from one another. Alarmed by what he saw as a vulnerable Union capital city, Halleck promptly ordered McClellan to return to Washington with his troops.

Once McClellan returned to the capital, Halleck intended to combine his army with the Union troops commanded by Pope. Lincoln's new general-in-chief knew that if these two armies were put together, the resulting military force would be much larger than General Lee's rebel Army of Northern Virginia. Halleck could then march after Lee and use the Union's superior firepower to smash the Confederate Army.

Unfortunately for Halleck and the Union cause, Lee acted before Pope and McClellan could bring their armies together. As McClellan gathered his troops for the long boat ride back to Washington, Lee sent a Confederate force under the command of Stonewall Jackson to test Pope's position, about fifty miles southwest of the U.S. capital. On August 9, Jackson whipped a detachment of Pope's army at Cedar Mountain. Lee then decided to bring the rest of his troops forward.

The Second Battle of Bull Run

After absorbing the beating at Cedar Mountain, Pope regrouped and prepared for the arrival of Lee's Confederate forces. But instead of meeting Pope's Union troops head-on, Lee devised a daring strategy in which he divided his army in two. Half of the rebel force stayed in position under the immediate command of Lee's trusted lieutenant, Major General James Longstreet (1821–1904). The other half of the Confederate Army, led by Stonewall Jackson, swooped around Pope's western flank.

Pope was very distracted by the presence of Longstreet's regiments. He did not realize that Jackson's twenty-four thousand–man force had glided by him until Jackson seized control of a Union supply base at Manassas Junction, site of the First Battle of Bull Run. Upon arriving at Manassas, Jackson's hungry and tired men immediately devoured large quantities of the Union provisions, which included everything from turkey and beef to lobster salad and wine.

News of Jackson's successful maneuver shocked and confused Pope, who nonetheless roused his army. Urged on by Pope, the Union troops set out for Manassas in hopes of defeating Jackson before Lee could send reinforcements. On August 29, Pope found Jackson's army, and the Union general launched an immediate attack. The advance failed, though, partly because Pope had come to the mistaken belief that Stonewall's troops were already in retreat, when in reality they had assumed strong defensive positions. Another reason for the failure of the Union attack was the poor performance of a number of Pope's lieutenants in the heat of battle. Finally, Northern military leaders in Washington were slow to send additional troops to help Pope, even though Mc-

Clellan's army had returned from the Virginia peninsula by this time. McClellan himself argued that his troops should remain in defense of the capital and that Pope should be left "to get out of his scrape by himself."

As the battle at Manassas continued during the afternoon of August 30, Pope became convinced that Jackson's outnumbered army was on the verge of collapse. He ordered his troops forward, unaware that Lee's forces had arrived the night before and taken up positions along the Union flank. As the Union Army launched its attack, a sudden eruption of Confederate artillery fire ripped into it, destroying the offensive.

The Union charge quickly turned into a retreat. Confederate troops gave chase, and by the end of the day Pope's army was in tatters. As the dust settled on Manassas Junction, it was clear that the Confederacy had won another major battle on its soil. This clash, called the Second Battle of Bull Run, resulted in more than sixteen thousand Union casualties. It also created more uncertainty about the North's military leadership. Lee's army suffered damage as well—more than ninety-one hundred men were killed or wounded in the battle. But in the aftermath of Second Bull Run, the South stood poised to invade the North.

Confederate victories in the West

News of Lee's triumph at the Second Battle of Bull Run sent a ripple of fear through the Lincoln administration, especially since victory suddenly seemed in doubt in the West as well. Only a few months earlier—in the spring of 1862—the Union had seemed ready to completely smash the rebels in the West. Federal forces had seized control of almost fifty thousand square miles of Confederate territory in the region, including such prized Southern cities as Nashville, New Orleans, and Memphis. Even the mighty Mississippi River had fallen into the hands of the North.

During the summer of 1862, however, the Union Army discovered how difficult it was to maintain control over such a large expanse of unfriendly territory. Confederate cavalry parties repeatedly raided Federal outposts and supply trains, and bridges and railroads utilized by the North were sabotaged (destroyed) on a regular basis. By August, these rebel activities had loosened the Union's hold on the West, paving the way for Confederate Army moves into Tennessee and Kentucky.

As Northerners digested the news of the Confederacy's sudden flurry of triumphs, a grim mood descended over the Union. All across the North, people realized that the South suddenly stood on the brink of victory. This possibility stunned everyone, and criticism of Lincoln and his generals became harsh through much of the North. Dispirited Union soldiers, most of whom had served with great bravery, felt as if the sacrifices made by them and their comrades were being wasted by mediocre Union generals.

Northern communities, meanwhile, were already mourning the deaths of friends, neighbors, and family members. Many people wondered if their sacrifices to "preserve the Union" would be in vain.

Lee advances into the North

In early September, Lee's army marched across the Potomac River and into Maryland. Lee made this advance into the North for several reasons. First, he knew that the Northern army was demoralized (weakened in spirit) and unprepared to offer immediate resistance. Moreover, he knew that the farmlands of Maryland and Pennsylvania held plenty of food and supplies that could be used by his hungry troops. He also thought that a successful campaign in the North might convince neutral European powers like Great Britain and France to finally acknowledge Confederate independence. But most of all, Lee believed that if the Confederate Army proved that it was capable of seizing control of regions of the North, Lincoln might be forced to negotiate a truce that would recognize the Confederacy.

President Lincoln, meanwhile, reluctantly turned command of the Union's battered and dispirited eastern troops over to General McClellan. Lincoln admitted that the decision "greatly distressed" him, because he viewed the general as a selfish and arrogant man with limited abilities as a battlefield leader. But the president recognized that McClellan's continued popularity with Union troops might enable him to improve their badly damaged morale. Lincoln hoped that the general's abilities as an organizer might improve the army's discipline and performance.

Antietam—the bloodiest day in American military history

A few days after Lee crossed into Maryland, McClellan left Washington with seventy-five thousand troops of the Army of the Potomac (which now included troops from Pope's disbanded Army of Virginia). McClellan traveled east in search of Lee, who had divided his fifty-two thousand–man army in order to attack the Federal armory at Harpers Ferry, Virginia (now in West Virginia), located just south of Maryland near the Potomac River. Led by Stonewall Jackson, the Confederate detachment captured the armory on September 15, seizing a huge number of weapons (13,000 rifles and 73 pieces of artillery) and 12,500 prisoners in the process. After grabbing everything that they could carry from Harpers Ferry, Jackson's troops moved back into Maryland in order to rejoin the rest of Lee's army at Sharpsburg, on Antietam Creek.

McClellan, meanwhile, continued to advance his Northern troops forward. He proceeded cautiously until September 13, when he received an incredible stroke of good luck. On that day, a Union soldier found a copy of Lee's military plans wrapped around three cigars lost by a careless Confederate officer. After reviewing

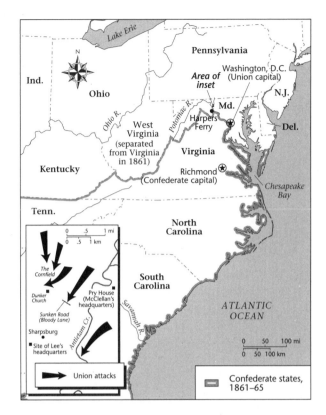

Antietam Creek, Maryland, site of the bloodiest one-day battle in American military history. *(Illustration by XNR Productions. Reproduced by permission of The Gale Group.)*

Lee's orders, an excited McClellan increased the speed of his advance in order to catch the Confederates before Lee could reunite his scattered forces.

McClellan's discovery of Lee's secret plans spurred him to close in on the Confederate Army more quickly, but many historians believe that the Union general was still too slow to act. By September 16, most of McClellan's forces had reached the vicinity of Antietam Creek. But he held off on launching a major attack until the next day, in part because he seriously overestimated the size of the Confederate Army stationed there. McClellan's decision to wait saved Lee from a complete disaster, for Stonewall Jackson's detachment did not return to Lee's camp until the evening of the sixteenth.

On the morning of September 17, the two armies finally converged in a vicious day-long battle that killed or wounded more than twenty-three thousand Union and Confederate soldiers. This one-day casualty toll marked the single bloodiest day in Civil War history. Throughout the morning and afternoon, Union regiments roared forward through a hail of rebel gunfire in brave attempts to break through the Confederate defenses. The Federal troops destroyed many Southern regiments, but Lee's men refused to give way. This desperate courage impressed even the Union soldiers who attacked them. "It is beyond all wonder," said one Union veteran of Antietam, "how such men as the rebel troops can fight on as they do; that filthy, sick, hungry, and miserable, they should prove such heroes in fight, is past explanation."

When darkness finally fell on the battlefield, both armies withdrew in exhaustion, leaving behind thousands of dead and wounded soldiers. The next morning Lee held his position, as if daring McClellan to resume the fight. But McClellan stayed put, and on the evening of September 18, Lee gathered the remains of his army together and slipped back into Virginia.

The Battle of Antietam (called the Battle of Sharpsburg in the South)

thus ended in a strangely inconclusive way, with neither side able to claim a clearcut victory. But while the battle itself had ended in a bloody draw, the clash marked a major turning point in the Civil War. Lee's invasion of the North had ended in failure, and his Army of Northern Virginia had sustained terrible damage. Moreover, the Battle of Antietam provided the people of the North with badly needed reassurance that the war might yet go their way. Finally, it gave Lincoln the opening he needed to issue his famous Emancipation Proclamation.

Lincoln's Emancipation Proclamation

A few days after the Battle of Antietam, Lincoln issued a document that changed the very nature of the Civil War. This preliminary Emancipation Proclamation, issued on September 22, stated that unless the seceded Confederate states voluntarily returned to the Union by January 1, 1863, all slaves within those states would be free. The historic declaration also called for the inclusion of blacks into the U.S. armed services.

Lincoln's desire to issue such a proclamation had been growing for some time. He believed that Northern support for the war would increase if its people came to believe that it was fighting not only to preserve the Union, but also on behalf of basic American principles of freedom and liberty for *all* men and women. In addition, he recognized that slaves remained a vital labor source for the

A view of the Antietam battlefield on the day of the battle. A man (right) uses binoculars to scout out the territory. *(Photograph by Alexander Gardner. Courtesy of the Library of Congress.)*

South, and that any loss of slaves would hurt its ability to continue its rebellion. As Lincoln later stated, "The moment came when I felt that slavery must die that the nation might live!"

By the summer of 1862, Lincoln was ready to issue his Proclamation. But Secretary of State William Seward (1801–1872) convinced him to wait. Seward pointed out that if the president issued the decree at a time when the war was going badly for the North, many people would dismiss it as a desperate attempt to avoid defeat. He encouraged Lincoln to wait until

his army registered a big victory before making his declaration.

The Union's ability to hold its own at Antietam gave Lincoln the opening he needed. His announcement triggered a storm of reaction all across the divided nation. In the North, most free blacks and abolitionists reacted with delight. Black leader Frederick Douglass (c. 1818–1895), for instance, wrote that "we shout for joy that we live to record this righteous decree." Many Northern newspapers praised Lincoln. But not everyone in the North embraced the Emancipation Proclamation. Some abolitionists complained that Lincoln's proclamation did not include slaves living in the Union slave states of Maryland, Delaware, Missouri, and Kentucky. Northerners opposed to the war—many of them members of the Democratic political party—also spoke out against Lincoln's stand, which they worried might extend the war.

In Richmond and other cities of the Confederacy, most people ridiculed Lincoln's Proclamation. They pointed out that the Union had no power to enforce the Proclamation in the Confederacy. Many Southerners viewed the announcement as an obvious attempt to trigger a slave rebellion in the South. In the days following Lincoln's announcement, countless Southern newspapers and lawmakers expressed renewed determination to resist the North.

As time passed, however, Lincoln's Emancipation Proclamation turned out to be an invaluable weapon in the Union arsenal. It dramatically broadened Northern civilian support for the war effort, and gave Union soldiers another noble cause for which to fight. It also helped convince Europe not to interfere in the war. As Bruce Catton wrote in *The Civil War,* the simplicity and, yet, dramatic impact of the Emancipation Proclamation "changed the whole character of the war and, more than any other single thing, doomed the Confederacy to defeat."

Lincoln fires McClellan

The autumn of 1862 brought about yet another change in the Union's military leadership. McClellan's failure to pursue Lee's retreating army at Antietam had infuriated Lincoln and many of his advisors. McClellan insisted that he had performed wonderfully. "Those on whose judgment I rely," he once stated, "tell me that I fought the battle splendidly and that it was a masterpiece of art." But the Lincoln administration believed that Lee's army could have been completely destroyed if McClellan had contested the Confederate retreat into Virginia.

Nonetheless, Lincoln did not remove McClellan from command of the Army of the Potomac until early November, after the general repeatedly ignored Lincoln's orders to launch another offensive into Virginia. Lincoln replaced McClellan with General Ambrose E. Burnside (1824–1881), who promptly devised a plan to march on Richmond.

The Battle of Fredericksburg

Burnside's advance on Richmond was halted at Fredericksburg, a Virginia town located near the Rappahannock River. As Burnside reached the outskirts of the city, he encountered seventy-five thousand Confederate troops under the direction of Lee, Jackson, and Longstreet. Burnside had a huge army of 120,000 men under his command, and he decided to launch a series of frontal assaults against the rebel positions.

As Burnside's December 13 attack on the Confederate's defensive positions unfolded, Union casualties mounted at a frightening pace. Lee's

"The Angel of Marye's Heights"

One of the true heroes of the Battle of Fredericksburg was Sergeant Richard R. Kirkland of the Second South Carolina Volunteers. On December 13, Union general Ambrose Burnside made repeated attempts to break through the Confederate defenses with frontal assaults. This foolish strategy failed, and with each withdrawal of Federal troops, they had to leave wounded comrades behind.

Burnside finally called a halt to the attacks, and quiet fell over the battlefield. After the fighting stopped, Confederate soldiers defending Marye's Heights and other rebel positions could hear the moans and cries of wounded Union soldiers out on the field. The suffering of the wounded Yankees became too much for Kirkland to bear. The young Confederate decided that he had to try and help the wounded soldiers.

Kirkland ran over to his commander and asked for permission to leave the safety of the Confederate line and carry canteens of water to the suffering Union soldiers. The commander granted Kirkland's request, even though everyone thought that Union troops would shoot him as soon as he left the protection of the wall at Marye's Heights.

Kirkland knew that he might be shot and killed, but he did not let fear prevent him from carrying out his mission of mercy. He jumped over the wall with an armful of canteens and ran out to the fallen wounded soldiers. Kirkland expected a rifle shot to ring out at any time, ending his life. But the amazed Union soldiers in the distance held

Confederate soldiers lie dead behind a stone wall at Marye's Heights in Fredericksburg, Virginia. *(Photograph by Andrew J. Russell. Courtesy of the National Archives and Records Administration.)*

their fire and stared as he comforted numerous Yankee soldiers. Both armies watched quietly as he went from soldier to soldier, the only moving form on a battlefield covered with dead and wounded men. Kirkland spent an hour and a half providing water and reassuring words to enemy soldiers before returning to the Confederate line.

Kirkland's heroism at Fredericksburg made a deep impression on both armies. They called him "the Angel of Marye's Heights" and "The Hero-Sergeant of Fredericksburg." After the battle, Kirkland continued to serve as a member of the Second South Carolina Volunteers. But he only lived for another ten months before being killed at the Battle of Chickamauga in Georgia.

Bodies of dead soldiers are gathered for burial following the Battle of Fredericksburg. *(Photograph by Timothy H. Sullivan. Courtesy of the Library of Congress.)*

Burnside and his lieutenants continued to order their men forward into a hail of gunfire. "[Union soldiers] fought until late in the afternoon under murderous fire, gaining little more than feet or yards," wrote Herman Hattaway in *Shades of Blue and Gray.* "It was a futile, wild, fantastic, direct slam against a well-entrenched enemy, and it failed miserably." As one Union officer later recalled, "the whole plain [at Fredericksburg] was covered with men, prostrate and dropping. . . . I had never before seen fighting like that—nothing approaching it in terrible uproar and destruction."

On December 14, Burnside called off the attack. A day later, he finally withdrew his forces from Fredericksburg and returned to Washington, where he reported to a disappointed Lincoln. The Battle of Fredericksburg had been a humiliating defeat for the Union. Burnside's Army of the Potomac suffered more than 12,500 casualties in the clash, while the rebel army had lost only 5,300 men to death or injury. But Lincoln wanted to give Burnside another chance, so he left him in command.

troops were well fortified and determined to protect their positions, but

1863: The Tide Turns

During the first half of 1863, doubts about the Federal army's ability to defeat the Confederate forces mounted across the North. And when Confederate general Robert E. Lee (1807–1870) led his troops to a spectacular victory at Chancellorsville, Virginia, the North grew increasingly anxious. In July, antiwar feelings combined with anger over many of the wartime actions of President Abraham Lincoln (1809–1865) led to a deadly riot in New York that took the lives of more than one hundred people.

But July 1863 also marked a significant turning point in the Civil War. During the first days of that month, the Union forces won two major battles. In the West, the North's successful siege of Vicksburg, Mississippi, enabled it to establish control over the entire length of the Mississippi River. In the East, the Union victory at the famous Battle of Gettysburg forced Lee to abandon his efforts to bring the war onto Northern soil. These victories encouraged Union troops across the country. They also increased public support for the Lincoln administration in the North, although opposition to the president's policies remained strong among many Northerners. A few months later, the South rebounded from these defeats

Words to Know

Blockade the act of surrounding a harbor with ships in order to prevent other vessels from entering or exiting the harbor; the word blockade is also sometimes used when ships or other military forces surround and isolate a city, region, or country

Civil War conflict that took place from 1861 to 1865 between the Northern states (Union) and the Southern seceded states (Confederacy); also known in the South as the War between the States and in the North as the War of the Rebellion

Confederacy eleven Southern states that seceded from the United States in 1860 and 1861

Conscription forced enrollment of able-bodied men into a nation's armed forces; also known as a draft

Draft see **Conscription**

Emancipation the act of freeing people from slavery or oppression

Federal national or central government; also refers to the North or Union as opposed to the South or Confederacy

Rebel Confederate; often used as a name for a Confederate soldier

Regiment a military unit of organized troops; regiments usually consisted of one thousand men and were divided into ten companies of one hundred men each

Siege surrounding and blockading of a city, town, or fortress by an army attempting to capture it

Union Northern states that remained loyal to the United States during the Civil War

with a dramatic triumph at the Battle of Chickamauga in Georgia. As the year drew to a close, however, a decisive Union victory at Chattanooga, Tennessee, provided further evidence that the war might finally be turning in the North's favor.

Rosecrans and Bragg duel in the West

The first major clashes of 1863 took place in the war's western theater

(military area), in central Tennessee. In the last months of 1862, the two sides had engaged in a number of battles for control of Kentucky and Tennessee. But while an indecisive battle at Perryville, Kentucky, in October 1862 had convinced Confederate general Braxton Bragg (1817–1876) to withdraw from that state, he still hoped to take control of middle Tennessee.

The struggle for possession of central Tennessee pitted Bragg's thirty-

People to Know

Braxton Bragg (1817–1876) Confederate general who led the Army of Mississippi and the Army of Tennessee; fought at Perryville, Chickamauga, and Chattanooga

Ambrose E. Burnside (1824–1881) Union general who commanded the Army of the Potomac at Fredericksburg; also fought at First Bull Run, Antietam, and in Ulysses S. Grant's Wilderness campaign

Jefferson Davis (1808–1889) president of the Confederate States of America, 1861–65

Ulysses S. Grant (1822–1885) Union general who commanded all Federal troops, 1864–65; led Union armies at Shiloh, Vicksburg, Chattanooga, and Petersburg; eighteenth president of the United States, 1869–77

Joseph Hooker (1814–1879) Union major general who commanded the Army of the Potomac at Chancellorsville; also fought at Second Bull Run, Antietam, Fredericksburg, Chattanooga, and Atlanta

Thomas "Stonewall" Jackson (1824–1863) Confederate lieutenant general who fought at First Bull Run, Second Bull Run, Antietam, Fredericksburg, and Chancellorsville; led 1862 Shenandoah Valley campaign

Joseph E. Johnston (1807–1891) Confederate general of the Army of Tennessee who fought at First Bull Run and Atlanta

Robert E. Lee (1807–1870) Confederate general of the Army of Northern Virginia; fought at Second Bull Run, Antietam, Gettysburg, Fredericksburg, and Chancellorsville; defended Richmond from Ulysses S. Grant's Army of the Potomac, 1864 to April 1865

Abraham Lincoln (1809–1865) sixteenth president of the United States, 1861–65

James Longstreet (1821–1904) Confederate lieutenant general in Robert E. Lee's Army of Northern Virginia for much of the war; fought at First Bull Run, Second Bull Run, Antietam, Fredericksburg, Gettysburg, Chickamauga, Knoxville, the Wilderness, and Petersburg

George G. Meade (1815–1872) Union major general who commanded the Army of the Potomac, June 1863 to April 1865; also fought at Second Bull Run, Antietam, Fredericksburg, and Chancellorsville

John C. Pemberton (1814–1881) Confederate lieutenant general who commanded Vicksburg defenses during the siege of Vicksburg

William Rosecrans (1819–1898) Union major general of the Army of the Mississippi and the Army of the Cumberland, 1861–63; fought at Corinth, Murfreesboro, and Chickamauga

Philip H. Sheridan (1831–1888) Union major general who commanded the Army of the Potomac's cavalry corps and the Army of the Shenandoah; also fought at Perryville, Murfreesboro, Chickamauga, and Chattanooga

ership of Rosecrans, Brigadier General Philip H. Sheridan (1831–1888), and Major General George H. Thomas (1816–1870) prevented a Confederate rout (overwhelming defeat) of the North. By the end of the day, Bragg was so certain of victory that he sent a report to the Confederate capital city of Richmond, Virginia, in which he boasted that "the enemy has yielded his strong point and is falling back. We occupy the whole field and shall follow. . . . God has granted us a happy new year."

But as the Battle of Stones River spilled into 1863, the Confederate commander realized that he had underestimated Rosecrans. The Union commander had not retreated. Instead, he had only fallen back to take up a stronger defensive position. When Bragg ordered an assault on the Union line on January 2, 1863, his charging troops were carved up by heavy artillery fire, and he was forced to call off the attack. Later that night, Bragg learned that Union reinforcements were on the way to help Rosecrans. This information, combined with several days of heavy rain that reduced the battlefield to mud, convinced the rebel commander to give up the fight. Only a few days after prematurely declaring victory, Bragg reluctantly removed his army from the region.

The Battle of Stones River took a heavy toll on both armies. Rosecrans reported more than thirteen thousand Union troops dead, wounded, or missing after the battle, while Bragg tallied more than ten thousand Confederate

Men repair a railroad track after the Battle of Stones River. *(Courtesy of the Library of Congress.)*

eight thousand–man Confederate Army of Tennessee against the Union's Army of the Cumberland, a forty-seven thousand–man force led by Major General William S. Rosecrans (1819–1898). The two sides met at Stones River, near the town of Murfreesboro, where Bragg had established a strong defensive position.

The battle between the two armies erupted on December 31, 1862. During the first day of fighting, the rebel troops threatened to overrun many Union positions. Only the lead-

casualties. These shocking losses badly damaged both armies. But although the battle itself ended in a stalemate (a contest that ends without an obvious winner), many Northern strategists regarded it as a victory. The Union stand at Stones River had halted the Confederate bid to regain control of middle Tennessee.

Lincoln signs the Emancipation Proclamation

Back in the East, President Lincoln opened the new year by formally signing the Emancipation Proclamation, first announced back in September 1862. This document freed all slaves located in the rebellious Southern states. It did not apply to slaves in the four "border states" that allowed slavery but remained loyal to the Union (Delaware, Kentucky, Maryland, and Missouri), or to those areas of the Confederacy that were already under Federal control.

Lincoln's Emancipation Proclamation proved to be one of the major events of the Civil War. It convinced thousands of slaves to flee the South for freedom in the North, which deprived the Confederacy of a vital source of labor. Even more importantly, however, it transformed the North's view of the entire war. Prior to Lincoln's Proclamation, the North had been fighting solely to preserve the Union. After Lincoln signed the Proclamation, the Northern cause included the abolishment of slavery. This moral dimension increased Northern support for the war effort among citizens and soldiers alike. It also discouraged the European powers from supporting the Confederate cause.

Burnside's "Mud March"

In January 1863, the Union's Army of the Potomac launched another campaign against General Lee's Confederate Army of Northern Virginia. Still stung by his disastrous defeat at Fredericksburg, Virginia, a month earlier, General Ambrose E. Burnside (1824–1881) planned to approach Lee's army from another direction. Burnside hoped to pry Lee out of the hills surrounding Fredericksburg, where he remained. But within hours of setting out, Burnside's advance was slowed by a heavy rainstorm. The storm lingered for days, transforming the surface of the roadways into nearly impassable mud pits. At first, Burnside ordered his troops on. But as soldiers sank into the mud up to their knees and supply wagons became hopelessly stuck in the quagmire, it became clear that the offensive was doomed. At one point, the army's helplessness became so great that Confederate soldiers on the other side of a river launched a volley of teasing laughter and jokes that further humiliated the hungry and tired Union troops.

Burnside finally called off the march. As the troops of the Army of the Potomac trudged back to camp, Lincoln decided that he needed to change generals once again. On January 25, 1863, Major General Joseph Hooker (1814–1879) replaced Burnside as commander of the Army of the Potomac.

Excerpt from a Union Soldier's Diary

Many Civil War soldiers left behind letters and diaries describing their experiences. One of these soldiers was Rice C. Bull, a private with the 12th Corps of the 123rd New York Volunteer Infantry Regiment of the Union Army. Bull joined the army in the fall of 1862. In the winter of 1863, his regiment marched southward into Virginia during a blizzard and set up camp in the small town of Stafford. In the following passage from his book *Soldiering: The Civil War Diary of Rice C. Bull,* Bull describes conditions at the camp and his experience with the disease typhoid:

The intention had been to march the 12th Corps to Fredericksburg [Virginia], but as the movement against the enemy had to be abandoned because of the storm, we were ordered to camp at Stafford. As the 11th Corps, formerly stationed here, was now at the front and would not return we were directed to move into their camp. Their cabins were well built and all we had to do was place our tent cloths over the rafters. Then we made great fires, dried out our blankets, and stood before the fire until the mud had hardened on our clothes. It looked like yellow plaster and when dry would peel off in flakes, and you could see the "army blue" underneath. The march had

been trying to us new soldiers, unused as we still were to such hardship.

It was unfortunate that we moved into this old camp, it proved to be a most unhealthy place. The 11th Corps had been there for some time and the stream from which they got their drinking water had been contaminated by their closets [latrines]. Typhoid fever soon developed in our Regiment and many men were ill. There were some who died, three were from our Company. We remained in this camp until March 1st; while there I had my only sickness while in the service. I remember how miserable I felt, feverish, faint, weak and with no desire for food. . . .

Conditions had become so bad by this time that we moved our camp a mile north on a hill which had not been occupied by troops. The ground was high and dry and there was water from a stream that had not been contaminated. All went to work with a will and we built new quarters. While they were not as fine as the ones we left they were comfortable and they were healthy. That winter we had already constructed winter camps at Harpers Ferry, Fairfax Station, and Stafford so we felt we were getting expert in that business. In this new camp the health of all improved at once and the depression that had settled on the Regiment passed away.

Hooker prepares for battle

Lincoln appointed Hooker as the new leader of the Union's main army of the East with some reluctance. Hooker had made public statements suggesting that he did not have a high opinion of the president, and many people believed that he had been disloyal to Burnside over the previous few months. Nonetheless, Lincoln viewed Hooker as a "a brave and skillful soldier" who could help restore battered Union morale.

Lincoln's faith in Hooker's ability to improve the Army of the Potomac's confidence and fighting spirit paid off. Hooker made sure that his troops were well fed, and he instituted a number of changes that improved his soldiers' health and the conditions in which they lived. He also boosted morale by displaying unwavering confidence in his own abilities. For example, at one point he reportedly said, "May God have mercy on General Lee, for I will have none." By April, when Hooker led a massive Union Army of more than 130,000 troops in a new offensive against Lee, the Army of the Potomac's new commander had become immensely popular with his men.

The Battle of Chancellorsville

Rather than engage in a disastrous frontal attack like the one that Burnside had tried a few months earlier, Hooker planned to launch an assault from two directions. As Hooker approached Lee's position around Fredericksburg, he divided his army into two main forces. He stationed a large section of troops directly across from the Confederate positions, but he also took another seventy thousand men around Lee's left flank (side) to a spot near the town of Chancellorsville, Virginia.

Lee knew that Hooker's Union Army posed a major threat to his own force, especially since his army was smaller than usual. Earlier in the

Union major general Joseph Hooker.
(Photograph by Mathew B. Brady. Courtesy of the Library of Congress.)

spring, Lieutenant General James Longstreet (1821–1904) had taken a corps of fifteen thousand rebels to gather food and supplies. This left Lee with only sixty thousand Confederate troops at his disposal, less than half the total number of soldiers under Hooker's command. The Confederate commander recognized that his only hope of victory was to devise a strategy that could neutralize the Union force's numerical advantage.

As Hooker moved his seventy thousand–man detachment around Lee's flank, Lee decided to launch his

Life in the Army Camps

Many people think that soldiers in the Civil War fought nearly every day. Actually, though, one of the main characteristics of daily life in the army camps was boredom. Soldiers in the Civil War spent an average of fifty days in camp for every one day they fought in battles. While in camp, they settled into a routine of training and relaxation. For soldiers in the Union Army, a typical day began with roll call early in the morning, followed by breakfast. Then the men spent most of the morning and early afternoon marching and performing drills. Most soldiers did not like the endless drilling, but it did help them learn to follow orders and work together as a unit.

In the late afternoon, Northern soldiers usually took some time to mend their uniforms and polish their boots for the daily inspection that took place after dinner. The standard Union Army uniform consisted of a blue cap with a black visor, a blue coat with a stand-up collar, light blue pants, and black shoes. Different colored stripes on the uniform indicated the branch of service to which the soldier belonged. For example, infantry (foot soldiers) uniforms had blue stripes, artillery uniforms had red stripes, and cavalry (soldiers on horseback) uniforms had yellow stripes. The soldiers' caps also had different symbols sewn onto them depending on their branch of service. The uniforms were made

of wool and were of high quality, especially after the first year of the war.

Union soldiers usually received adequate amounts of food. Their diet consisted mainly of meat, coffee, and bread, although fresh fruits and vegetables were sometimes available. Most soldiers did not like the thin, cracker-like bread they received, which they called "hardtack." They usually soaked it in water or coffee to soften it up before eating it. After dinner and the evening inspection, the soldiers usually relaxed by singing songs, writing letters to their families, and playing games, including an early version of baseball. This routine tended to change for a few days every other month, when the soldiers received their pay. Some of them used their money for gambling, buying alcohol, or visiting prostitutes.

Daily life in the army camps was very similar for Confederate soldiers. The main differences occurred due to the shortages of food, clothing, and other necessities that plagued the South during the war years. Prior to the Civil War, the Northern economy was based on manufacturing, while the Southern economy was based on farming. The North also had more railroads, canals, and roads to aid in the transportation of supplies. As a result, the South had

Soldiers relax after a drill. *(Courtesy of the National Archives and Records Administration.)*

problems obtaining supplies and distributing them to its troops throughout the war.

The chronic shortages affected Confederate soldiers in many ways. For example, the shortage of cloth meant that there were not enough uniforms for all the troops. The standard Confederate uniform consisted of a gray coat and pants and black shoes. But many soldiers were forced to make their own uniforms, so the Southern troops often appeared ragged and inconsistent. Later in the war, even the gray dye for the uniforms was in short supply. The soldiers began using a homemade dye on their clothing, which turned it a yellow-ish-brown color they called "butternut." Some men had to march and fight barefoot until they could take a pair of shoes from a Union soldier they captured or killed. The Confederate Army also had a shortage of tents, which meant that many soldiers slept out in the open under a blanket.

Food was in short supply as well. Even though the farms and plantations of the South could produce enough to feed the Confederate Army, the limited transportation system made it difficult to send the food where it was needed before it spoiled. In addition, some Southern farmers found that their crops were ruined by violent battles and military movements. As a result of these factors, the Confederate soldiers ate mostly cornbread and beef and were hungry much of the time. The men sometimes gambled their paychecks for extra food rations and could trade food for such luxuries as tobacco or stationery. Despite the hardships they faced, however, the troops from both the North and the South managed to keep their spirits up. "On each side the soldier realized that he personally was getting the worst of it, and when he had time he felt very sorry for himself," Bruce Catton wrote in *The Civil War.* "But mostly he did not have the time, and his predominant [most frequent] mood was never one of self-pity. Mostly he was ready for whatever came to him."

twenty-six thousand men. All during the day of May 2, Jackson marched his troops around the unsuspecting Union Army. By late afternoon, Jackson's force was in position in the woods along the Federal army's right flank. Two hours before dusk, Jackson attacked with brutal force. His assault shattered the right side of Hooker's force and destroyed the Yankee position. Nonetheless, the successful attack ended in tragedy for the South. As evening fell over the battlefield, a group of Confederate soldiers accidentally shot Jackson, who had been riding ahead of his troops.

When the Confederate hero died a few days later, the entire South went into mourning.

Lee's greatest triumph

The Battle of Chancellorsville continued for another two days, but the Union proved unable to recover from Jackson's deadly surprise attack. On May 6, Hooker finally disengaged his troops from the area and retreated after suffering more than seventeen thousand casualties. Lee's Army of Northern Virginia, on the other hand, had lost fewer than thirteen thousand troops despite having a far smaller force.

Lee's victory at Chancellorsville was his greatest triumph yet. Using his own mastery of tactics to deadly effect, he had whipped an army more than twice the size of his own Confederate force. But the victory came at a great price. Lee had lost his best general (Jackson) and more than

Confederate lieutenant general James Longstreet. *(Courtesy of the National Archives and Records Administration.)*

own surprise attack. Using Confederate cavalry under the command of Jeb Stuart (1833–1864) to mask his movements, Lee took forty-five thousand men to Chancellorsville. The two armies met on May 1 on the outskirts of the town. By this time, however, Confederate movements had confused Hooker, and he held off on calling a full-scale assault.

After a day of skirmishing, Lee ordered Lieutenant General Thomas "Stonewall" Jackson (1824–1863) to circle around Hooker's force with

20 percent of his army in the clash. But, as James M. McPherson noted in *Battle Cry of Freedom,* the Confederates' victory at Chancellorsville "bred an overconfidence in their own prowess and a contempt for the enemy that led to disaster. Believing his troops invincible, Lee was about to ask them to do the impossible."

Lee invades Pennsylvania

In the days following his triumph at Chancellorsville, Lee decided to invade the North again. He made this choice for several reasons. For one thing, he knew that the rich farm country of southern Pennsylvania contained plenty of food and supplies that his troops could take for themselves. In addition, Lee and other Confederate leaders still held out hope that a successful campaign in the North might convince England or France to support them in their bid for independence from the Union. Finally, Lee knew that a successful invasion of Pennsylvania would increase antiwar sentiments in the North. If such feelings grew strong enough, President Lincoln would have no choice but to negotiate a peace agreement with the South.

In early June, Lee moved forward at the head of an army that had been reinforced to a strength of seventy-five thousand men. By mid-June, his Army of Northern Virginia had crossed the Potomac River and entered southern Pennsylvania, where it raided farms and seized numerous black people. The rebel army transported many of these men and women to the South, claiming that they were escaped slaves.

The Union reacted cautiously to this invasion. Following Lincoln's orders, Hooker shadowed Lee's movements. But Hooker's army stayed to the east, where it could shield Washington, D.C., and other Northern cities along the East Coast from Lee's forces. On June 27, Lincoln appointed yet another officer to take command of the Army of the Potomac. Disappointed in Hooker's performance, the president replaced him with Major General George G. Meade (1815–1872).

As the Confederate Army roamed through the Pennsylvania countryside, Jeb Stuart's cavalry went on a mission that took the horsemen miles from Lee's troops. Lee relied heavily on Stuart's units to scout out enemy locations and movements, so their absence hindered the Confederate general. As Lee moved deeper into Union territory, he became increasingly uncertain about the strength and whereabouts of Union forces in the region.

The Battle of Gettysburg

On the morning of July 1, 1863, advance scouting parties from the two armies stumbled into one another near the small Pennsylvania town of Gettysburg. When Lee learned of this skirmish, he suddenly realized that the Union Army was very close. He hurriedly ordered his army of seventy-five thousand men to gather around Gettysburg before the Federal army could attack. Meade, mean-

Major General George Meade and fellow Union officers. *(Photograph by William Morris Smith. Courtesy of the Library of Congress.)*

while, ordered his army of ninety thousand troops forward to engage the rebel invaders. But the size of his army made it difficult to move quickly, so only a fraction of Meade's full force reached Gettysburg that day.

Throughout the day of July 1, Lee's men punished their outnumbered Yankee foes. The Confederates pushed the Union troops back to a field outside of Gettysburg known as Cemetery Ridge, where the Federals managed to hold their ground. The following day, Lee ordered a major attack on the Union position. He directed troops led

by Stonewall Jackson's replacement, Richard S. Ewell (1817–1872), and Jubal Early (1816–1894) to keep the Union's center and right flanks occupied at the same time that Longstreet's corps smashed into the Federal Army's left flank.

As the rebel attack unfolded, it appeared that Lee's plan might work. The Union's left side absorbed terrific punishment from Longstreet's troops, who pushed on through hails of Yankee gunfire. But the attack fizzled, stopped by Union reinforcements and the heroism of Federal soldiers like

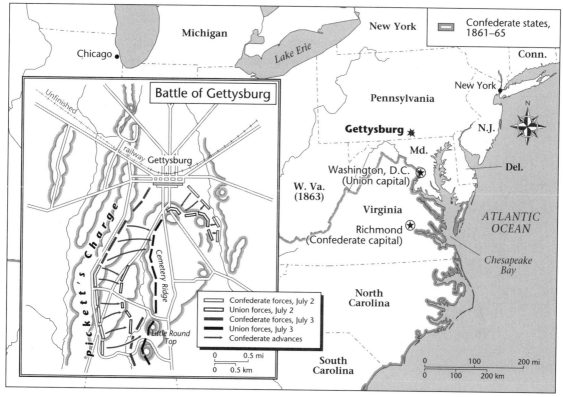

Gettysburg, Pennsylvania, site of Pickett's Charge at the Battle of Gettysburg in 1863.
(Illustration by XNR Productions. Reproduced by permission of The Gale Group.)

Joshua Lawrence Chamberlain (1828–1914). Chamberlain and his men of the Twentieth Maine Regiment had been ordered to keep a strategic position known as Little Round Top out of Confederate hands. Chamberlain's regiment stopped repeated attacks, only to run out of ammunition. In a desperate move, Chamberlain ordered a bayonet attack. His men rushed forward to engage in hand-to-hand combat with the enemy, using the sharp bayonets on the ends of their guns like swords. This tactic stunned his rebel foes and assured the North's continued posses-

sion of Little Round Top. Chamberlain's heroic defense of that position remains one of the most legendary feats in Civil War history.

Lee orders "Pickett's Charge"

On July 3, the battle resumed, as Lee made one final attempt to grasp the big victory that he so desperately wanted. As the clash spilled into the afternoon, Lee ordered a risky assault on the center of the Union's defenses. Lee's plan called for fifteen thousand men under the command of James J. Pettigrew (1828–1863) and George E.

Pickett (1825–1875) to rush Cemetery Ridge, the heart of the Northern defenses. Noting that these divisions would have to cross a mile of open ground to reach the Union line, Longstreet repeatedly urged Lee to reconsider his plan. But the Confederate general refused to change his strategy, and at 3 P.M. Longstreet reluctantly relayed Lee's order to attack.

In the hours prior to the attack, Confederate artillery units had directed a torrent of shellfire at Union positions in hopes of knocking out Federal cannons. Lee knew that if those weapons were disabled, it would be much easier for his troops to reach Cemetery Ridge. At first, the Union had responded to the South's bombardment with a major artillery attack of its own. As time passed, however, most of the Union guns fell silent. Lee hoped that their silence meant that they had been knocked out of action. But as Pickett and Pettigrew launched their assault—which came to be known as "Pickett's Charge"—the Union cannons came to life once again, repeatedly hitting the advancing rebel soldiers with a hail of deadly fire.

Pickett and Pettigrew pushed their troops forward, but as they rushed over the unprotected hillside toward Cemetery Ridge, Northern cannons and gunfire took a fearsome toll. By the time the first Confederate soldiers reached the low walls of Cemetery Ridge, several of the attacking rebel divisions had been destroyed. Union troops easily disposed of the few hundred soldiers who reached the wall. The other remnants of the assault force limped back to Confederate positions.

Lee's decision to attack the center of the Union's defenses had resulted in disaster. Of the fifteen thousand troops who had taken part in Pickett's Charge, only half returned. Pickett's division suffered particularly heavy losses. He lost two-thirds of his men in the attack, and only one of his thirty-five officers escaped the charge without being killed or wounded. Horrified by his misjudgment, Lee admitted to the survivors that he was to blame. He then gathered his bloodied troops together and retreated back to Virginia, haunted by the knowledge that his invasion of the North had ended in failure.

The Battle of Gettysburg took an awful toll on both armies. Meade's Army of the Potomac sustained more than twenty-three thousand casualties in the three days of fighting, while the Confederates lost approximately twenty-eight thousand troops. But while both sides suffered enormous losses in the clash, it was clear that the Union had won a major victory. Gettysburg had reduced the size of Lee's Army of Northern Virginia by one-third at a time when Confederate efforts to recruit new soldiers were faltering. Moreover, the battle had driven the Confederates out of the North. Finally, Meade's victory showed Northern soldiers and civilians alike that Lee could be beaten on the field of battle.

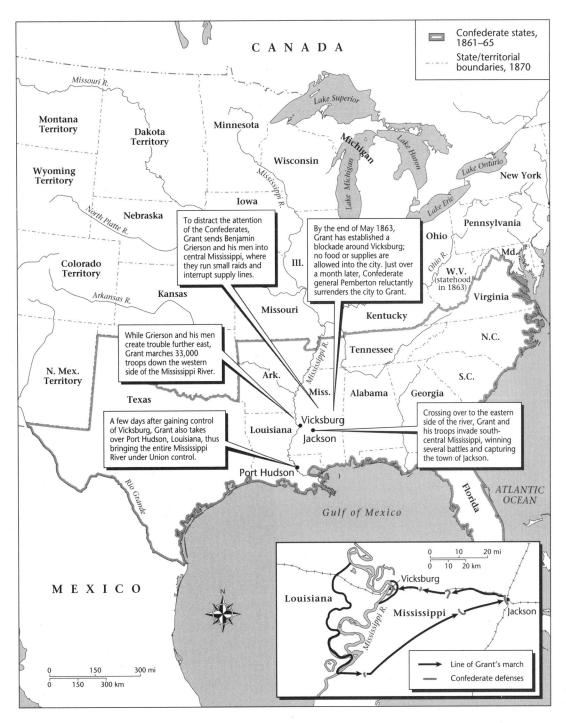

Key moments in the Union's attempt to gain total control of the Mississippi River. *(Illustration by XNR Productions. Reproduced by permission of The Gale Group.)*

Union general Ulysses S. Grant. *(Courtesy of the National Archives and Records Administration.)*

Grant's fight for possession of the Mississippi River

Back in the West, meanwhile, most military activity centered around the Union's efforts to seize control of the entire length of the Mississippi River. If the North could accomplish this, it would be able to use the waterway freely to transport troops and supplies from the border states of Missouri and Kentucky all the way to the Gulf of Mexico. In addition, total Union control of the river would cut Texas, Louisiana, and Arkansas off from the other Confederate states.

By late 1862, Union general Ulysses S. Grant (1822–1885) had managed to seize control of the entire river, except for two hundred miles below Vicksburg, Mississippi. But Vicksburg was heavily fortified with artillery and troops commanded by Confederate general John C. Pemberton (1814–1881). During the first few months of 1863, Grant made several unsuccessful attempts to neutralize the rebel stronghold. Finally, in April 1863, the Union general launched a daring and brilliant plan to capture the city.

First, Grant sent a brigade of cavalrymen under the command of Benjamin Grierson (1826–1911) deep into the heart of the state of Mississippi. Over the next two weeks, Grierson caused trouble wherever he roamed, destroying Confederate supply lines and conducting successful raids on small rebel military units. Grierson's actions distracted the Confederates, who repeatedly failed in their attempts to stop him.

As Confederate attention turned to Grierson, Grant marched thirty-three thousand troops southward through a maze of swamps and bayous (marshy inlets) on the western side of the Mississippi River. The route was very difficult, but by sticking to the Louisiana side of the river he was able to avoid attracting fire from the cannons of Vicksburg, perched high on the Mississippi's opposite shore. In late April, these troops met up with a fleet of Union vessels that had made a midnight dash down the river past Vicksburg's thundering guns. Grant used these ships to transport his men back to the eastern side of the river on April 30.

During the first two weeks of May, Grant's army swept through southcentral Mississippi with devastating effectiveness, stealing supplies and destroying rebel railroads. The Union invaders won five different clashes during this time, defeating a variety of Confederate opponents. By mid-May, Grant had captured the town of Jackson, chased off a rebel army under the command of General Joseph E. Johnston (1807–1891), and completely encircled the Confederate defenses at Vicksburg. Johnston's rebel army remained in the area, but Grant knew that Confederate losses had reduced the force to only thirty thousand men, many of whom were recent draftees. Grant's army, by comparison, had grown to include more than seventy thousand battle-hardened troops, thanks to reinforcements from Memphis and other areas under Union control.

The Siege of Vicksburg

Shortly after surrounding Vicksburg, Grant made two attempts to storm the city's defenses. But Pemberton's troops beat back both assaults. In the final days of May, the Union general decided to change tactics. Grant posted several divisions to keep an eye on Johnston, then told the rest of his men to prepare for a long siege of the city. The Union Army quickly established a blockade around Vicksburg, stopping all shipments of food or supplies into the city. Grant's plan was to starve the city into surrendering.

During the first weeks of the siege, spirits remained high among Pemberton's troops and Vicksburg's civilian population. People stayed upbeat even though Union artillery and gunboat fire forced many of them to flee their homes for caves on the outskirts of the city. Convinced that Johnston would eventually break Grant's grip on them, the soldiers and civilians tried not to think about their rapidly fading supplies of food. Johnston's army never mounted a serious threat to Grant's position, however, despite the repeated urgings of Confederate president Jefferson Davis (1808–1889).

During the last weeks of June, confidence in Johnston dried up around the city. At this point, rations became so small in Vicksburg that people were forced to eat rats, cats, and dogs. In addition, the pressure of living under the growing threat of starvation drove some people to nervous breakdowns. Medical supplies vanished as well, even as the number of sick and wounded continued to rise. Chaplain William Lovelace Foster (1830–1869) of the Thirty-Fifth Mississippi Infantry recalled the awful conditions under which Confederate doctors and nurses were forced to treat these patients: "On passing through the hospital what a heart-rending spectacle greets the eyes! Here we see the horrors of dreadful war! . . . The weather is excessively hot and the flies swarm around the wounded—more numerous where the wound is severest. In a few days the wounds begin to be offensive and horrid. . . . Never before did I have such an idea of the cruelty and the barbarism of war."

On June 28, Pemberton received a letter addressed from "many soldiers" that begged him to give in to Grant's stranglehold on the city. "If you can't feed us, you had better surrender, horrible as the idea is, than suffer this noble army to disgrace themselves by desertion," stated the starving soldiers. "This army is now ripe for mutiny, unless it can be fed." A few days later, on July 4, Pemberton reluctantly surrendered the city to Grant, and Union troops moved in. As the Yankee soldiers took up positions throughout Vicksburg, many of them rushed to share their rations with the city's starving people. Grant, meanwhile, allowed Pemberton's battered troops to scatter for their homes across the South. A few days later, Grant took control of Port Hudson, Louisiana, the last Confederate presence on the Mississippi. The entire Mississippi River Valley now belonged to the North.

Grant's grim victory at Vicksburg shook the Confederacy to its core. Combined with Lee's defeat at Gettysburg, Grant's triumph on the Mississippi deflated Southern expectations of victory and forced many Southerners to consider the possibility of an ultimate Union triumph. "One brief month ago we were apparently at the point of success," lamented Confederate officer Josiah Gorgas (1818–1883) in July 1863. "Now the picture is just as sombre as it was bright then. . . . It seems incredible that human power

could effect such a change in so brief a space. Yesterday we rode on the pinnacle of success—today absolute ruin seems to be our portion. The Confederacy totters to its destruction."

Lincoln's troubles on the home front

The Union victories at Gettysburg and Vicksburg in July 1863 came just in time for President Lincoln. In the first half of 1863, political and popular opposition to Lincoln's wartime policies had mounted all across the North. Democrats accounted for a good deal of this criticism. They opposed the Republican president on the war, emancipation, and a wide range of other issues. But many other people had emerged as critics of Lincoln as well.

The reasons for this unhappiness with the president varied. Many Northerners believed that the Lincoln administration's determination to win the war had led it to take illegal measures to silence its opponents. These measures included putting people in jail without trial and closing newspapers that were critical of the administration. Other opponents argued that wartime inflation (increases in the cost of food, clothing, and other goods) was destroying the Northern economy. Another reason for Lincoln's unpopularity in some regions was his decision to institute the Conscription Act in March 1863. This law required all male citizens between the ages of twenty and forty-five to enlist in the Union Army.

Lincoln's conscription law infuriated many people. Large numbers of people opposed a military draft because it forced thousands of young men to join a fight that had already claimed the lives of tens of thousands of other young men. Democrats, meanwhile, charged that one of the law's provisions—which enabled enlistees to avoid serving by hiring a substitute or paying a $300 fee—meant that the ranks of the Federal Army would be filled mostly by poor people. These critics complained that the draft would force white laborers to fight for the freedom of blacks, who would then come to the North and take their jobs.

Democratic anger about Lincoln's policies became so great that many of the party's leaders and organizations threatened to defy the president. Members of one Democratic convention even pledged that "we will not render support to the present Administration in its wicked Abolition crusade [and] we will *resist* to the *death* all attempts to draft any of our citizens into the army." These tensions over the draft ultimately sparked an ugly riot in New York City that left 105 people dead in July 1863. Many of the rioters targeted black people in the violence. Black homes and an orphanage for black children were burned to the ground, and several blacks were hung from street lampposts. The unrest ended only after the mob clashed with a detachment of Federal troops from the Army of the Potomac.

The single greatest problem that confronted Lincoln during the first half of 1863, however, was the lack of progress in the war. Many Northerners had come to the gloomy conclusion that the North could not beat the South. Others believed that the Union would eventually win, but only after enduring many years of war and sacrificing thousands and thousands of young men. The president himself confessed similar fears from time to time.

Nevertheless, Lincoln managed to maintain a steady guiding hand over the troubled nation throughout this period. He kept various political factions working together to advance the Federal war effort. He also used all his skills as a leader and communicator to keep the majority of the Northern people united behind his vision of a restored United States. But sooner or later, he knew that domestic support for the war effort would die if the Union Army could not produce victories in the field.

The nearly simultaneous Union victories at Vicksburg and Gettysburg thus came at an ideal time for Lincoln. As he had anticipated, Union victories in the field triggered renewed support for the war effort among the North's civilian population. In fact, news of the Federal triumphs instantly transformed the atmosphere across much of the North from one of discouragement to one of confident determination.

Rosecrans occupies Chattanooga

In the months following the clashes at Vicksburg and Gettysburg,

Bread Riots in Richmond

By the middle of 1863, shortages of food and supplies had become so severe in some parts of the Confederacy that riots broke out. Hungry mobs invaded stores and food warehouses in more than a dozen Southern cities during the spring and summer, including Augusta, Georgia, and Mobile, Alabama.

The largest and most alarming of these riots was the one that erupted in the Confederate capital of Richmond, Virginia. Richmond was very vulnerable to food shortages for two major reasons. First, it had to feed both the Confederate armies and the city's own growing population. Second, many farmers in northern Virginia had a difficult time harvesting their crops because of the large number of battles that took place in the region.

By the spring of 1863, constant fighting elsewhere in Virginia had reduced Richmond's food supply to very low levels. At the same time, the cost of the few food items left on store shelves jumped to shockingly high levels. On April 2, a few hundred women gathered at a Baptist church to talk about the growing crisis. They then marched to the mansion of Governor John Letcher (1813–1884) to express their concern, but he basically ignored them. From that point on, the group grew in size and became an unruly mob. It turned to an area of Richmond that housed shops and bakeries.

Within a short period of time, the mob grew to more than a thousand people. Women made up most of the crowd, but some men and boys joined in as well. The mob broke into several food warehouses and shops, taking bread and flour and other food items for their hungry families. Some rioters then moved on to other

the Union and Confederate forces that had been involved in those fights spent most of their time resting and rebuilding their armies. In middle Tennessee, though, the war continued. In late June, Union general William S. Rosecrans had moved his Army of the Cumberland against General Braxton Bragg's Confederate Army of Tennessee. Rosecrans directed his sixty thousand–man army forward throughout the summer of 1863 in a brilliant campaign that completely confused Bragg. By early September, Rosecrans' maneuvers had convinced Bragg to abandon the southeastern Tennessee city of Chattanooga, even though it was a major Confederate railroad center and supply depot. When Jefferson Davis learned that Bragg had fled Chattanooga without a fight, he confessed that "we [the Confederate states] are now in the darkest hour of our political existence."

stores, stealing jewelry, clothing, and other items in the confusion.

When Richmond mayor Joseph C. Mayo (1795–1872) learned of the riot, he quickly mobilized a company of militia to stop the mob. But the crowd ignored his warnings to go back to their homes. The members of the mob knew that the militia contained friends and neighbors, and they did not believe that the soldiers would ever attack them.

Finally, President Jefferson Davis arrived at the scene. Davis knew that the mob's conduct could not be allowed to continue, and at first he tried to convince them to leave voluntarily. The rioters responded with hostility, though, and Davis decided that he needed to take stronger measures. He told the mob that if it did not leave the area in five minutes, he would order the militia to fire into the crowd. The rioters did not budge for four minutes. But when Davis looked at his watch and said, "My friends, you have one minute more," the mob broke up, and the people returned to their homes.

Confederate officials later arrested several leaders of the mob, and a few of them even went to prison for a short time. But the riot convinced city officials and merchants that they needed to take additional steps to relieve the people's hunger. The local government increased their distribution of food to needy citizens, and local merchants dropped their prices. These changes helped the people of Richmond, but finding enough food for their families continued to be a problem throughout the rest of the war.

Bragg's evacuation of Chattanooga convinced Rosecrans that his Army of the Cumberland could acquire additional Confederate territory. After stationing a garrison of soldiers in Chattanooga, the overconfident Rosecrans resumed his pursuit of Bragg's Army of Tennessee. But Bragg had stopped retreating. Instead, he established a strong position in northern Georgia, where large numbers of Confederate reinforcements joined him from as far away as Virginia. These reinforcements included two divisions commanded by Longstreet, who had been one of Rosecrans' roommates at West Point, the prestigious New York military training academy.

Unaware of Bragg's decision to make a stand, Rosecrans pushed his troops forward. Bragg, meanwhile, sent a number of Confederate soldiers directly to the Union camp, where they pretended to be deserters. Their false tales of Confederate retreat further boosted Rosecrans' overconfidence.

The Battle of Chickamauga

By mid-September, Bragg's army had grown to seventy thousand men, and the Confederate general decided to launch a major attack on Rosecrans' widely dispersed troops. Rosecrans learned of the attack just in time, and he hurriedly gathered his army together near Chickamauga Creek in Georgia. The brutal Battle of Chickamauga erupted on the morning of September 19. Both sides engaged in bitter struggles for small pieces of land, but neither army could gain a big advantage. At one point, Confederate troops under the direction of Major General John B. Hood (1831–1879) registered significant gains on their Yankee foes. But their advance disintegrated when Hood and his lieutenants stumbled into an angry nest of stinging hornets.

On September 20, the battle resumed. This time, however, Rosecrans' Army of the Cumberland wilted under heavy pressure from Bragg's troops. Rather than attempt to hold his position, Rosecrans called a panicky retreat. Many of Rosecrans' divisions promptly fled the field of battle, and Bragg's triumphant soldiers immediately gave chase. The entire Union Army might have been destroyed were it not for the heroics of Major General George H. Thomas. The courageous Federal officer used his

troops to establish a defensive shield around the fleeing Union soldiers. Thomas's brave stand enabled the Army of the Cumberland to withdraw to Chattanooga without being cut to pieces by their pursuers. Even so, Rosecrans lost sixteen thousand men in the struggle.

Over on the Confederate side, meanwhile, casualties numbered more than eighteen thousand. In addition, Bragg was harshly criticized in Richmond and by his own officers in the days following the battle. These critics argued that if Bragg had pursued Rosecrans more vigorously, the Army of the Cumberland could have been wiped out before it reached the safety of Chattanooga.

Nonetheless, the Battle of Chickamauga was a major triumph for the South. It gave the Confederacy something to cheer about after the disasters at Vicksburg and Gettysburg. Moreover, it sent a strong message to the North that the South remained a strong foe on the field of battle.

Federal victory at Chattanooga

In October 1863, the South tried to finish off the Union's Army of the Cumberland. Bragg's forces formed a heavily armed circle around the city of Chattanooga. This line of rebel troops made it impossible for the North to deliver supplies to Rosecrans's soldiers, and prevented the Union Army from making an escape. The Confederates hoped to starve the Union troops into surrendering, just

Lookout Mountain, near Chattanooga, Tennessee. *(Courtesy of the Library of Congress.)*

as Grant had done to them during the siege at Vicksburg.

The situation at Chattanooga deeply alarmed the Lincoln administration. Lincoln viewed Rosecrans's behavior as "confused and stunned like a duck hit on the head." The president's military advisors warned him that the siege of Chattanooga might ruin the Army of the Cumberland. As the Confederate stranglehold over the city tightened, Federal troops under the command of Joseph Hooker and William T. Sherman (1820–1891) were ordered to travel to the area to give assistance. In mid-October, Lincoln appointed Ulysses S. Grant to take control of all Union troops in the entire West.

As soon as Grant received his promotion, he replaced Rosecrans with Thomas as commander of the Army of the Cumberland. He then took action to deliver supplies to the Union troops trapped in Chattanooga. By the end of October, a series of maneuvers enabled the North to open a supply route into the city, and morale among the troops in the Army of the Cumberland rose dramatically.

During the first few weeks of November, the situation at Chattanooga continued to sour for the South. Bragg's relationships with his officers and troops worsened to the point that Jefferson Davis actively considered replacing him. In addition, more than twelve thousand Confederate troops were sent to Knoxville, Tennessee, as part of a failed attempt to pry the city loose from Union control. This departure of troops reduced Bragg's army to

less than fifty thousand men. In the meantime, the swift arrival of Sherman's and Hooker's Union divisions pushed the Federal troop strength to more than fifty-six thousand.

On November 24, Grant ordered an attack on Bragg's army, which was concentrated along Missionary Ridge and Lookout Mountain near Chattanooga. Union troops first attacked Lookout Mountain, taking control of the position with surprising ease. The following day, Grant moved to take Missionary Ridge, the rebels' lone remaining stronghold. Thomas's Army of the Cumberland led the attack. Forced to endure weeks of teasing from Sherman's and Hooker's troops because of their defeat at Chickamauga, Thomas's troops entered the field of battle in an angry mood. After seizing a row of Confederate rifle pits, they charged up the mountain slope to attack the rebel position at the top of Missionary Ridge. Grant watched this development with alarm, for no one had ordered such a charge. But the brave assault was successful. As the Army of the Cumberland drove into the Confederate lines, the rebels broke into a complete retreat.

The Union victory at Chattanooga was a very important one. The Confederate withdrawal into Georgia served as a strong signal that Federal control of the West could not be broken by the rebels, and it reassured Northern public opinion. In addition, the ragged Confederate retreat convinced Davis that Bragg needed to be removed from his command. Davis quickly replaced him with General Joseph E. Johnston, even though the Confederate president strongly disliked Johnston. Finally, the campaign once again displayed the military talents and leadership of Ulysses S. Grant. Taking note of Grant's many triumphs of the previous few years, Lincoln named him general-in-chief over all Union troops a few months later.

Women in the Civil War

The Civil War had a greater effect on American women than any other conflict in the nation's history. Women from both the North and the South played a wide range of roles during the war. "Although conditioned in contrasting environments and schooled in opposing philosophies, women stepped forward as defenders of their respective causes," Mary Elizabeth Massey wrote in *Women in the Civil War*. "Emotions, energies, and talents that even they did not realize they possessed were unleashed."

Many women made direct contributions to the war effort as nurses, spies, government employees, factory workers, and members of aid societies. Some even hid their identities in order to join the fight as soldiers. In order to serve their country, these women had to overcome traditional attitudes that had limited them to roles as homemakers and mothers in the past. Many other women became involved in the war against their will. They spent long hours worrying about the safety of their loved ones in battle, writing letters to boost soldiers' spirits, and taking care of their homes and children in the absence of men. Especially in the South,

Words to Know

Civil War conflict that took place from 1861 to 1865 between the Northern states (Union) and the Southern seceded states (Confederacy); also known in the South as the War between the States and in the North as the War of the Rebellion

Confederacy eleven Southern states that seceded from the United States in 1860 and 1861

Union Northern states that remained loyal to the United States during the Civil War

education or to become politically active. Famous Civil War nurse Clara Barton (1821–1912) once claimed that the war placed women fifty years ahead of where they would have been otherwise in American society.

A time of hardship and grief

The Civil War placed a terrible emotional burden on women on both sides of the conflict. Those who were left at home worried constantly about the safety and comfort of the husbands, fathers, and sons they had sent to battle. They followed reports of the war in the newspapers and waited anxiously for word about their loved ones. Throughout the war years, women often gathered at train stations across the country to hear the names of the dead called, and to comfort those who were grieving afterward. The endless fear and sadness took a heavy toll on them. As diarist Mary Boykin Chesnut (1823–1886) wrote, "Does anybody wonder why so many women die? Grief and constant anxiety kill nearly as many women as men die on the battlefield."

women faced extreme shortages of food and clothing, and many were forced to leave their homes as enemy troops arrived.

When the war ended, life did not return to normal for most American women. Over six hundred thousand men died, and many of those who did return home had physical or emotional scars. Many families lost their homes and property and struggled to make ends meet, especially in the South. Such hardships forced some women to begin working outside the home. Other women found that they enjoyed the freedom and independence they had discovered through their wartime experiences. Many of these women refused to return to traditional roles after the war, and instead chose to continue their

Many women found that keeping busy helped ease their anxiety. In the North, some women passed the time by sewing and knitting furiously in order to produce warm clothing for the soldiers. Some formed aid societies, which were groups that raised money and collected food, clothing, medicine, and other supplies for the troops or for wounded soldiers and their families. Other Northern women took jobs outside the home in order to support their families and contribute to the war effort. Since many men had left factory jobs to enlist in the army, over one hundred thousand industrial positions opened up for women during the war years. Thousands more women became "government girls" by taking office jobs as civil service workers (employees in government administration). Free black women formed groups to help former slaves who had escaped to the North.

The Civil War was more difficult for Southern women in some ways, because most of the major battles took place on Southern soil. "Although women in both camps shared many of the same problems and experiences, one very important distinction existed," Massey explained. "This 'woman's war' was being fought by Southerners on their own doorsteps and the women had to battle the enemy as best they could." In addition to worrying about the safety of their loved ones, Southern women also had to worry about protecting their homes and getting enough food for their children.

During the course of the war, Northern troops conquered many major Southern cities, including Nashville, New Orleans, Atlanta, and Richmond. When some of these cities were captured, particularly towards the end of the war, large numbers of women and children were forced to leave their homes and become refugees. The Northern troops often took whatever food and valuables they could find, either for their own

 People to Know

Dorothea Dix (1802–1887) educator who fought for humane treatment of the mentally ill

Rose O'Neal Greenhow (1817–1864) Washington socialite who was a spy for the Confederacy

Florence Nightingale (1820–1910) nurse who dedicated her life to the care of the sick and those wounded in war

Elizabeth Van Lew (1818–1900) Virginian who was a spy for the Union

use or to keep them from falling into enemy hands. After the Union troops left, many Southern women returned to find their homes destroyed and their fields burned. In this way, a once-wealthy woman might suddenly find herself poor and homeless.

To make matters worse, basic necessities of life such as food and clothing were in very short supply throughout the South during the war years. Northern ships had blocked the flow of goods into Southern ports, and many farmers either left their fields unplanted or saw their crops seized for the war effort. Prices rose quickly on the goods that were available. Southern women had to be very resourceful in order to make ends meet. Some traded fancy dresses, jewelry, and

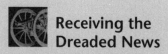

Receiving the Dreaded News

Many women who remained at home during the war lived in constant fear of receiving bad news about the fathers, husbands, and brothers who served as soldiers in the conflict. In *Reminiscences of the Women of Missouri during the Sixties,* Mrs. P. G. Robert of Richmond, Virginia, described the shock one of her young neighbors experienced upon learning that her new husband had been killed in action:

> A bride of six weeks, going to the door on her way out, returned to tell her mother that the next door neighbor's son had been killed and was being carried into the mother's house. Her mother hastened with her to the door, only to find that the soldiers had mistaken the house, retraced their steps, and were coming up their own steps, bearing the groom who but six weeks before, in the pride and strength of manhood, went to join his regiment; although he held in his pocket a furlough [leave of absence] for several days, he could not let his regiment go into active service without him. The mother, taking in the incident, caught her daughter in her arms and bore her into the parlor and laid her on the floor on the identical spot where six weeks before she had stood as a bride.

other items for food. Others set up small businesses in their homes, making soap or candles.

Life was difficult for black women in the South, too. Many chose to remain with their masters even though the Emancipation Proclamation had technically set them free. Most of these women stayed where they were because they felt safer in familiar surroundings than in a war zone. Some continued to work in the fields, while others cooked or cleaned for Confederate troops.

Because many battles were near their homes, Southern women also came into more direct contact with the horrors of war than did most Northern women. For example, major fighting took place just outside of Richmond, Virginia, in May and June 1862. During this time, twenty-one thousand wounded Confederate soldiers were brought into the city for medical attention. "We lived in one immense hospital," a Richmond woman said. Churches, hotels, warehouses, barns, and even homes throughout the South were turned into temporary hospitals, and hundreds of women were pressed into service as nurses.

Women's roles in the war

Not all American women remained at home while the men fought the Civil War. Some wives, particularly those of officers, followed their husbands to the front lines of battle and lived with them at soldiers' camps. Some unmarried women spent time at the soldiers' camps as well, cooking, doing laundry, and sometimes serving as prostitutes—even though the traditional values of society frowned upon this practice. In addition, approximately four hundred women posed as men in order to fight in the war as soldiers. Some of these women were inspired by their strong feelings about the cause, while others were merely looking for adventure. Many of the female soldiers managed to serve for two or more years before their gender was discovered, usually after they were wounded.

Nurses and aid workers

Over three thousand American women acted as paid nurses during the Civil War, and thousands more performed nursing duties as volunteers. Women chose to contribute to the war effort as nurses for a wide variety of reasons. Some became nurses out of compassion—they saw that the wounded soldiers needed help and were determined to provide it. Others were looking for excitement or for an opportunity to be independent and make themselves useful. Still others became nurses so that they could be near their loved ones or because they needed the money.

In the early days of the war, both the Union and Confederate armies actively discouraged women from serving as nurses. Many men of that time felt that nursing was not an appropriate activity for women. They did not want "refined ladies" to be subjected to the horrors of war by treating sick, wounded, and dying soldiers in army hospitals. "No one denied that most women had an aptitude for nursing, that many had gained experience from tending their families and friends, and that necessity had required those in rural areas to be amateur pharmacists, yet public opinion doubted the [suitability] of their nursing in army hospitals," Massey noted. "It was permissible for white women to nurse the sick at home or even in the slave quarters, but they had no business in the masculine [environment] of an army hospital which presented sights that no lady should see," according to James M. McPherson in *Battle Cry of Freedom*. "[Most men felt that] women should stay at home and make bandages, knit socks for soldiers, and comfort the menfolk when they returned from the rigors [hardships] of battle."

But many women chose to become nurses anyway, ignoring the opinions of their fathers, husbands, or brothers. Some of them were inspired by Florence Nightingale (1820–1910), the Englishwoman who had revolutionized British Army medical services during the Crimean War (1853–56) a few years earlier. Many American women viewed Nightingale as a hero for her wartime service and for building the world's first nursing school in 1860. Unfortunately, there were no formal training programs for nurses in the United States at that time. As a result, the word "nurse" applied to many people who performed different functions in the early years of the Civil War. Some women nurses wrote letters for bedridden soldiers, prepared their meals, or entertained them with music or stories. Others changed bandages, disinfected wounds, and assisted in operations.

Nursing efforts were generally better organized among Northern

Dorothea Dix, Superintendent of Female Nurses for the Union

Dorothea Lynde Dix was born in Hampden, Maine, in 1802. She worked as a schoolteacher for many years before turning her attention to the treatment of the insane. In the early 1800s, people who were deaf, could not speak, or had psychological problems were treated as outcasts in American society. They were often sent to asylums (institutions for the mentally ill) where they endured inhumane treatment by uncaring workers. In 1843, Dix published a report describing the terrible abuse mentally ill people suffered in such places. She claimed that they were treated like animals—left unclothed, sometimes chained to a bed or wall, in small, dark, unsanitary rooms. She argued that the insane deserved special facilities staffed by caring, trained personnel. In the pre-war years, Dix took her case to state legislatures all over the country and succeeded in convincing many of them to build special hospitals for the treatment of the insane.

Over the years, Dix gained a reputation as an important social reformer. In the 1850s, she traveled to Europe to visit Florence Nightingale, the Englishwoman who had revolutionized British Army medical services during the Crimean War and later established the world's first nursing school. At the beginning of the Civil War, it became clear that the Federal government needed an efficient, qualified woman to supervise the female nurses who would be working with the Union Army. Dix was appointed superintendent of female nurses on June 10, 1861.

Dix—who was a proper, matronly woman at the age of fifty-nine—immediately began outlining qualifications and rules for women nurses. Like many other people of her time, she believed that nursing was not an appropriate occupation for young, unmarried women. She thought that attractive female nurses would be harassed by soldiers, would not be taken seriously by doctors, and would have their morality questioned by the larger society. As a result, she set a minimum age of thirty for women nurses, and also required appli-

women than Southern women. Northern women enjoyed greater independence at the beginning of the Civil War, and many had formed or joined groups to support the abolition of slavery. As a result, they became involved in nursing earlier and in greater numbers. Women throughout the North organized local aid societies to collect supplies and distribute them to Union troops. In 1861, several of these local societies combined forces under the U.S. Sanitary Commission, which was created by an order of President Abraham Lincoln (1809–1865). The mission of this government

Dorothea Dix. *(Reproduced by permission of AP/Wide World Photos, Inc.)*

cants to be "plain in appearance." Women who met these requirements and completed the formal training were allowed to take paying jobs as nurses at army hospitals. While they worked, Dix required them to wear simple, hoopless dresses, and no jewelry or makeup. Although some nurses initially objected to this rule, they soon realized that fancy clothing would only get in the way of doing their jobs.

Dix had equal numbers of admirers and enemies during her time as superintendent of female nurses for the Union. She could be soft-spoken and gentle at times, but at other times she was abrasive (harsh) and opinionated, especially when she had to defend her nurses from discrimination. "It is not always clear whether the men resented Miss Dix because she was dictatorial or because she was more efficient than many of them," Mary Elizabeth Massey wrote in *Women of the Civil War.* "The nurses' opinions of their superintendent were mixed; the new ones almost invariably were afraid or awed, but after a time most came to respect her and many were sincerely devoted." When the Civil War ended, Dix resigned from her post and returned to her humanitarian work on behalf of the insane. She continued working up until her death in 1887, at the age of eighty-five.

agency was to establish training programs for nurses and to improve sanitary conditions for the Union Army.

By 1863, the Sanitary Commission had seven thousand affiliated local organizations and tens of thousands of women volunteer workers. These volunteers raised money and sent food, medicine, and clothing to army camps and hospitals. They also provided meals and lodging to soldiers coming and going from the battle lines. The Sanitary Commission provided training for women nurses and sent them to areas where they were

Appreciation for the Contributions of Women in the Civil War

By the time the Civil War ended, most people recognized that women had made immense contributions to the war effort. President Abraham Lincoln was one of many men who expressed their appreciation:

> I am not accustomed to use the language of eulogy. I have never studied the art of paying compliments to women. But I must say that, if all that has been said by orators and poets since the creation of the world in praise of women was applied to the women of America, it would not do them justice for their conduct during this war. I will close by saying, God bless the women of America!

needed. Women nurses were particularly important on hospital ships—large, specially equipped boats that evacuated wounded Union soldiers from Southern ports and took them to civilian hospitals in New York and Washington. These ships often faced enemy fire as they carried out their missions. Another important role of the Sanitary Commission involved inspecting army camps and recommending changes that would improve the health of the soldiers. These inspections were important because poor hygiene at army camps—including contaminated water supplies and unsanitary cooking practices—contributed to widespread illness and disease among the soldiers.

In contrast to these organized efforts in the North, most Southern women entered nursing independently. Some chose to become nurses, while others were pressed into service when their homes were turned into makeshift hospitals. The early efforts of these women nurses were recognized in September 1862, when the Confederate Congress passed a law allowing civilian nurses to work in army hospitals. Many Southern women became part of the official Confederate Army medical service under this law.

Confederate nurses faced special problems. Since most of the fighting took place in the South, they were often forced to move patients and entire hospitals in order to remain behind the battle lines. When Confederate troops made a sudden retreat, some women nurses risked their lives to stay with patients who could not be moved.

Since Southern white women had tended to lead sheltered lives before the war, many people were surprised at the nurses' courage and ability to recover quickly during the war. Kate Cumming, a young woman from Mobile, Alabama, served as a nurse in a hotel that had been turned into a hospital. "Nothing that I had ever heard or read had given me the faintest idea of the horrors witnessed here," she wrote in her memoir, *Kate: The Journal of a Confederate Nurse*. "The foul air from this mass of human beings at first made me giddy and sick, but I soon got over it. We have to walk and, when we give the men anything, kneel in blood and water; but we think nothing of it."

The service of women nurses during the Civil War helped change traditional attitudes about women as the "weaker sex." It also helped turn nursing into a respectable profession for women. "Despite the early skepticism [doubting attitude] of the surgeons and the general public about the propriety as well as the ability of women to serve as nurses during the Civil War, some 3,000 women showed the world they had the stamina [endurance], the commitment, the organizational abilities, and the talent to become a vital force in the Nation," Marilyn Mayer Culpepper wrote in *Trials and Triumphs: Women of the American Civil War.*

Spies, scouts, couriers, and saboteurs

American women also played other, less visible, roles in the Civil War—for example, by helping their side gain information as spies, scouts, and couriers (messengers carrying information). "Many spirited girls and imaginative women were challenged by the opportunity to perform daring deeds for their cause," Massey noted. Some women became spies out of strong feelings of patriotism—they wanted to do their part to help their own side win the war. Others became spies for the opposite reason—they wanted to help the other side win. For example, the wife of one Confederate officer had been born and raised in the North, and she passed informa-

Nurses and officers of the U.S. Sanitary Commission. *(Photograph by James Gardner. Courtesy of the Library of Congress.)*

tion about the South's plans to her father and brothers in the Union Army.

Since many women in both the North and the South had friends or family fighting for the other side, rumors about spying activities circulated from the earliest days of the Civil War. Newspapers often printed such rumors, which forced some women to live under clouds of suspicion. In some cases, neighbors turned on women whose loyalty they questioned. Women accused of spying were often banished from the region where they lived and forced to make dangerous journeys to the other side of the battle lines. Many of the women accused of spying were innocent, but some women actively gathered and carried secret information during the war. Most women who became involved in these activities counted on receiving less severe punishment if they were caught because of their gender.

In general, the Union did a better job of detecting and punishing enemy agents than did the Confederacy. Even before the Civil War began, the Federal government had taken steps to silence people who favored secession in Washington, D.C., and other areas. Many Southern sympathizers and suspected spies were either arrested and put in prison or banished from the Union. However, officials on both sides were reluctant to believe that women would act as spies. They often refused to consider women dangerous until after they had transmitted secret military information to the other side.

There were many successful women spies on both sides of the Civil War. One of the most effective Union spies was Elizabeth Van Lew (1818–1900) of Richmond, Virginia, who became known as "Crazy Bet." Throughout the war years, she pretended to be an eccentric (odd character) so that Confederate officials would view her as "crazy but harmless." In the meantime, she helped Federal prisoners escape from Richmond and provided Union general Ulysses S. Grant (1822–

1885) with information that helped him capture the Confederate capital city. After the war ended, Grant arranged for guards to protect Van Lew's house and later appointed her postmistress of Richmond.

Black women also made effective spies during the war. In fact, Van Lew received much of her secret information from her former slave, Mary Elizabeth Bowser. Van Lew had sent Bowser to Philadelphia for schooling prior to the war. Once the war started, she arranged for Bowser to become a servant to President Jefferson Davis (1808–1889) in the Confederate White House. Bowser pretended that she could not read, then stole glances at confidential memos and orders while she was cleaning. She also eavesdropped on conversations between Confederate officials while she served dinner. Bowser passed information about troop movements and other Confederate Army plans along to Van Lew, who sent it on to Union officials. Bowser's activities as a Union spy went undetected throughout the war.

An early Confederate spy was Rose O'Neal Greenhow (1817–1864), a Washington socialite who used her prominent position to extract information from Union officials. The secret messages she sent to friends in the South helped turn the First Battle of Bull Run (also called the First Battle of Manassas) into a Confederate victory in 1861. Afterward, she was placed under house arrest, and her home was turned into a prison for other women spies. Greenhow still managed to send messages outside, however, so after a brief stay in a Federal prison, she was sent behind Confederate lines in 1862. President Davis greeted her warmly and told her, "But for you there would have been no Battle of Bull Run."

Many other women acted as couriers during the war, smuggling money, weapons, or messages in their hair or in the lining of their hoop skirts. Still others committed acts of sabotage in support of their cause. For example, one Southern woman and her daughter destroyed several bridges in Tennessee to slow a Union advance. Other women helped prisoners escape, destroyed enemy property, and cut telegraph wires.

Changes in attitudes after the war

The Civil War inspired many American women to move beyond the comfort of their traditional roles. Before the war, only 25 percent of white women worked outside the home before marriage. Taking care of a home and raising a family were considered the ideal roles for women, while men increasingly worked outside the home. This situation created separate spheres for men and women in American society. During the war, however, women often worked alongside men as equals in hospitals, offices, factories, and political organizations. In addition, many women began paying attention to current events because many issues had a direct impact on their lives. They began speaking out about military and political matters, proving that they were literate and had the capacity to form well-reasoned opinions. As a result, women were generally taken more seriously in society. "By the end of the war, gone or at least fast disappearing was the typical stereotype of women as delicate, submissive [docile or yielding] China dolls," Culpepper wrote. "The change was a welcome one for many women who savored their newly acquired independence and emerging feelings of self-worth."

But the end of the war brought other problems for some women, particularly in the South. Many soldiers returned home defeated and disheartened, while others faced severe physical or emotional problems. Many families had lost their homes and property during the war. To make matters worse, Confederate money suddenly became worthless, which left many families with heavy debts.

In families where the men had been killed or disabled, women were often required to enter the work force. As a result, the social restrictions that had prevented many women from working outside the home gradually relaxed. Some women chose to continue their volunteer work at hospitals and veterans' rehabilitation centers, while others turned their attention to new causes, such as women's rights. Greater numbers of women sought higher education, and many colleges and universities around the country began admitting women.

1864: The North Tightens Its Grip

In early 1864, the Federal Army made plans to destroy the Confederate military once and for all. Union armies led by Ulysses S. Grant (1822–1885) and William T. Sherman (1820–1891) launched offensives deep into Confederate territory with the specific purpose of wiping out the South's major remaining armies. This strategy enjoyed support throughout the North, which had become confident of victory after the Union triumphs of 1863. By midsummer, however, Northern confidence wavered as Confederate defiance stayed strong. Dissatisfaction with Grant's campaign was particularly strong, since he racked up very high casualty rates in his effort to break the Confederate Army of Northern Virginia, led by Robert E. Lee (1807–1870).

As the 1864 U.S. presidential elections drew near, many people believed that war-weary Northerners would vote to replace President Abraham Lincoln (1809–1865) with Democratic candidate George B. McClellan (1826–1885), the former general of the Army of the Potomac. If McClellan won the election, many citizens believed he would enter into peace negotiations to end the war and provide the Confederacy with the independence it wanted. But a late flurry of Union victo-

Words to Know

Blockade the act of surrounding a harbor with ships in order to prevent other vessels from entering or exiting the harbor; the word blockade is also sometimes used when ships or other military forces surround and isolate a city, region, or country

Civil War conflict that took place from 1861 to 1865 between the Northern states (Union) and the Southern seceded states (Confederacy); also known in the South as the War between the States and in the North as the War of the Rebellion

Confederacy eleven Southern states that seceded from the United States in 1860 and 1861

Federal national or central government; also refers to the North or Union as opposed to the South or Confederacy

Guerrillas small independent bands of soldiers or armed civilians who use raids and ambushes rather than direct military attacks to harass enemy armies

Rebel Confederate; often used as a name for a Confederate soldier

Siege surrounding and blockading of a city, town, or fortress by an army attempting to capture it

Union Northern states that remained loyal to the United States during the Civil War

Grant takes control

In the early months of 1864, the Lincoln administration took advantage of a quiet winter in the war to prepare the Union Army for the coming year. For example, Lincoln called for an additional five hundred thousand enlistees to join the military and appointed Ulysses S. Grant as commander of all Union forces.

Grant officially assumed his new position of lieutenant general on March 12. He immediately made big changes in the Union's war strategy. Convinced that Union military superiority had too often been wasted on unimportant missions in the past, Grant made it clear that he wanted to take a different approach. Rather than weaken his armies by diverting divisions all over Confederate territory, Grant proposed to keep his two primary armies together. These armies were the Army of the Potomac in the East, led by George Meade (1815–1872), and the newly created Military Division of the Mississippi in the West, led by William Sherman. Grant wanted to use these armies for the sole purpose of hammering the Confederate military to pieces.

The two primary rebel armies in 1864 were Robert E. Lee's famous Army of Northern Virginia and the Army of Tennessee, commanded by Joseph E. Johnston (1807–1891). Grant knew that these armies were dangerous. But both forces were operating under increasingly severe troop and supply limitations, and Grant wanted to squeeze the remaining life

ries vaulted Lincoln to victory in the November elections and smashed Confederate hopes of avoiding ultimate defeat.

out of them. The Union commander recognized that if he could wreck these Confederate armies, the South would have no choice but to return to the Union under conditions set by the North.

The North launches twin offensives

In early May 1864, the primary Union armies of the East and West rolled forward in search of forces commanded by Lee and Johnston. Sherman's army in the West pushed toward Atlanta, Georgia, in hopes that Johnston would use his army to defend the city. Grant, meanwhile, rode with the Army of the Potomac as it began its march on the Confederate capital of Richmond, Virginia. (George Meade remained the official head of the Army of the Potomac, but Grant exercised ultimate control over its actions.)

Grant knew that Lee would have to use his army to defend Richmond from invasion. The Union general reasoned that once the two sides met, his force of 115,000 soldiers would eventually crush Lee's army of 75,000 men. But before Grant could use his numerical superiority on an open field, Lee rushed to meet the advancing Union Army in a rugged northern Virginia region known as the Wilderness. Lee recognized that the Wilderness' dense woods, thick underbrush, and winding ravines would make it very difficult for Grant to make full use of his cavalry, artillery, and other advantages in firepower.

Battle of the Wilderness

On May 5, the two armies clashed in the brambles (prickly shrubs) and ravines of the Wilderness. The battle lasted for two days, as both sides engaged in a vicious struggle for survival. Desperate combat erupted all throughout the woods as opposing divisions crashed blindly into one another. A forest fire added to the terror and confusion of the battle. Many wounded men burned to death in the blaze, and billowing smoke made it even harder for the exhausted soldiers to find their way through the Wilderness.

The Battle of the Wilderness ended on May 7 in a virtual stalemate, with neither side giving ground. Lee's Army of Northern Virginia suffered losses of ten thousand soldiers in the fight, further weakening that valiant force. But the Union Army suffered more than seventeen thousand casualties in the clash without getting a mile closer to Richmond.

When Grant ordered his troops to prepare to pull out on the evening of May 7, depressed Federal soldiers assumed that they were going to retreat back to the North once again. After all, previous Union commanders of the Army of the Potomac had always retreated to lick their wounds after clashing with Lee. But as the Union Army left their camp, the soldiers suddenly realized that they were marching deeper into Confederate territory rather than retreating back to the North. Excited cheers broke out all along the Federal line. The soldiers who comprised the Army

People to Know

Jefferson Davis (1808–1889) president of the Confederate States of America, 1861–65

Jubal Early (1816–1894) Confederate lieutenant general who led the 1864 campaign in Shenandoah Valley; also fought at First Bull Run, Second Bull Run, Antietam, Fredericksburg, Chancellorsville, Gettysburg, the Wilderness, and Spotsylvania

David Farragut (1801–1870) Union admiral who led naval victories at New Orleans and Mobile Bay

Ulysses S. Grant (1822–1885) Union general who commanded all Federal troops, 1864–65; led Union armies at Shiloh, Vicksburg, Chattanooga, and Petersburg; eighteenth president of the United States, 1869–77

John B. Hood (1831–1879) Confederate general who commanded the Army of Tennessee at Atlanta in 1864; also fought at Second Bull Run, Antietam, Fredericksburg, Gettysburg, and Chickamauga

Joseph E. Johnston (1807–1891) Confederate general of the Army of Tennessee who fought at First Bull Run and Atlanta

Robert E. Lee (1807–1870) Confederate general of the Army of Northern Virginia; fought at Second Bull Run, Antietam, Gettysburg, Fredericksburg, and Chancellorsville; defended Richmond from Ulysses S. Grant's Army of the Potomac, 1864 to April 1865

Abraham Lincoln (1809–1865) sixteenth president of the United States, 1861–65

George McClellan (1826–1885) Union general who commanded the Army of the Potomac, August 1861 to November 1862; fought in the Seven Days campaign and at Antietam; Democratic candidate for presidency, 1864

George G. Meade (1815–1872) Union major general who commanded the Army of the Potomac, June 1863 to April 1865; also fought at Second Bull Run, Antietam, Fredericksburg, and Chancellorsville

Philip H. Sheridan (1831–1888) Union major general who commanded the Army of the Potomac's cavalry corps and the Army of the Shenandoah; also fought at Perryville, Murfreesboro, Chickamauga, and Chattanooga

William T. Sherman (1820–1891) Union major general who commanded the Army of the Tennessee and the Military Division of the Mississippi, October 1863 to April 1865; led the famous "March to the Sea"; also fought at First Bull Run, Shiloh, and Vicksburg

George H. Thomas (1816–1870) Union major general who commanded the Army of the Cumberland to victories at Chattanooga, Atlanta, and Nashville; also fought at Perryville and Chickamauga

of the Potomac were sick of losing to Lee. They viewed Grant's decision to continue his push to Richmond as a vote of confidence in their abilities. Many of them vowed that the campaign would not end until Lee's army was broken.

The Battle of Spotsylvania

As the Army of the Potomac pushed forward, it moved around Lee's right flank and drew near a small Virginia village called Spotsylvania. But Lee quickly mobilized his troops and launched a night march that enabled the Confederates to reach the village first. The rebel army immediately prepared a system of trenches and other fortifications, then settled in to await the arrival of the Union Army.

Lee's troops did not have to wait very long. Grant's Union forces attacked Lee's defenses on May 8, and for the next several days the two sides repeatedly clashed together in deadly fighting. On May 12, the Union forces managed to break through the Confederate defenses at a point that came to be called Bloody Angle. But rebel troops rushed forward to close the breach (opening), and for eighteen solid hours the two sides struggled for control of the trenches. Their desperate rushes often ended in brutal hand-to-hand combat. By midnight, when the Confederate forces finally withdrew to newly built defenses to their rear, the trenches at Bloody Angle were piled with dead bodies. "I never expect to be fully believed when I tell what I saw of

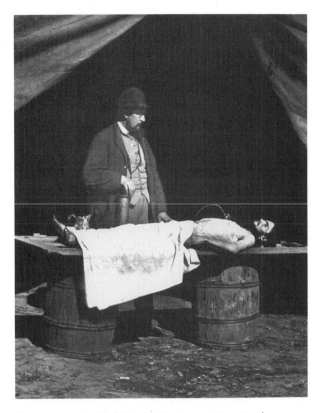

The corpse of a Civil War soldier is embalmed.

the horrors of Spotsylvania," admitted one Union officer after the war.

The fight for Spotsylvania lessened somewhat after the nightmarish struggle at Bloody Angle, but skirmishes continued for another week before Grant decided to move on. He resumed his march southward, pushing for Richmond while simultaneously looking for an opportunity to smash Lee's army, which escaped Grant's efforts to trap them in open-field combat.

Two wounded armies

By the end of May, Grant's plan to exert continuous pressure on

Illness and Disease Take a Toll on Soldiers

Approximately 359,000 Union soldiers and 258,000 Confederate soldiers lost their lives during the war. Although many of these men died on the battlefield, almost twice as many died of disease as were killed in combat. Part of the problem was that the science of medicine was not very advanced in the 1860s. "The unfortunate Civil War soldier, whether he came from the North or from the South, not only got into the army just when the killing power of weapons was being brought to a brand-new peak of efficiency; he enlisted in the closing years of an era when the science of medicine was woefully, incredibly imperfect, so that he got the worst of it in two ways," historian Bruce Catton explained. "When he fought, he was likely to be hurt pretty badly; when he stayed in camp, he lived under conditions that were very likely to make him sick; and in either case he had almost no chance to get the kind of medical treatment which a generation or so later would be routine."

During the Civil War years, doctors did not know what caused disease or why wounds became infected. The war occurred just before scientists discovered the microscopic organisms, like bacteria and viruses, that can infect food and water or enter the human body through wounds. As a result, doctors did not sterilize surgical instruments, bandages, or wounds. Vaccinations and antibiotics did not exist. Soldiers in army camps did not practice basic hygiene in cooking or disposing of waste. They thought that water was safe to drink unless it smelled bad or had garbage floating in it.

Disease hit soldiers the hardest right after joining the army. When thousands of men from different areas and

---

the Army of Northern Virginia was taking a heavy toll on the rebels. In mid-May, Lee lost legendary cavalryman Jeb Stuart (1833–1864) in a battle with Union cavalry led by Philip H. Sheridan (1831–1888). In addition, some of Lee's most important officers died from illnesses or had nervous breakdowns. Even Lee was not immune to Grant's relentless pressure. At one point the Confederate general contracted a severe case of flu that left him too weak to mount his horse. Finally, Grant's aggressive style was slowly eating away at Lee's army. Each battle and skirmish added to the Confederate death toll and deepened the mental and physical exhaustion of survivors.

But the fighting took a heavy toll on the Union Army, too. From May 5 to May 12 alone, the Army of the Potomac suffered thirty-two thousand casualties. Continual skirmishes pushed the casualty rate ever higher.

Hospital tents in Washington, D.C. *(Courtesy of the Library of Congress.)*

tonsillitis, and smallpox. Although most men eventually recovered from these diseases, the outbreaks reduced the strength of military units. To make matters worse, the poor sanitation in army camps led to numerous cases of dysentery, typhoid, pneumonia, and other illnesses. Maintaining the health of the troops was a major problem for both the North and the South throughout the war. "Disease was a crippling factor in Civil War military operations," historian James M. McPherson wrote. "At any given time a substantial proportion of men in a regiment might be on the sicklist. Disease reduced the size of most regiments from their initial complement of 1,000 men to about half that number before the regiment ever went into battle."

backgrounds crowded together in army camps, large numbers of them contracted common diseases like measles, mumps,

Grant pushed forward, however, and at the end of May he prepared for another major clash with Lee at a place called Cold Harbor, located ten miles northeast of Richmond.

The Battle of Cold Harbor

Lee adopted a defensive position at Cold Harbor. Recent reinforcements from other Confederate positions had increased the size of his army to almost sixty thousand men,

but Lee knew that Grant's approaching force was much larger. The rebel army's only hope was to build defensive fortifications that could withstand a full assault from the Yankees.

Armed with reinforcements that increased the size of his army to almost 110,000 troops, Grant tried to use brute force to pry the Confederates out of their positions at Cold Harbor. On the evening of June 2, he ordered his troops to prepare for a

Confederate general Robert E. Lee on horseback. *(Courtesy of the Library of Congress.)*

full frontal assault on the rebel defenses the following morning. A ripple of fear and apprehension ran through the Federal camp when the soldiers learned of this plan, for they knew that many of them would be killed or wounded in the attack. In the hours leading up to the assault, hundreds of Union soldiers pinned pieces of cloth and paper with their names and addresses to their uniforms so their bodies could be identified after the battle.

Grant launched his assault on Cold Harbor on the morning of June 3. The decision was possibly the worst of his entire military career. The Confederate Army shattered the advance in a hail of gunfire, and the Union Army never came close to breaching the rebel defenses. By the early afternoon Grant had lost more than seven thousand men. The Confederates, on the other hand, lost fewer than fifteen hundred in the clash. Years later, Grant admitted that his order to attack had been a terrible decision. "I have always regretted that the last assault at Cold Harbor was ever made," he wrote. "At Cold Harbor no advantage whatever was gained to compensate for the heavy loss we sustained."

Grant targets Petersburg

After the Union defeat at Cold Harbor, Grant changed tactics. He assigned two Union detachments under the command of David Hunter (1802–1886) and Philip Sheridan to undertake raids designed to cripple Confederate railroads and supply lines. He then removed the remainder of the Army of the Potomac from Cold Harbor and slipped southward across the James River. Grant's swift move to the south brought him close to Petersburg, Virginia, a city that supplied Richmond with much of its food and supplies. Grant knew that if the Union Army could capture the railroad yards of Petersburg, the Confederacy would have to abandon its capital city or risk mass starvation.

Once again, though, Lee's army reached Grant's target just in time to establish defensive positions. Grant tested the Confederate defenses, then ordered his men to prepare for a siege of the city. This siege began in mid-June 1864. It would not end until April 1865, when Lee finally abandoned the city.

Northern disillusionment with Grant's campaign

By midsummer 1864, many Northerners were questioning Grant's Petersburg strategy. At the beginning of the year, most Northern communities assumed that Grant would be able to destroy Lee's army and capture Richmond within a matter of weeks. But as the summer rolled by, the Army of the Potomac had not accomplished either goal.

The shockingly high casualty toll was another reason for Northern disillusionment with Grant's campaign. Within a month of setting out in pursuit of Lee's army, Grant's force had suffered sixty thousand casualties (Lee's Army of Northern Virginia lost approximately thirty-five thousand troops during this same period). These losses had a dreadful impact on public support for the war, for the release of each new casualty list triggered a new wave of heartbreak and mourning in hundreds of communities across the North. With each passing day, greater numbers of Northerners expressed doubts about the wisdom of continuing the war against the South. *New York Tribune* editor Horace Greeley (1811–1872) spoke for hundreds of thousands of Northerners when he stated in a letter to President Lincoln that "our bleeding, bankrupt, almost dying country . . . longs for peace—shudders at the prospect of fresh conscription [military draft], of further wholesale devastations, and of new rivers of blood."

Sherman chases Johnston

Over in the western theater, meanwhile, Sherman's initial attempts to demolish Joseph Johnston's Confederate Army of Tennessee also failed. Armed with nearly one hundred thousand troops, Sherman's force was considerably larger than the one led by Johnston. This advantage in firepower encouraged the Union commander to

Songs Reflect War Weariness

During the summer of 1864, several songs about the Civil War became very popular across the North. But unlike the patriotic war songs of previous years, these songs reflected widespread unhappiness with the war. As the casualty lists continued to grow with no end to the war in sight, many Northerners turned to songs like "Tenting on the Old Camp Ground." This song included lyrics sadly saying that "Many are the hearts that are weary tonight, Wishing for the War to cease."

Other popular antiwar songs of 1864 included "Tell Me, Is My Father Coming Back?" and "Yes, I Would the War Were Over." Millions of copies of sheet music to these songs were sold all across the North. Perhaps the best-known of these war-weary songs was "When This Cruel War Is Over." This song reflected the fears of countless women that their husbands and boyfriends might die on the field of battle.

Sheet music for the Civil War ballad "When This Cruel War Is Over." *(Courtesy of Duke University, Rare Book, Manuscript, and Special Collections Library.)*

Dearest Love, do you remember, when we last did meet,

How you told me that you loved me, kneeling at my feet?

Oh! How proud you stood before me, in your suit of blue,

When you vow'd to me and country, ever to be true.

CHORUS:

Weeping, sad and lonely, hopes and fears how vain!

When this cruel war is over, praying that we meet again.

When the summer breeze is sighing, mournfully along,

Or when autumn leaves are falling, sadly breathes the song.

Oft in dreams I see thee lying on the battle plain,

Lonely, wounded, even dying, calling but in vain.

CHORUS

If amid the din of battle, nobly you should fall,

Far away from those who love you, none to hear you call—

Who would whisper words of comfort, who would soothe your pain?

Ah! The many cruel fancies, ever in my brain.

CHORUS

But our Country called you, Darling, angels cheer your way;

While our nation's sons are fighting, we can only pray.

Nobly strike for God and Liberty, let all nations see

How we loved the starry banner, emblem of the free.

make repeated attempts to engage his Confederate foe on the field of battle.

But Johnston refused to be pinned down. Sometimes he used strategic retreats to avoid his Yankee pursuers. On other occasions, he stationed his rebel troops in strong defensive positions that could only be attacked with great difficulty and loss of life. By early summer, the Army of Tennessee had been pushed all the way from the Tennessee border to the outskirts of Atlanta, Georgia, but Johnston's sly maneuvering kept his army largely intact.

Hood assumes command in the West

Johnston's strategy of evasion frustrated Sherman, who knew that a big Union victory would help reassure unhappy Northerners that a Confederate collapse was near. But while Johnston's retreats enabled him to avoid a showdown, they also angered Confederate president Jefferson Davis (1808–1889). Davis had long disliked Johnston, and he believed that battlefield victories were the best way to increase Northern dissatisfaction with the war and improve Southern morale. President Davis thus decided to replace Johnston with Lieutenant General John B. Hood (1831–1879), a battle-hardened officer with a reputation as a bold and aggressive leader.

Hood took over on July 17 and immediately went on the offensive. In the last two weeks of July, he ordered three different assaults on Union forces threatening Atlanta. All three attacks failed though, and Hood suffered thousands of casualties in the process. By August, Hood's tired army was trapped in the city of Atlanta, and Sherman had gained control of most of the surrounding countryside. Unwilling to order a full-scale assault on the city's defenses, Sherman decided instead to try to bomb and starve the city into submission.

Democrats nominate McClellan for president

Back in the North, meanwhile, President Lincoln's chances of winning the upcoming presidential election seemed to grow dimmer with each passing day. Taking advantage of widespread disgust and discontent with the war, the Democrats promised voters that they would put an end to the bloodshed if their candidate—former Union general George McClellan—was elected president. The party was dominated by antiwar Democrats known as "Copperheads," possibly because some members wore buttons made from copper coins with a picture of the goddess of liberty. They declared the war a failure and made it clear that it was willing to give up on efforts to restore the shattered Union in return for peace.

McClellan objected to some elements of his party's campaign platform (statement of policies and actions that will be taken). "The Union must be preserved at all hazards," he wrote in a letter accepting the Democratic nomination for president. "I

Former Union general George B. McClellan ran unsuccessfully as a Democrat in the 1864 presidential election. *(Courtesy of the National Archives and Records Administration.)*

could not look in the face of my gallant comrades of the army and navy, who have survived so many bloody battles, and tell them that their labor and the sacrifice of so many of our slain and wounded brethren had been in vain." Despite such statements, however, most Northerners believed that a vote for McClellan in the upcoming election would be a vote for ending the war.

By August, Lincoln himself was certain that he would not be re-elected. At that time, neither Grant nor Sherman had succeeded in destroying their enemies, and both Petersburg and Atlanta remained in Confederate hands. Moreover, news from other regions of the country deepened the feeling that a final Union victory was as distant as ever. In Louisiana, Confederate forces smashed a Union bid to invade Texas. Over in northern Mississippi and southern Tennessee, Confederate cavalry raiders led by Nathan Bedford Forrest (1821–1877) tormented Union forces throughout the summer. Further north, in the Shenandoah Valley of Virginia, fourteen thousand Confederate troops under the command of Jubal Early (1816–1894) marched to within a dozen miles of Washington, D.C., before being turned back.

Certain that Northern disillusionment and sorrow had finally exhausted the nation's will to fight, Lincoln prepared for the November elections with a heavy heart. His dream of restoring the Union and ending slavery seemed doomed. But then, within the space of a few weeks, the military situation in the South changed in dramatic fashion.

Farragut captures Mobile Bay

During the course of the Civil War, the North's naval blockade of Southern ports had choked off most Confederate efforts to obtain badly needed supplies from Europe and elsewhere. But a few Confederate ports remained open to rebel blockade runners (ships that tried to carry supplies through gaps in the Union's naval

Lincoln Comes Under Enemy Fire

In July 1864, fourteen thousand Confederate troops under the command of Lieutenant General Jubal Early marched through the Shenandoah Valley and across the Potomac River into Maryland. After crossing the Potomac, Early marched toward Washington, D.C. This movement shocked and worried lawmakers in the capital. After all, most Union forces at this time were far away, fighting Robert E. Lee's Army of Northern Virginia for possession of Petersburg and Richmond.

By July 11, Early's army had reached the outer defenses of Washington. The Confederate force halted, but it tested the Union defenses on several occasions during the next couple of days. On July 12, President Abraham Lincoln decided to visit Fort Stevens, which was one of the capital's primary defensive strongholds. Shortly after Lincoln arrived at the fort, it came under fire from Early's troops. The Federal soldiers within the fortress immediately ducked behind walls to avoid getting shot. But according to witnesses, Lincoln repeatedly popped his head over the fort's walls to get a look at the enemy sharpshooters. Finally, a Union captain stationed further along the wall noticed what Lincoln was doing. Unable to recognize the president at a distance, he gruffly yelled at him to keep his head down "before you get shot!" Lincoln was reportedly amused at being addressed in such a rough fashion, but he immediately obeyed. The shooting ended a short time later, and Lincoln returned to the White House.

The advance of Early's army into Maryland scared many Northerners. But the Confederate troops proved unable to slip past the capital's outer defenses. A few days after Early's troops fired on Lincoln, additional Union soldiers arrived in the area. Outnumbered, Early ordered his army to withdraw back into the woodlands of Virginia's Shenandoah Valley.

blockade). One of the most important of these ports was located on the Gulf of Mexico at Mobile, Alabama. By the summer of 1864, the Union Navy had neutralized every Confederate port along the Gulf of Mexico except for the harbor at Mobile. The port thus became a Union target of prime importance, and in August the Yankees moved to shut it down.

On the morning of August 5, Rear Admiral David Farragut (1801–1870)—the hero of the Battle of New Orleans—led a fleet of fourteen ships and four heavily armored warships known as monitors into Mobile Bay. Farragut knew that his mission to seize control of Mobile Bay would not be easy. Confederate defenses in the bay included Fort Morgan, three gun-

David Farragut. *(Courtesy, National Archives.)*

boats, an armored vessel called the C.S.S. *Tennessee,* and a deadly underwater minefield. As Farragut's fleet cruised up the bay, the guns from Fort Morgan and the rebel ships opened fire on the invaders. The Union fleet returned fire, and the smoke from the guns became so thick that Farragut lashed himself to a mast high above the deck of his ship so that he could see what was going on.

As the Union fleet plowed through the bay, one of its four monitors—the *Tecumseh*—struck an underwater mine. The mine (then known as a torpedo) blew a huge hole in the ship, and it quickly sank to the bottom of the bay with its captain and ninety-two sailors still trapped on board. The other Union vessels hesitated when the *Tecumseh* went down, but Farragut ordered them forward, shouting "Damn the torpedoes! Full speed ahead!"

Farragut's charge eventually pushed the other Union ships through the minefield and out of the range of Fort Morgan's guns. He quickly defeated the outnumbered Confederate ships. Over the next three weeks, Union forces took control of Fort Morgan and two other rebel strongholds on Mobile Bay. The city of Mobile remained in Confederate hands, but Farragut's capture of the bay effectively ended its usefulness as a blockade-running port.

Atlanta falls to Sherman

A few weeks after Farragut's dramatic victory, disaster struck the Con-

Burned-out buildings can be seen following Union general William T. Sherman's capture of Atlanta. *(Courtesy of the Library of Congress.)*

federacy again as Atlanta fell into Union hands. Throughout the month of August, Sherman's siege of the city had made life very difficult for the citizens and troops huddled behind its fortifications. But Atlanta resisted Sherman's forces until the end of the month, when Yankee troops seized control of the last of the railway lines providing supplies to Atlanta. Hood launched a desperate offensive to regain control of the rail line, only to receive a sound thrashing at the Battle of Jonesboro.

Sherman's capture of the last rail line connecting Atlanta to the rest of the Confederacy signaled the end of that city's resistance to the Yankee invaders. Hood hastily evacuated his army from the city on September 1, and the Union Army marched down its streets a day later. Within hours of his arrival in Atlanta, Sherman issued a series of harsh orders designed to evict all of the city's citizens and transform it into a Union stronghold. "If the people [of Atlanta] raise a howl against my barbarity and cruelty," wrote Sherman, "I will answer that war is war, and not popularity-seeking. If they want peace, they and their relatives must stop the war."

Atlanta mayor James Calhoun tried to convince Sherman to change his mind, but the Union general did not budge. "War is cruelty, and you cannot refine it," he told Calhoun. "You might as well appeal against the thunderstorm as against these terrible hardships of war. They are inevitable [unavoidable], and the only way the people of Atlanta can hope once more to live in peace and quiet at home, is to stop the war, which can only be done by admitting that it began in error and is perpetuated in pride."

Northern confidence returns

When Northerners first learned of Farragut's dramatic victory, they did not react with great emotion. They recognized that the seizure of Mobile Bay would make it much more difficult for the South to obtain desperately needed provisions. But the public's attention remained focused on Petersburg and Atlanta, where Union military progress seemed hopelessly stalled.

Given this state of affairs, it is not surprising that news of Sherman's capture of Atlanta electrified communities all across the North. Only days before, public opposition to the Civil War had been so great that even some fierce Lincoln supporters expressed doubts about continuing the fight. But the victory at Atlanta revived Northern confidence and dramatically enhanced Lincoln's prospects for reelection. Sherman's triumph also triggered a reassessment of Farragut's exploits in Mobile Bay. Before the

victory in Atlanta, most people viewed the victory in Alabama as an isolated win of no real importance. After Atlanta fell, however, Northerners referred to the triumph at Mobile Bay as a sure sign that the Confederacy was finally crumbling.

In the South, meanwhile, the loss of Atlanta stunned war-weary Confederate citizens. Many of them had come to believe that they would gain independence from the Union only if Lincoln was defeated in the upcoming presidential election. They recognized that defeats such as the one at Atlanta not only hurt the Confederate Army and citizenry, but also improved the Republican's chances of retaining his office. "Since Atlanta I have felt as if all were dead within me, forever," lamented Southern diarist Mary Boykin Chesnut (1823–1886). "We are going to be wiped off the earth."

Sheridan goes to the Shenandoah Valley

Even as Southerners tried to come to grips with the disasters at Mobile Bay and Atlanta, Confederate misfortunes spread into the Shenandoah Valley, a longtime rebel stronghold. The Confederate Army had used the Shenandoah Valley to their advantage ever since the war began. Stretching across northern Virginia between the Blue Ridge and Appalachian mountains, the valley's abundant farmlands had been tapped by Robert E. Lee and other Southern commanders to feed their armies. In addition, rebel armies had often traveled through the heavily

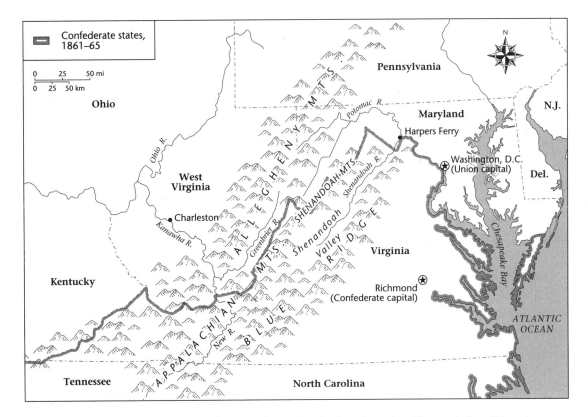

The Shenandoah Valley in Virginia. *(Illustration by XNR Productions. Reproduced by permission of The Gale Group.)*

forested valley on their way to conduct raids of Northern farms, towns, and supply centers. Finally, the valley had twice been used by the Confederates as an invasion route into the North.

The Confederates made skillful use of the Shenandoah Valley during the summer of 1864 as well. After conducting a series of raids on Union positions, a rebel army under the direction of Lieutenant General Jubal Early retreated into its dense woodlands to hide. A Federal force of forty-five thousand men spent a good part of the summer chasing Early around the valley, but with little success.

Grant then ordered General Philip H. Sheridan to take command of the Union troops and pursue Early until his army was destroyed. In addition, he instructed Sheridan to demolish the fields and farms of the valley so that they would be of no use to future Confederate forces. This grim order, which Sheridan executed with cold efficiency, marked the beginning of the "total warfare" phase of the Civil War.

"Total warfare" was a phrase used to describe the Union's emerging military philosophy, which called for the destruction of Southern fields, factories, and supplies. It reflected the

Excerpt from a Confederate Soldier's Diary

On the whole, Confederate soldiers fought under more difficult conditions than their Union counterparts during the Civil War. Widespread shortages of food, medicine, clothing, and other supplies often left Confederate troops desperately cold and hungry. This situation sometimes determined the outcome of battles.

In October 1864, Confederate troops under Lieutenant General Jubal Early fought Union troops under General Philip H. Sheridan for control of the Shenandoah Valley in northern Virginia. When it appeared certain that Sheridan's forces would defeat the rebels, Sheridan rode off to Washington to report on his progress. Early's troops launched a surprise attack during Sheridan's absence and overtook a Union Army camp, sending the Union soldiers running into the woods in a disorganized retreat. But rather than pressing their advantage, the Confederate forces gave in to their basic human needs. Private John Worsham described the scene in his diary:

The world will never know the extreme poverty of the Confederate soldier at this time. Hundreds of men who were in the charge were barefooted. Every one of them was ragged. Many had on everything they had, and none had eaten a square meal for weeks. As they passed through Sheridan's camp, a great temptation was thrown in their way. Many of the tents were open, and in plain sight were rations, shoes, overcoats, and blankets. The fighting continued farther and farther, yet some of the men stopped. They secured well-filled haversacks [knapsacks] and, as they investigated the contents, the temptation to stop and eat was too great. Since most of them had had nothing to eat since the evening before, they yielded. While some tried on shoes, others put on warm pants in place of the tattered ones. Still others got overcoats and blankets—articles so much needed for the coming cold.

The Confederate troops were not able to enjoy these items for long. Sheridan met his fleeing Union troops on his way back from the capital and quickly reorganized them for a counterattack. They destroyed the unsuspecting Confederate forces and claimed the Shenandoah Valley for the Union.

North's growing belief that the South could not carry on the fight if its civilian population lost the will to continue.

Total warfare

During the month of September, Sheridan scored two significant victories over Early's forces. Neither of these battles destroyed the rebel army, but they forced Early to lay low for several weeks. In the meantime, Sheridan went about the process of burning the Shenandoah Valley countryside. Throughout September and early October, Sheridan's Union force—which

Ulysses S. Grant. *(Courtesy of the National Archives and Records Administration.)*

had been designated the Army of the Shenandoah—destroyed everything in its path. Sheridan proclaimed that "the people [of the Shenandoah Valley] must be left [with] nothing but their eyes to weep with over the war." Wherever they went, Sheridan's troops destroyed crops, burned barns, and drove off livestock. Small bands of Confederate guerrillas harassed Sheridan's troops, but their occasional raids and sniper attacks could not stop the destructive Union advance.

By mid-October, Sheridan's army appeared to have established complete control over most of the valley, and Sheridan made a quick visit to Washington to report on the progress of his campaign. While he was gone, however, Early launched a surprise attack on October 19 that caught his Yankee foes completely off-guard. The entire Union Army quickly broke into a disorganized retreat, leaving behind a large number of artillery guns and various supplies.

As the Union troops fled down the valley, however, they were met by Sheridan, who was returning from the capital. Sheridan stopped the panicky retreat and swiftly reorganized his army for a counterattack. A few hours later, the Army of the Shenandoah roared back into their camp in a rush of hoofbeats and gunfire. Early's troops were completely unprepared for Sheridan's attack, and the Union assault destroyed the rebel army. By the time Early managed to withdraw his army from the area, it had been cut to pieces.

Lincoln wins reelection

Sheridan's decisive victory over Early destroyed any hopes that the Confederacy might have had of regaining control of the Shenandoah Valley. Moreover, it provided further evidence to Northern voters that the Confederacy was finally falling apart after years of struggle and bloodshed. "Coming on the heels of Mobile Bay and Atlanta, Sheridan's conquest was a tonic that checked war weariness and created a new spirit of optimism [in the North]," wrote Bruce Catton in *The Civil War*. "The war was visibly being won, and although the price remained high, it was obvious that the last crisis had been passed. Sherman, Farragut, and Sheridan were winning Lincoln's election for him."

In November 1864, the Union held its national elections, and the people of the North returned Lincoln to office for a second term by a comfortable margin. He received half a million popular votes more than McClellan, and won 212 of the 232 available electoral votes. Perhaps the most impressive aspect of Lincoln's reelection was the strong support he received from Union soldiers in the field. Nearly 80 percent of soldiers who voted cast their ballots for Lincoln, despite their deep war weariness and enduring affection for McClellan.

Lincoln's reelection demolished Confederate hopes that they might somehow achieve independence through a negotiated settlement. Moreover, it signaled a renewed Northern willingness to support Lincoln's war

The Sons of Liberty

The Sons of Liberty was a secret organization that developed in midwestern Union states during the Civil War. Members of this strange organization, which was also sometimes known as the Order of American Knights and the Knights of the Golden Circle, were dedicated to "states' rights" and fiercely opposed to the Republican Party. Its members claimed that the organization was devoted to legitimate causes such as promotion of civil rights and providing political support for antiwar politicians. Investigators into their activities, however, claimed that the group's activities were treasonous. They claimed that the organization's efforts to drain Northern support for the war effort sometimes strayed into active support for the Confederacy. In any event, the active membership of the Sons of Liberty remained small throughout the war, and the organization's plots almost always failed or fell apart in the planning stages.

The Sons of Liberty sometimes worked with Confederate spies based in Canada and extremist members of the Copperhead wing of the Democratic Party. Plotting together, these men devised a wide range of actions that were meant to create chaos in the North. These plots included schemes to rob Northern banks, burn New York City, support anti-Lincoln newspapers, and capture a Union warship patrolling the Great Lakes.

Most of these plots collapsed, however. One major reason for their failure was the fact that everybody knew that the Sons of Liberty existed. As Northern police and military organizations mounted efforts to stop the organization, they discovered that it was easy to place spies within the disorganized group. When these spies learned of Sons of Liberty plots, they passed the information on to Northern law enforcement officials. As a result, the Sons of Liberty had to abandon many of their schemes before ever trying them.

Some people in the North harbored deep fears about the Sons of Liberty and similar secret organizations. In a few places, this fear was well-founded. In Missouri, for example, the Sons of Liberty allied itself with bands of Confederate guerrillas that terrorized the state. For the most part, however, the Sons of Liberty did little damage to the North, and President Abraham Lincoln never really viewed the group as a major threat.

policies, which remained focused on obtaining an unconditional Confederate surrender. "I am astonished at the extent and depth of [the North's] determination . . . to fight to the last," wrote a reporter for the *London Daily News.* "[The people of the North] are in earnest in a way the like of which the world never saw before, silently, calmly, but desperately in earnest."

Sherman begins his "March to the Sea"

Lincoln's victory in the 1864 election further battered the morale of war-weary Southerners. Jefferson Davis responded to Lincoln's reelection by proclaiming that the South stood as "defiant as ever" thanks to the "indomitable valor [intense bravery] of its troops" and the "unquenchable [unable to be satisfied] spirit of its people." But Northern military leaders sensed that the Southern willingness to continue the fight was wavering. In the final weeks of 1864, General Sherman set out to break the spirit of the Southern people once and for all.

Sherman rolled out of Atlanta in mid-November with sixty thousand troops, leaving the city's factories and public buildings in smoking ruins so that they could not be used by the Confederacy. His sights set on the coastal city of Savannah, Sherman marched eastward through the heart of Georgia. He moved his army forward at a leisurely pace, confident that the Confederacy did not have the military capacity to stop his progress. Over the next few weeks, Sherman fed and supplied his troops by seizing whatever he needed from Georgia's farms and villages. His army then systematically destroyed any crops and supplies that it did not use. "We cannot change the hearts of those people of the South," stated Sherman. "But we can make war so terrible and make them so sick of war that generations would pass away before they would again appeal to it."

As Sherman's "March to the Sea" continued through the Confederate heartland, his army left a path of sorrow and ruin in its wake. The Yankee invaders razed (leveled to the ground) hundreds of farms and plantations, determined to hammer the Southern people into submission. Georgia's suffering was made even worse by a lawless group of thieves and deserters who followed behind Sherman's force. These wild hooligans, known as "bummers," robbed and burned anything that the army left behind, terrorizing the local people in the process.

Sherman completed his March to the Sea in mid-December, and he took immediate steps to take Savannah from Confederate control. He captured the city within a few days, and on December 22 he sent a telegram to Lincoln offering Savannah as a "Christmas gift." The seizure of Savannah thus ended one of the most successful Union campaigns of the entire war. As Paul M. Angle pointed out in *A Pictorial History of the Civil War Years,* Sherman's push to Savannah brutalized both Southern morale and Southern military capacity: "With fewer than 2,000 casualties he had destroyed a large portion of the war potential of the deep South, he had demonstrated that a large section of the Confederacy was a defenseless shell, and he had placed his army in a position from which he could move north and cooperate with Grant in a final campaign against Lee."

Thomas crushes Hood in Tennessee

At the same time that Sherman made his fearsome march through Georgia, Hood moved into Tennessee in a desperate gamble. The Confederate commander hoped that by threatening Nashville, which the North had captured in 1862, he might somehow lure Sherman out of Georgia or regain rebel control of central Tennessee. But Sherman ignored Hood's offensive, and Union general George H. Thomas (1816–1870) quickly moved against the rebel army.

As Hood traveled through southern Tennessee, the Confederate general understood that his chances of waging a successful attack on Nashville were very slight. After all, his army had been reduced to fewer than forty thousand men, and Thomas had assembled fifty thousand Union troops to defend the city. But he pressed forward, unable to devise any other plan of action.

On November 30, Hood attacked Union troops under the command of Major General John Schofield (1831–1906) in the town of Franklin, twenty-five miles south of Nashville. But the entrenched Federal troops turned back the Confederate assault, inflicting terrible damage on Hood's valiant but exhausted men in the process. Two weeks later, Thomas finished the job at the Battle of Nashville. This clash, fought on December 15 and 16, shattered Hood's dreams of conquering Nashville. It also removed the Confederate Army of Tennessee from active participation for the remainder of the war.

Blacks in the Civil War

Black people from both the North and the South participated in the Civil War in a variety of ways. Free blacks from the North tried to join the fight as soldiers from the earliest days of the conflict. These men not only wanted to help free the slaves in the South, but also felt that they could improve their chances of gaining equal rights in American society by proving their patriotism and courage on the battlefield. But prejudice (unfair treatment because of their race) prevented blacks from enlisting in the Union Army until late 1862. It also created racial conflicts with working-class whites in many Northern cities during the war years.

In the South, black slaves performed much of the heavy work that was required to prepare the Confederacy for war. They built forts, dug trenches, hauled artillery and supplies, set up army camps, and acted as cooks and servants for Confederate soldiers. Some free blacks in the South even fought for the Confederacy in the early years of the Civil War. However, after President Abraham Lincoln (1809–1865) issued the Emancipation Proclamation, which freed the slaves in 1863, Southern blacks increasingly realized what a Union

Words to Know

Abolitionists people who worked to end slavery

Civil War conflict that took place from 1861 to 1865 between the Northern states (Union) and the Southern seceded states (Confederacy); also known in the South as the War between the States and in the North as the War of the Rebellion

Confederacy eleven Southern states that seceded from the United States in 1860 and 1861

Discrimination unfair treatment of people or groups because of their race, religion, gender, or other reasons

Emancipation the act of freeing people from slavery or oppression

Union Northern states that remained loyal to the United States during the Civil War

ination. For example, they received lower wages than white soldiers who held the same rank, they did more than their fair share of heavy labor, and they were not allowed to become officers. Despite these problems, more than two hundred thousand black men fought bravely for the Union. Their courage and determination on the battlefield earned the respect of many white Americans and helped the North win the Civil War. As a result, black Americans were able to break down many barriers of discrimination after the war ended.

Northern blacks want to join the fight

Many free blacks in the North were happy when Southern states began seceding from (leaving) the United States in 1860. In fact, some black leaders had been suggesting the separation of Northern free states from Southern slave states for many years. These black leaders believed that the U.S. government was obligated to protect slavery under the Constitution. They had seen the number of blacks held in slavery increase from seven hundred thousand to four million since the United States had been formed almost nine decades earlier. They knew that the federal government had enforced the Fugitive Slave Laws, which required people in the North to help Southern slave owners find and capture their escaped slaves. Finally, black leaders believed that the federal government would call out the military to crush any major slave rebellions in the South. For these rea-

victory would mean for them. Thousands of slaves escaped and took refuge behind Union lines, and many of those who remained in the Confederacy stopped cooperating with Southern whites. Some Southern blacks even aided the Union cause by destroying Confederate property, spying on troop movements, or helping Union prisoners escape.

When black Americans were finally allowed to join the Union Army in 1862, they still faced discrim-

sons, many free blacks felt that the institution of slavery would be more likely to end if the South did not have the support of the Union.

When the Civil War began with the Confederate attack on Fort Sumter in 1861, thousands of black men volunteered to become soldiers in the Union Army. They cited two main reasons for wanting to join the fight. First, they wanted to help put an end to slavery. Second, they believed that proving their patriotism and courage on the field of battle would help improve their position in American society. "Once let the black man get upon his person the brass letters, U.S., let him get an eagle on his button, and a musket on his shoulder and bullets in his pocket, and there is no power on earth which can deny that he has earned the right to citizenship in the United States," said black abolitionist Frederick Douglass (c. 1818–1895).

But Federal law prohibited black men from joining state militias or the Union Army, and many Northern whites wanted to keep it that way. For one thing, they claimed that the Civil War was not about slavery. They called it a "white man's war" and said that its purpose was to restore the Union rather than to settle the issue of slavery. And since the war was not about slavery, they felt that there was no need to change the law so that black people could join the fight. In reality, the dispute between North and South involved a number of different issues, including the question of how much power should be granted to the

 People to Know

John Andrew (1818–1867) governor of Massachusetts, 1860–66; organized the Fifty-fourth Massachusetts Regiment, the first Northern black unit in the Civil War

Frederick Douglass (c. 1818–1895) abolitionist who was the first African American leader of national stature in U.S. history

Thomas Wentworth Higginson (1823–1911) abolitionist who led the First South Carolina Volunteers, the first regiment of former slaves in the Union Army

Abraham Lincoln (1809–1865) sixteenth president of the United States, 1861–65

Robert Gould Shaw (1837–1863) Union colonel of the Fifty-fourth Massachusetts Regiment, the famous all-black unit in the Civil War

individual states and how much should be held by the federal government. But in the end, slavery was the one issue upon which the two sides could not compromise.

Another reason that many Northern whites did not want black men joining the army was deep-seated racial prejudice. Some whites believed that they were superior to blacks and did not want to fight alongside them. They also thought that black men, particularly those who had been slaves, would be too cowardly and subservient (helpful in an inferior capacity) to make good soldiers. Finally, they worried that allowing blacks to fight in the war would have negative political implications. Several states along the border between North and South allowed slavery, but remained part of the Union anyway. Some Northern political leaders thought that these border states would join the Confederacy if the Union Army admitted black soldiers.

Black leaders in the North were outraged at the policies and prejudices that prevented them from fighting in the Civil War. They pointed out that black soldiers had fought for the United States in both the American Revolution (1775–83) and the War of 1812 (June 1812 to December 1814). Frederick Douglass charged that black men "were good enough to help win American independence, but they are not good enough to help preserve that independence against treason and rebellion." Many Northern blacks signed petitions asking the Federal government to change its rules, but the government refused. In the meantime, some light-skinned black men passed for white and enlisted in the army anyway. Thousands of other blacks provided unofficial help for the cause by serving as cooks, carpenters, laborers, nurses, scouts, and servants for the Union troops. In addition, about twenty-nine thousand black men served in the Union Navy, which never had a policy against blacks becoming sailors.

Prejudice leads to race riots in the North

Racial prejudice caused other problems for Northern blacks during the Civil War, in addition to preventing them from serving their country as soldiers. At that time, many immigrants from Germany, Ireland, Italy, and other European countries worked in industrial factories in the North. Working conditions in the factories were not good in those days, and many people worked long hours for low wages. Some workers formed groups called labor unions in order to negotiate with their employers for better working conditions and higher pay. Most labor unions did not allow black people to become members. When employers did not meet the demands of the unions, the members would often refuse to work—or go on strike—as a form of protest. Then the factory owners would hire black workers, who were not part of a union, to take the place of striking workers. This practice made many working-class white people angry and resentful. But instead of taking out their anger on their employers, they targeted black workers.

In 1862 and 1863, the job competition between European immigrants and Northern blacks sparked race riots in several major cities. Some of the most destructive riots occurred in Cincinnati, Ohio, in July 1862. Angry groups of Irish and German laborers set fires and attacked people in the black part of town, and then groups of black workers retaliated the next day. The mob violence continued for five days, and large sections of the city were destroyed. Similar events took place in New York City; Chicago, Illinois; and Detroit, Michigan, over the next few months. The situation grew even more tense once President Abraham Lincoln granted freedom to black slaves in the South in 1863. Working-class whites in the North worried that emancipation would create a flood of Southern blacks who would work for low wages and take their jobs.

Blacks in the Confederacy

In the early years of the Civil War, black slaves performed much of the hard labor that was required to prepare the Confederacy for war. They built forts and dug trenches, transported artillery and unloaded shipments of arms, set up army camps and acted as cooks and servants for the soldiers. They also continued to work in the fields, growing food and cotton to be used in the war effort. The prevailing attitude in the South was that "every Negro who could wield [handle] a shovel would release a white man for the musket [gun]," according to Charles H. Wesley and Patricia W. Romero in *Afro-Americans in the Civil War: From Slavery to Citizenship*. Most slaves who worked for the Confederate troops found conditions difficult. Food and clothing were scarce, living conditions were cramped and unsanitary, and doctors rarely came to treat sick and injured slaves.

In some cases, free black men volunteered to serve in the Confederate Army. Although it might seem strange for black people to fight in support of slavery, there were several reasons for such wartime service. Some free blacks believed that they would receive better treatment from Southern whites if they fought for the Confederacy. Others were afraid that they would be forced to join if they did not do so voluntarily. Finally, some free blacks in the South fought due to feelings of patriotism toward their state or city. But most Southern whites did not like the idea of black men serving in the Confederate Army. They did not trust black soldiers, even when they had volunteered, and were always suspicious that their true loyalties lay with the North. They worried that giving weapons to free black men would lead to widespread slave rebellions. In fact, the Confederate government enacted strict laws to restrict the activities of free blacks during the war.

As the Civil War dragged on, life became chaotic through much of the South. Large numbers of people were forced to leave their homes, as Union forces captured Southern cities. White men were usually too busy fighting the war to pay much attention to the behavior of their slaves. Over time, many Southern blacks took advantage of this situation. Some slaves remained in the South but became less willing to submit to the authority of whites. For example, large networks of slaves formed to help Union soldiers escape from prison and find their way back to safety in the North. These slaves brought the soldiers food and water, helped them hide from Confederate forces, and

Freed male slaves look for work opportunities. *(Courtesy of the U.S. Signal Corps, National Archives and Records Administration.)*

served as guides through the forests and countryside.

Other slaves took their first opportunity to escape to the North. "During the first two years of the War, most slaves were loyal to their masters in the lower South," Wesley and Romero explained. "After 1863, however, when the news and the meaning of freedom spread, there were many instances of disloyalty and dissatisfaction. . . . As the word revealing freedom reached the South, slaves ran away from the plantations to join the advancing Union troops."

Word of emancipation spreads in the South

President Lincoln's Emancipation Proclamation put an end to slavery in the United States on January 1, 1863. Word of emancipation spread slowly among slaves in the South, however. Mail delivery, telegraph lines, and other forms of communication were disrupted during the war. In addition, many Southern whites attempted to prevent the information from getting around. They worried that slaves would rebel and become violent upon hearing the news. But most slaves eventually learned of their freedom. Free blacks within the Union passed word to others in the South. Some slaves were able to read about the Proclamation in Southern newspapers, and others were simply informed by their masters.

Free blacks in both the North and South celebrated the end of slavery and looked forward to the time when they would be treated equally in American society. Most slaves were thrilled to learn that they were free, although some recognized that freedom brought uncertainty and new responsibilities. Since many slaves had not received basic education and were not trained in any special skills, they were concerned about how they would make a living and take care of their families.

Educator Booker T. Washington (1856–1915) remembered first hearing about the Emancipation Proclamation with other slaves in Virginia: "For some minutes there was great rejoicing, and thanksgiving, and wild scenes of ecstasy. But there was no feeling of bitterness. In fact, there was pity among the slaves for our former owners. The wild rejoicing on the part of the emancipated colored people lasted but for a brief period, for I noticed that by the time they returned to their cabins there was a change in their feelings. The great responsibility of being free, of having charge of themselves, of having to think and plan for themselves and their children, seemed to take possession of them."

As slaves in the South heard about the Emancipation Proclamation, they began to recognize what the Civil War meant for their future. If the

Booker T. Washington was six years old when President Abraham Lincoln issued the Emancipation Proclamation in 1863. *(Courtesy of the Library of Congress.)*

North won, slavery would be abolished throughout the land. As a result, some slaves began to rebel against their masters and to help the Union cause. Some simply refused to work, while others started fires to destroy property belonging to whites. In addition to fighting the North, Southern whites increasingly had to worry about fighting slave uprisings.

Escaped slaves move north

About five hundred thousand slaves escaped from the South and

Union major general Benjamin F. Butler.
(Photograph by Mathew B. Brady. Courtesy of the Library of Congress.)

crossed the battle lines into Union territory during the Civil War. Prior to mid-1862—when black men were not allowed to be soldiers, and many Northern whites claimed that it was a "white man's war"—some Union generals returned fugitive slaves to their owners in the South. But before long, some Union officials began welcoming escaped slaves, partly because they often brought useful information about enemy troop numbers and positions. Keeping fugitive slaves became the official Union policy in 1861. A small group of escaped slaves approached Union general Benjamin F.

Butler (1818–1893) that May, and he refused to return them to Confederate hands. He argued that the Fugitive Slave Act—which required Americans in free states to help slave owners retrieve their property—no longer applied because the Confederacy was a foreign country. He called the escaped slaves "contraband [captured goods] of war" and declared his intention to keep them. In August, the U.S. Congress passed the Confiscation Act, which allowed the Union Army to seize any property used "in aid of the rebellion," including slaves.

At first there was no clear Federal policy regarding "contrabands," as the escaped slaves came to be known. Eventually, most Union Army units set up contraband camps and provided food, clothing, and shelter to the former slaves. The residents of many Northern cities organized freedmen's aid societies and sent volunteers to teach the contrabands to read and write. One of the earliest contraband communities was established on the Sea Islands off the coast of South Carolina. Volunteers provided the former slaves with education and land and helped them make the transition to freedom. Following emancipation, some free Northern blacks started schools in the South to educate freed slaves.

Some of the escaped slaves who came through Union lines stayed to become cooks or laborers for the soldiers. Others were put to work on abandoned plantations to grow food and cotton for the troops. In addition,

Northerners Organize to Help the "Contrabands"

Thousands of slaves escaped from plantations in the South during the Civil War and made their way to the North, particularly after President Abraham Lincoln's Emancipation Proclamation set the slaves free in 1863. Many former slaves crossed the battle lines to join the advancing Union troops, where they were accepted as "contraband of war." Most of the "contrabands," as the escaped slaves came to be called, were poor and uneducated and arrived with only the possessions they could carry on their backs. At first, the Union Army did not have any systems in place to deal with the contrabands.

Before long, however, many Northern cities organized freedmen's aid societies to collect money and supplies for the former slaves. They also sent volunteers to teach the contrabands how to read and write and help them make the transition to working for pay. Many of the early teachers and aid workers were Northern whites who had supported the abolition of slavery. But large numbers of free blacks became involved in helping the contrabands after emancipation. The following statement from the Reverend Henry McNeal Turner (1834–1915), pastor of Israel Bethel Church in Washington, D.C., shows how black leaders throughout the North rallied people to the cause:

Reverend Henry McNeal Turner.

The time has arrived in the history of the American African, when grave and solemn responsibilities stare him in the face. . . . The great quantity of contrabands (so-called), who have fled from the oppressor's rod, and are now thronging Old Point Comfort, Hilton Head, Washington City, and many other places, and the unnumbered host who shall soon be freed by the President's Proclamation, are to materially change their political and social condition. The day of our inactivity, disinterestedness, and irresponsibility, has given place to a day in which our long cherished abilities, and every intellectual fibre of our being, are to be called into a sphere of requisition [a formal demand or request]. . . . Thousands of contrabands, now at the places above designated, are in a condition of the extremest suffering. We see them in droves every day perambulating [walking around] the streets of Washington, homeless, shoeless, dressless, and moneyless. . . . Every man of us now, who has a speck of grace or bit of sympathy, for the race that we are inseparably identified with, is called upon by force of surrounding circumstances, to extend a hand of mercy to *bone of our bone and flesh of our flesh.*

A poster urges black men to join the Union Army.

some former slaves served as spies for the North. They traveled through the South, pretending to be slaves on their way from one plantation to another, and gathered information from slaves and free blacks. Then they came back and told Union officials about the location and size of the enemy forces. Spying was dangerous work for blacks, because anyone who was caught could be killed or returned to slavery.

Union Army finally accepts black soldiers

In 1862, the Union Army suffered a series of defeats at the hands of the Confederates. This led to low morale among the troops and difficulty attracting white volunteers. As a result, public opinion about allowing blacks to fight gradually began to change. By this time, several Union generals had tried to set up black regiments despite the lack of government approval, including General James Lane (1814–1866) in Kansas, General David Hunter (1802–1886) in South Carolina's Sea Islands, and General Benjamin Butler in New Orleans. On July 17, 1862, the U.S. Congress passed two new laws that officially allowed black men to serve as soldiers in the Union Army. But they were only allowed to join special all-black units led by white officers.

The first black regiment (unit), the First South Carolina Volunteers, was formed in August 1862. Massachusetts abolitionist Thomas Wentworth Higginson (1823–1911) was appointed colonel of this regiment. In January 1863, he led his troops on a raid along the St. Mary's River, which formed the border between Georgia and Florida. He reported back to his superior officers that he was very pleased by his unit's performance. "The men have been repeatedly under fire; have had infantry, cavalry, and even artillery arrayed against them, and have in every instance come off not only with unblemished honor, but with undisputed triumph," General Higginson wrote. "Nobody knows anything about these men who has not seen them in battle. I find that I myself knew nothing. There is a fiery energy about them beyond anything of which I have ever read." In March, Higginson's regiment and another black regiment under James Montgomery (1814–1871) joined forces to capture Jacksonville, Florida. As the success stories of black troops in battle began rolling in, several more black regiments were organized.

Although some black men were eager to join the Union Army, those in Northern cities tended to be more reluctant to enlist than they had been earlier in the war. For one thing, they were able to find good jobs in factories that were busy producing goods for the war effort. In addition, some

black men worried about what would happen to them if they were captured by the Confederates. The Confederate government had said that it intended to ignore the usual rules covering the treatment of prisoners of war and deal with captured black soldiers in a harsh manner. It issued a statement saying that black soldiers would be "put to death or be otherwise punished at the discretion [judgment] of the court," which might include being sold into slavery. Many people thought that the Confederacy was just trying to discourage blacks from joining the Union Army, but a few well-publicized incidents convinced other people that they were serious.

One such incident was the "Fort Pillow massacre" of 1864. Fort Pillow was a Union outpost on the Mississippi River, north of Memphis, Tennessee. Half of the 570 Union soldiers stationed there to guard the fort were black. On April 12, the fort was captured by Confederate forces led by General Nathan Bedford Forrest. An unknown number of black soldiers (estimates range from twenty to two hundred) and a few white officers were killed after they had surrendered, in violation of the basic rules of war. This incident received a great deal of news coverage in the North. While it made some black men hesitant to volunteer, it made others determined to fight in order to take revenge on the Confederates.

Another reason that some black men were reluctant to enlist in the Union Army was that the army

The Fifty-Fourth Massachusetts Regiment

In January 1863, the U.S. government authorized Governor John Andrew (1818–1867) of Massachusetts to put together a regiment of black soldiers from his state. Since there were not enough black men living in Massachusetts at that time, Andrew called upon prominent abolitionists and black leaders to recruit men from all over the North to form the Fifty-Fourth Massachusetts Regiment. The Fifty-Fourth Massachusetts would be the first all-black regiment to represent a state in battle during the Civil War. Many white people in the North were opposed to allowing black soldiers to fight for the Union Army, so Governor Andrew and his recruiters staked their reputations on the success or failure of the regiment. "Rarely in history did a regiment so completely justify the faith of its founders," James M. McPherson wrote in *The Negro's Civil War.*

Since black men were not allowed to become officers in the Union Army, the governor selected several white men to lead the Fifty-Fourth Massachusetts. Andrew knew that the regiment would receive a great deal of publicity, so he chose these officers carefully. He asked a young, Harvard-educated soldier named Robert Gould Shaw (1837–1863) to become colonel of the regiment. Shaw accepted the position and immediately began training his troops for battle. "May we have an opportunity to show that you have not made a mistake in entrusting the honor of

the state to a colored regiment—the first state that has sent one to the War," Shaw wrote to Andrew.

The Fifty-Fourth Massachusetts got an opportunity to prove itself on July 18, 1863. The regiment was chosen to lead an assault on Fort Wagner, a Confederate stronghold that guarded the entrance to Charleston Harbor in South Carolina. The soldiers had marched all of the previous day and night, along beaches and through swamps, in terrible heat and humidity. But even though they were tired and hungry by the time they arrived in Charleston, they still proudly took their positions at the head of the assault. The Fifty-Fourth Massachusetts charged forward on command and were hit with heavy artillery and musket fire from the Confederate troops inside the fort. Colonel Shaw was killed, along with nearly half of his six hundred officers and men. But the remaining troops kept moving forward, crossed the moat surrounding the fort, and climbed up the stone wall. They were eventually forced to retreat when reinforcements did not appear in time, but by then they had inflicted heavy losses on the enemy.

The next day, Confederate troops dug a mass grave and buried Shaw's body along with his fallen black soldiers, despite the fact that the bodies of high-ranking officers were usually returned by both sides. The Confederates intended this action to be an insult, since they believed that whites

Actors Jihmi Kennedy (left) and Denzel Washington in *Glory*, a 1989 film about the Fifty-Fourth Massachusetts Regiment. *(Reproduced by permission of AP/Wide World Photos, Inc.)*

were superior to blacks and thus deserved a better burial. Several weeks later, when Union forces finally captured Fort Wagner, a Union officer offered to search for the grave and recover Shaw's body. But Shaw's father, a prominent abolitionist, refused the offer. "We hold that a soldier's most appropriate burial-place is on the field where he has fallen," he wrote.

Even though the Fifty-Fourth Massachusetts did not succeed in capturing Fort Wagner, their brave performance in battle was considered a triumph. "In the face of heavy odds, black troops had proved once again their courage, determination, and willingness to die for the free-

dom of their race," McPherson wrote. Newspapers throughout the North carried the story, even those that had opposed the enlistment of blacks in the Union Army. As abolitionist Angelina Grimké Weld (1805–1879) said of the regiment: "I have no tears to shed over their graves, because I see that their heroism is working a great change in public opinion, forcing all men to see the sin and shame of enslaving such men." The success of the Fifty-Fourth Massachusetts and other black regiments not only helped the North win the Civil War, but also led to greater acceptance of blacks in American society.

In 1989, director Edward Zwick turned the story of the Fifty-Fourth Massachusetts Regiment into a major movie called *Glory*, starring Matthew Broderick (1962–) as Colonel Shaw and Morgan Freeman (1937–) and Denzel Washington (1954–) as two of his soldiers. Based in part on Shaw's letters and diaries, *Glory* traces the opposition to blacks serving as soldiers in the Civil War, follows the recruitment and training of the historic regiment, and ends with the assault on Fort Wagner. It was nominated for an Academy Award as Best Picture of 1989 and won Oscars for Best Cinematography, Best Sound, and Best Supporting Actor (Washington). In his book *Drawn with the Sword: Reflections on the American Civil War*, James M. McPherson praised the movie's realistic combat footage and called *Glory* "the most powerful movie about [the Civil War] ever made."

Two black soldiers sit outside their tent. *(Courtesy of the Library of Congress.)*

still had policies that discriminated against blacks. For example, black soldiers were not allowed to be promoted to the rank of officer, meaning that they were stuck being followers rather than leaders. Black regiments were always led by white officers. In addition, black soldiers received lower pay than white soldiers of the same rank. Black soldiers with the rank of private were paid $10 per month, with $3 deducted for clothing. But white privates received $13 per month, plus an additional $3.50 for clothing. Finally, black soldiers often performed more than their fair share of hard labor and fatigue duty, such as pitching tents,

loading supplies, and digging wells and trenches. These policies began to change when black regiments proved themselves in battle. But it took a protest by two black regiments from Massachusetts—who refused to accept any pay until they were treated equally with white soldiers—to convince the War Department to make the changes official in June 1864.

By late 1864, the Union Army included 140 black regiments with nearly 102,000 soldiers—or about 10 percent of the entire Northern forces. Black men fought in almost every major battle during the final year of the Civil War and played an important role in achieving victory for the Union. Approximately 37,300 black men died while serving their country, and 21 received the Congressional Medal of Honor for their bravery in battle.

The black regiments fighting for the Union were so successful that the Confederates even considered arming slaves late in the war. Most Southern whites opposed this idea because they believed that blacks were inferior and worried that it would promote slave rebellions. But as the Union Army advanced through the South, the Confederate government became desperate enough to consider it. In 1865, the Confederate Congress passed the Negro Soldier Law and established a few companies of black soldiers in Richmond, Virginia. But the Union won the Civil War before any of these troops could be used in battle.

Blacks' wartime service breaks barriers of discrimination

As black soldiers helped the Union achieve victory in the Civil War, some white people began to reconsider their earlier beliefs that blacks were inferior and should be kept separate from whites. "The performance of Negro soldiers on the front lines in the South helped make things easier for colored civilians in the North," James M. McPherson noted in *The Negro's Civil War*. During the war years, the U.S. government passed several new laws designed to reduce discrimination against blacks. For example, one law allowed blacks to carry the U.S. mail, and another permitted blacks to testify as witnesses in federal courts.

A major turning point for blacks came in 1865, when John S. Rock (1825–1866) became the first black lawyer allowed to argue cases before the U.S. Supreme Court. Just eight years earlier, the Supreme Court had ruled in the *Dred Scott* case that blacks did not have the rights of citizens of the United States. The government took a number of other important measures to reduce discrimination and provide equal rights for black people after the Civil War ended.

1865: Victory for the North

The North continued to roll toward victory during the first months of 1865. Exhausted by the long war, the South's military and civilian population proved powerless to stop the Union forces as they moved across the Confederate countryside. In early April, the South suffered two crushing blows when Federal troops captured both Petersburg and Richmond in Virginia. Rebel general Robert E. Lee (1807–1870) surrendered a few days later, ending the South's bid for independence.

People of the North joined together in tremendous celebrations when they learned of Richmond's capture and Lee's surrender. But their joy at winning the war turned to sorrow on April 14, 1865, when John Wilkes Booth (1838–1865) assassinated President Abraham Lincoln (1809–1865). Lincoln had successfully guided the Union through the most troubled period in its history. His death plunged the North into an angry and mournful mood.

Last days of the Confederacy

By the beginning of 1865, most Southerners recognized that a Union victory seemed inevitable. The Southern

Words to Know

Blockade the act of surrounding a harbor with ships in order to prevent other vessels from entering or exiting the harbor; the word blockade is also sometimes used when ships or other military forces surround and isolate a city, region, or country

Civil War conflict that took place from 1861 to 1865 between the Northern states (Union) and the Southern seceded states (Confederacy); also known in the South as the War between the States and in the North as the War of the Rebellion

Confederacy eleven Southern states that seceded from the United States in 1860 and 1861

Enlistment the act of joining a country's armed forces

Federal national or central government; also refers to the North or Union, as opposed to the South or Confederacy

Rebel Confederate; often used as a name for a Confederate soldier

Siege surrounding and blockading of a city, town, or fortress by an army attempting to capture it

Treason betrayal of one's country

Union Northern states that remained loyal to the United States during the Civil War

economy was in ruins, destroyed by the North's naval blockade and its occupation of large sections of Confederate territory. This economic collapse made it a struggle for Southerners to obtain food and clothing for themselves and their families.

Battlefield losses and supply shortages also took their toll on Confederate armies, which decreased in size with each violent clash. Depressed and exhausted by long months of fighting, many Southern soldiers deserted their units. Others stayed with the army, but their hunger and weariness made it difficult for them to be effective. The morale of these valiant but battered soldiers plummeted even lower in February, when Union general William T. Sherman (1820–1891) resumed his destructive march through the South.

Lee remains trapped in Petersburg

On February 1, 1865, General Sherman marched his sixty thousand–man army northward out of Savannah, Georgia. His goal was to move all the way up the Atlantic coastline to Petersburg, Virginia, where Union general Ulysses S. Grant (1822–1885) awaited his arrival.

Months earlier, Robert E. Lee and his Army of Northern Virginia had been forced to retreat to Petersburg in order to prevent Grant's Army of the Potomac from capturing the Confederate capital of Richmond. Richmond received most of its food and supplies from railroads that passed through Petersburg, which is twenty-three miles south of the capital city. If those railways were captured, the capital would have to surrender or face starvation.

Lee's defense of Petersburg prevented the Army of the Potomac from swooping in and capturing Richmond. But Grant's decision to lay siege to Petersburg prevented the Confederate defenders from moving anywhere else for the rest of 1864. Grant's siege kept Lee's troops trapped in Petersburg for month after month, even as Union armies in the West carved up large sections of Confederate territory.

Sherman moves through South Carolina

Grant's continued siege of Petersburg made it impossible for Lee to send the Army of Northern Virginia against Sherman's invasion. Lee could only stand by helplessly as Sherman left Georgia and plowed northward through South Carolina, leaving a trail of ruined crops and burning buildings in his wake.

Sherman's march through South Carolina resembled his late-1864 invasion of Georgia in some ways. Just as in Georgia, his Union troops fed and clothed themselves by taking whatever they needed from Southern homeowners, farmers, and shopkeepers. In addition, Sherman's army continued to destroy unused crops and set fire to buildings, just as it had done during its "March to the Sea" a few months before.

People to Know

John Wilkes Booth (1838–1865) actor who assassinated Abraham Lincoln

Jefferson Davis (1808–1889) president of the Confederacy, 1861–65

Ulysses S. Grant (1822–1885) Union general who commanded all Federal troops, 1864–65; led Union armies at Shiloh, Vicksburg, Chattanooga, and Petersburg; eighteenth president of the United States, 1869–77

Joseph E. Johnston (1807–1891) Confederate general of the Army of Tennessee who fought at First Bull Run and Atlanta

Robert E. Lee (1807–1870) Confederate general of the Army of Northern Virginia; fought at Second Bull Run, Antietam, Gettysburg, Fredericksburg, and Chancellorsville; defended Richmond from Ulysses S. Grant's Army of the Potomac, 1864 to April 1865

Abraham Lincoln (1809–1865) sixteenth president of the United States, 1861–65

Philip H. Sheridan (1831–1888) Union major general who commanded the Army of the Potomac's cavalry corps and the Army of the Shenandoah; also fought at Perryville, Murfreesboro, Chickamauga, and Chattanooga

William T. Sherman (1820–1891) Union major general who commanded the Army of the Tennessee and the Military Division of the Mississippi, led famous "March to the Sea"

Union general William T. Sherman (leaning against the back of a cannon) discusses strategy with his staff. *(Photograph by George N. Barnard. Courtesy of the Library of Congress.)*

But Sherman's troops treated South Carolina even more harshly than they had treated Georgia. South Carolina had been the first state to secede from the United States, and Sherman and the members of his army wanted to punish it for its leading role in establishing the Confederacy. As a result, the invading Union army looted South Carolina homes and burned South Carolina farmlands with great enthusiasm. The state capital of Columbia went up in flames, too, although people continue to disagree about how the fire got started. Some observers insisted that Federal troops purposely set the city on fire, but others called the fire an accident or blamed it on fleeing Southerners. In any event, Sherman's march through South Carolina left the state in ruins. "All is gloom, despondency [loss of hope or courage], and inactivity," admitted one South Carolina native. "Our army is demoralized and the people panic stricken. To fight longer seems to be madness."

Desperation in the Confederacy

In March, Sherman's Army of the Mississippi left South Carolina and

Union major general Philip H. Sheridan sits in front of his tent with his staff. *(Courtesy of the National Archives and Records Administration.)*

entered North Carolina. Meanwhile, Confederate defenses continued to crumble elsewhere in the South. Over in Virginia, Union troops under the direction of General Philip H. Sheridan (1831–1888) conducted a series of successful raids as they moved eastward to join Grant at Petersburg. In Alabama and Georgia, a young Union general named James H. Wilson (1837–1925) defeated Confederate cavalry forces led by the legendary Nathan Bedford Forrest (1821–1877) to take control of several important cities. And in North Carolina, Union forces captured the port city of Wilm-

ington, which had been the last remaining Confederate port open to blockade runners (supply ships that tried to carry provisions past the Union's naval blockade).

As Sherman's troops pushed through North Carolina, they were reinforced by twenty thousand troops under the command of John Schofield (1831–1906). The addition of Schofield's men increased the size of Sherman's army to more than eighty thousand troops, far bigger than any Confederate army in the region. Confederate general Joseph E. Johnston

Union major general John M. Schofield.
(Photograph by Mathew B. Brady. Courtesy of the Library of Congress.)

(1807–1891) tried to halt Sherman's progress with a force of twenty thousand troops. But the Union commander brushed him aside with ease as he continued his march for Petersburg.

The Confederacy considers using blacks as soldiers

As Union victories piled up during 1864 and early 1865, a small number of Southern lawmakers and community leaders suggested adding slaves to the Confederate Army. At first, whites across the Confederacy voiced strong objections to the idea of fighting side-by-side with blacks. Much of this resistance came from deep-seated racism. These bigoted critics argued that slaves did not have the intelligence or discipline to be good soldiers, and they declared that they would be deeply offended if blacks were asked to help defend the Confederacy.

Other Southerners objected to the idea of enlisting slaves for more practical reasons. They noted that few slaves would willingly join the Confederate Army unless they were promised their freedom. They warned that the South's slave-based economy might be permanently damaged if large numbers of slaves were freed. Still other critics worried that if the South voluntarily armed blacks, the slaves might revolt against their owners. More than anything else, though, white opposition to the idea of adding blacks to the Confederate Army stemmed from the belief that fighting with blacks would spoil the nobility of the Southern cause. "Many Southerners apparently preferred to lose the war than to win it with the help of black men," observed James M. McPherson in *Battle Cry of Freedom*.

By February 1865, however, important Confederate leaders like President Jefferson Davis (1808–1889) and General Lee announced their support for the use of black troops. "The negroes, under proper circumstances, will make efficient soldiers," wrote Lee on February 18. "I think we could at least do as well with them as the enemy." The general added that blacks who fought under the Confederate flag should be given their freedom after the war. "It would be neither just nor wise . . . to require them to serve as slaves [after the war]," he said.

In mid-March, Confederate lawmakers passed several preliminary bills designed to legalize the use of African Americans as Confederate soldiers. The Virginia legislature even passed a state law calling for the enlistment of black soldiers. Virginia managed to organize two companies of black soldiers to fight on behalf of the South within a few weeks of passing the law. But as it turned out, the war ended before they or any other black Confederate soldiers could take the field of battle.

Passage of the Thirteenth Amendment

At the same time that Confederate lawmakers debated about using slaves in their army, President Lincoln pushed for passage of the Thirteenth Amendment to the U.S. Constitution. This amendment abolished slavery all across the nation.

Lincoln knew that passing an amendment to the U.S. Constitution required a great deal of work. For any amendment to become law, it has to be approved by both the U.S. Senate and the U.S. House of Representatives. It then has to be ratified (approved) by three-fourths of the states before it can become law. Despite these obstacles, however, Lincoln offered strong support for the amendment after his 1864 reelection.

The U.S. Senate had passed the amendment back in December 1863, but it had stalled in the House of Representatives. Lincoln and other amendment supporters worked hard to send the bill back to the House, and on January 31, 1865, the U.S. House of Representatives passed it despite opposition from many Democrats. After the vote, representatives who had supported the amendment burst into celebration. "Some [members] embraced one another, others wept like children," recalled Indiana congressman George W. Julian (1817–1899). "I have felt, ever since the vote, as if I were in a new country."

The House's passage of the amendment cleared the way for individual states to vote on the bill. Ten months later, on December 18, 1865, the Thirteenth Amendment became law, ending slavery on American land forever.

Grant increases pressure on Petersburg

By the end of March, Northern military actions and occupations had reduced the Confederacy to tatters. The only remaining Confederate army of any significance was Lee's Army of Northern Virginia, numbering fewer than fifty thousand troops. But it remained trapped in Petersburg, surrounded by an army more than twice its size.

Lee recognized that his army would be destroyed if it remained in Petersburg. Sherman's army was drawing ever closer. The Confederate general knew that the addition of those eighty thousand troops to Grant's Army of the Potomac would make his foe even more powerful. Reviewing the situation, Lee decided to strike before Sherman arrived. On March 25, he ordered a desperate attack on Fort Stedman, a Union position outside of Petersburg. He hoped to punch a hole through Grant's line so that he could escape Petersburg and join forces with Johnston's small army to the south.

The Army of Northern Virginia fought valiantly, but Grant's forces pushed back the assault. As Lee's weary soldiers retreated back to their former positions, Grant decided to launch a strike of his own. On April 1, twelve thousand Federal troops led by General Sheridan defeated a small rebel force commanded by George Pickett (1825–1875) at a place called Five Forks, fifteen miles west of Petersburg. Sheridan's victory enabled the North to seize the last remaining railway line that had been providing supplies to Petersburg and Richmond.

Grant captures Petersburg and Richmond

When Grant learned of the Union victory at Five Forks, he knew that the South's last hope of saving Petersburg and Richmond had been crushed. Eager to press his advantage, he ordered a full assault on the Confederate defenses at Petersburg. The Union offensive forced the Confederates to evacuate both Petersburg and Richmond. Before fleeing Richmond,

Southern mobs looted and burned large sections of the city.

As Richmond went up in flames at the hands of its own citizens, Jefferson Davis and a number of important Confederate officials fled for North Carolina. They stopped in Danville, where Davis proclaimed that "I will never consent to abandon to the enemy one foot of the soil of any of the States of the Confederacy. Let us . . . meet the foe with fresh defiance, with unconquered and unconquerable hearts." Danville was named the new capital of the Confederacy, but it held the title for just one week before Davis was forced to flee again. Acknowledging that the North had taken control of most Confederate land east of the Mississippi River, Davis decided to make a run for Texas.

Lee surrenders to Grant

General Lee and his dispirited Army of Northern Virginia also evacuated Petersburg and Richmond on April 2. Lee moved his exhausted army southward in a desperate bid to join forces with Johnston's twenty thousand–man force, but the Army of the Potomac immediately gave pursuit. Lee's reduced army of thirty-five thousand men pushed on, spurred by their deep devotion to their commander. But on April 7, Union cavalry under the direction of Sheridan stopped their progress near the little town of Appomattox (pronounced app–uh-MAT-tux). As tens of thousands of additional Federal troops closed in from all sides, Lee finally acknowledged that the war had been lost.

On April 8, General Grant sent Lee a note asking him to surrender. Looking over the brave but battered remnants of his Army of Northern Virginia, Lee realized that he had no other choice. Writing in *The Civil War,* historian Bruce Catton noted that Lee's decision to surrender "came just as Federal infantry and cavalry were ready to make a final, crushing assault on the thin lines in Lee's front. Out between the lines came a Confederate horseman, a white flag fluttering at the end of a staff, and a sudden quiet descended on the broad field. While the soldiers in both armies stared at one another, unable to believe that the fighting at last was over, the commanding generals made their separate ways into the little town to settle things for good."

On the morning of April 9, Lee and Grant met at a small farmhouse to discuss the terms of surrender. Guided by Lincoln's instructions and his own strong desire to begin healing the North's tattered relationship with the South, Grant offered generous terms. He guaranteed that Confederate soldiers who put down their weapons and went home would not be prosecuted for treason in the future. Grant also agreed to Lee's request that Confederate soldiers be allowed to keep the horses that they owned in order "to put in a crop to carry themselves and their family through the next winter." Finally, Grant ordered his army to give food and medicine to Lee's sick and hungry troops.

On April 8, 1865, Union general Ulysses S. Grant asked Confederate general Robert E. Lee to surrender. *(Photograph by Mathew B. Brady. Courtesy of the Library of Congress.)*

After Lee and Grant signed the papers explaining the terms of surrender, the two legendary military leaders saluted one another and left the farmhouse to rejoin their armies. Grant later recalled that as he watched Lee leave to go comfort his men, "I felt . . . sad and depressed at the downfall of a foe who had fought so long and valiantly, and had suffered so much for a cause, though that cause was, I believe, one of the worst for which a people ever fought."

Wilmer McLean Witnesses History—Twice

During the course of the Civil War, an elderly Virginian named Wilmer McLean found himself in the thick of two of the conflict's most significant events.

When the Civil War first erupted in the spring of 1861, McLean owned land near the town of Manassas, Virginia. In mid-July, armies from both sides ventured into the area, and Confederate general Pierre G. T. Beauregard (1818–1893) took over McLean's house as his headquarters. A few days later, on July 21, the Civil War's first major military battle took place. This clash at Manassas, commonly known as the First Battle of Bull Run, ended in a decisive Confederate victory.

Beauregard's victory at Bull Run pleased McLean. But the fight also convinced the old man to move elsewhere. Union artillery fire had ripped through McLean's home during the battle, and the elderly Virginian worried that the region might attract other armies in the future.

McLean then moved his family to Appomattox County in southern Virginia, where they spent the next four years in peace. On the morning of April 9, 1865, though, McLean was approached by two mounted soldiers representing the armies of Union general Ulysses S. Grant and

Wilmer McLean's home in Appomattox County, Virginia, site of the Confederates' official surrender to the Union. *(Photograph by Timothy H. Sullivan. Courtesy of the Library of Congress.)*

Confederate general Robert E. Lee. The two riders explained that they were looking for a place where the two military leaders might discuss terms of surrender. McLean took them to an empty building in the area, but the riders rejected the site. The elderly Virginian then offered the generals the use of his own home. The two representatives accepted this suggestion, and a few hours later, the two generals entered his parlor to negotiate an end to the long and bloody war.

Lee's surrender signaled the end of the Confederacy's long fight for independence. The Army of

Northern Virginia had always been the South's greatest army, and its defeat made it clear to everyone that the South could no longer resist Lincoln's Union armies. In the meantime, Confederate president Jefferson Davis and several other members of the government had fled from Richmond, and then from Danville. Upon learning of Lee's defeat, Davis initially vowed to continue the fight and made plans to establish a new Confederate capital in Texas. But in the weeks following Lee's surrender at Appomattox, the remaining Confederate armies laid down their weapons. The rebel soldiers then wandered back to their homes, saddened by their defeat but relieved that they had survived a war that had killed so many of their countrymen.

Union celebrates victory

The first days of April produced great excitement and joy in the North. Each day seemed to bring news of another great Union victory, from Sheridan's win at Five Forks to the capture of Richmond. But the Union's greatest celebration came after its people learned that Lee had finally surrendered. "From one end of Pennsylvania Avenue to the other, the air seemed to burn with the bright hues of the flag," wrote one reporter who watched the festivities in Washington. "Almost by magic the streets were crowded with hosts of people, talking, laughing, hurrahing and shouting in the fullness of their joy. Men embraced one another, 'treated' one another, made up old quarrels, renewed old friendships, marched arm-in-arm singing." Similar celebrations erupted all across the North.

The North's happiness lasted only a few days, however, before turning to rage and sorrow. On April 15, 1865, the man who had skillfully guided the United States through the worst crisis in its history died at the hands of a deranged (insane) Southern sympathizer.

Lincoln is assassinated

On the evening of April 14, 1865, Lincoln and his wife, Mary Todd Lincoln (1818–1882), attended a performance of a comedy called *Our American Cousin* at Ford's Theatre in Washington, D.C. The president and his wife were joined in their private balcony box by a young Union officer and his fiancée. Shortly after ten o'clock, an actor named John Wilkes Booth slipped into the rear of Lincoln's balcony with a pistol. He shot the president in the back of the head, then leaped from the balcony down to the stage. He broke his leg in the fall, but still managed to escape the area on horseback. Stunned theater patrons rushed to Lincoln's side. They carried him from the theatre to a boarding house across the street, where the president died at 7:22 on the morning of April 15. Booth, meanwhile, remained uncaptured until April 26, when he was cornered in a barn in Virginia. In an attempt to force the fugitive out, soldiers set the barn ablaze. A defiant Booth refused to come out. He was found dead of a gunshot wound; it is unclear whether Booth shot himself or whether one of the soldiers shot him.

Major Anderson Returns to Fort Sumter

One event that powerfully symbolized the Union's victory over the Confederacy was a ceremony that took place at Fort Sumter, South Carolina, in April 1865. Four years earlier, Federal troops under the command of Major Robert Anderson (1805–1871) had been forced to lower the American flag and surrender the fort to Confederate attackers. That April 1861 assault on Fort Sumter had marked the beginning of the American Civil War.

By April 14, 1865, however, the Union had regained control of the battle-scarred walls of Fort Sumter. On that day, Union officials led by Anderson returned to the fortress to raise the same torn American flag that had waved above Charleston Harbor on the night of the Confederate attack. As thousands of soldiers, officials, and citizens looked on, Anderson raised the American flag over the fort once again. "I thank God that I have lived to see this day," An-

The U.S. flag is raised again at Fort Sumter, four years after the Confederate assault on the fort. *(Courtesy of the Library of Congress.)*

derson said, "and to be here, to perform this, perhaps the last act of my life, of duty to my country."

News of Lincoln's assassination shocked the North. The Union's triumph over the Confederacy in the Civil War had dramatically increased Lincoln's popularity in Northern communities. In addition, his steady leadership during the war had led many Union soldiers to develop a deep loyalty and devotion to their president. The loss of Lincoln at the hands of a raving assassin thus plummeted the nation into a dark mood of despair and anger.

The nation spent the next few weeks saying goodbye to the man who had successfully guided it through the worst years of crisis in its history. On April 19, thousands of mourners filed past Lincoln's body at the White House. These mourners ranged from ordinary citizens to General Grant, who broke down and wept at the sight of his slain president. One day later, Lincoln's body was placed on a train that took him to his hometown of

A painting shows John Wilkes Booth aiming at Abraham Lincoln at Ford's Theatre. Mary Todd Lincoln and another couple are seated next to the president. *(Courtesy of the Library of Congress.)*

Springfield, Illinois, for burial. Along the way, millions of Americans gathered along the train's route to view Lincoln's funeral car as it passed by.

Davis is captured and imprisoned

As the North mourned the death of President Lincoln, Jefferson Davis continued his desperate dash for Texas, where he hoped to rebuild the Confederate government. But Federal troops stayed in constant pursuit. They finally captured him on May 10, 1865, in Georgia. Davis's captors then

transported him to a prison cell in Fort Monroe in Virginia.

Davis's future remained in doubt for quite awhile. Many Northerners thought that he should be put on trial for treason, since he had been the leader of the Confederate government during the Civil War. Some people also thought that he had been involved in Lincoln's assassination. But after two years of imprisonment, the authorities decided to release him from jail. They knew any attempt to convict Davis would put further strain on the wounded relationship between

His Name Was Mudd

One of the most controversial figures in the assassination of President Abraham Lincoln was Samuel A. Mudd (1833–1883). Mudd was a Maryland physician who had left his career in medicine for a life as a farmer. Early in the morning of April 15, 1865, Lincoln assassin John Wilkes Booth and an accomplice named David Herold came to his door to seek medical attention. Booth had broken his leg after shooting Lincoln at Ford's Theatre in Washington, D.C. He managed to escape the capital, but the assassin knew that he would be captured quickly if his leg was not set.

Mudd invited Booth and his companion inside and treated the injured man. Booth and Herold then left the house. A few hours later, Federal investigators arrived at Mudd's house and arrested him as a conspirator (participant) in the Lincoln assassination. During the interrogation of Mudd, the retired doctor claimed that he had not even known that Lincoln had been shot when Booth showed up at his door. He also claimed that Booth's use of a phony beard prevented him from recognizing the assassin, even though he had met the actor on at least two previous occasions.

Mudd continued to proclaim his innocence, but he was eventually found guilty of aiding Booth in his escape. (Federal authorities caught up to both Herold and Booth ten days after they left Mudd's farmhouse; Herold surrendered, but Booth died in a violent clash with his pursuers.) Unlike some other people who were convicted of being involved in the plot to kill Lincoln, Mudd was not executed. But he was sentenced to life in prison at Fort Jefferson in Dry Tortugas, Florida, and the name "Mudd" took on negative associations that persist today.

As soon as Mudd entered the prison, guards and other staff members singled him out for mistreatment. Within months of Mudd's arrival, however, a fearsome outbreak of yellow fever swept through the penitentiary. When all the prison's army doctors died as a result of the

America's Northern and Southern sections. Davis returned to the South after his release from prison. Settling in his home state of Mississippi, he remained a major symbol of the Confederate cause until his death in 1889.

disease, Mudd volunteered to treat inmates and prison employees alike. His subsequent work to contain the yellow fever outbreak caught the public's attention. His wife, Sarah Frances Mudd, then launched a campaign to gain her husband's freedom.

In February 1869, President Andrew Johnson (1808–1875) pardoned (officially forgave) Doctor Mudd and two other men who had been convicted of helping with the assassination plot. Johnson's pardon allowed Mudd to leave prison, even though his conviction was not overturned. Mudd returned home to Maryland in March 1869. He continued to proclaim his innocence until his death in 1883.

Since Mudd's death, the debate over the physician's role in Booth's escape has not died away. Instead, new generations of the Mudd family have worked hard to clear his name. These campaigns have gained considerable support over the years. Former president Jimmy Carter (1924–) expressed support for their efforts,

and in 1992 the Army Board for Correction of Military Records recommended that Mudd's conviction be set aside. But an Army assistant secretary refused to set aside the conviction, claiming it was not the Board's role to attempt to settle historical disputes. Finally, in October 1998, a U.S. district judge ordered the U.S. Army to reconsider the conviction of Dr. Mudd, following a lawsuit filed by Richard Mudd, the doctor's grandson. In February 1999, Michigan senator Carl Levin (1934–) urged Army secretary Louis Caldera to clear Mudd's name once and for all.

Despite these recent developments, however, historians continue to disagree about whether Mudd was involved in the conspiracy. Some experts believe that Mudd's conviction was unjust, and that his treatment of Booth's injury was simply the act of a good person. But other experts remain convinced of his guilt, and argue that he might also have been involved in a number of failed plots to kidnap the president.

1865–1877: Reconstruction

Reconstruction was the period in American History immediately after the Civil War. The physical rebuilding of Southern cities, ports, railroads, and farms that had been destroyed during the war was only a small part of the Reconstruction process. The major work of Reconstruction involved restoring the membership of the Southern states in the Union.

The Civil War ended on April 9, 1865, when Confederate general Robert E. Lee (1807–1870) surrendered to Union general Ulysses S. Grant (1822–1885) at Appomattox Courthouse in Virginia. The North's victory settled two important issues. First, it established that states were not allowed to leave, or secede from, the United States. Second, it put an end to slavery throughout the country. But the end of the war also raised a whole new set of issues. For example, federal lawmakers had to decide whether to punish the Confederate leaders, what process to use to readmit the Southern states to the Union, and how much assistance to provide in securing equal rights for the freed slaves.

Because these complicated issues carried a great deal of importance for the future of the nation, Reconstruction was a

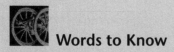

Words to Know

Black Codes series of harsh laws passed by white legislators in Southern states during Reconstruction that discriminated against black people; the Black Codes returned black people to a condition very close to slavery

Civil War conflict that took place from 1861 to 1865 between the Northern states (Union) and the Southern seceded states (Confederacy); also known in the South as the War between the States and in the North as the War of the Rebellion

Confederacy eleven Southern states that seceded from the United States in 1860 and 1861

Discrimination unfair treatment of people or groups because of their race, religion, gender, or other reasons

Emancipation the act of freeing people from slavery or oppression

Federal national or central government; also refers to the North or Union, as opposed to the South or Confederacy

Impeachment formal accusation of wrongdoing made by Congress against an elected official in an attempt to re-move him or her from office; the term usually includes both the bringing of charges by the House of Representatives and a trial by the Senate

Pardon to forgive and release from punishment

Reconstruction the period from 1865 to 1877 in which the Confederate states were readmitted into the United States

Secession the formal withdrawal of eleven Southern states from the Union in 1860–61

States' rights the belief that each state has the right to decide how to handle various issues for itself without interference from the national government

Union Northern states that remained loyal to the United States during the Civil War

Veto a power held by the U.S. president to stop a legislative bill passed by Congress from becoming a law; a bill can become law without the president's approval only if two-thirds of each chamber of Congress vote again in favor of it; such a vote is known as overriding the president's veto

time of great political and social turmoil. President Andrew Johnson (1808–1875), who took office after Abraham Lincoln (1809–1865) was assassinated in 1865, controlled the earliest Reconstruction efforts. But the U.S. Congress felt that the president's Reconstruction policies were too lenient (easy) on the South. Led by members of the Republican Party, Congress enacted stricter Reconstruction policies beginning in 1866 and sent in federal troops to enforce them. The ongoing dispute between Johnson and Congress led to the president's impeachment (a trial to decide whether to remove him from office) in 1868.

Under Congressional Reconstruction, the Southern states adopted new constitutions and formed governments that allowed the participation of black people. These states were then permitted to rejoin the Union. But it did not take long for the process to begin to fall apart. Many Southern whites continued to believe that blacks were inferior to them and should not have equal rights. Violence erupted throughout the South as whites rebelled against Congress's Reconstruction policies. Blacks were intimidated and terrorized so that they would not vote, and political leadership in the South gradually returned to the hands of whites. Reconstruction officially ended in 1877, when President Rutherford B. Hayes (1822–1893) withdrew federal troops from the South. But even though Reconstruction failed to ensure equality for black citizens in the United States, it set the stage for the Civil Rights Movement that would take place nearly a century later.

End of the war raises new issues

By winning the Civil War, the North achieved the two main things it had fought for—the Southern states remained part of the Union, and slavery was abolished throughout the land. But the end of the war also raised many difficult new questions.

People to Know

Ulysses S. Grant (1822–1885) Union general who commanded all Federal troops, 1864–65; led Union armies at Shiloh, Vicksburg, Chattanooga, and Petersburg; eighteenth president of the United States, 1869–77

Rutherford B. Hayes (1822–1893) nineteenth president of the United States, 1877–81

Andrew Johnson (1808–1875) seventeenth president of the United States, 1865–69

Abraham Lincoln (1809–1865) sixteenth president of the United States, 1861–65

For example, Northern lawmakers had to decide whether to punish the leaders of the Confederate rebellion. Some people in the North wanted the Confederate leaders to face harsh punishment for committing treason (betraying the United States). They believed that the Confederates should go to prison, give up their property, and be prohibited from voting or holding public office. These feelings intensified after Lincoln was assassinated. Other people in the North just wanted things to return to normal as soon as possible. They worried that punishing Confederate leaders would only stir up additional anger and resentment in the South.

Northern leaders also had to decide how and when the Southern states should be readmitted to the Union. Some people wanted the North to establish strict conditions for the states to meet before they could rejoin the Union. They felt that this was the only way to ensure the states' loyalty and to protect the rights of former slaves and Union supporters in the South. Other people thought that the North had already achieved its main goals, and believed that the federal government should not interfere with the states' internal issues. These people wanted the Southern states to be readmitted as quickly as possible.

One of the most pressing issues to arise at the end of the Civil War involved race relations. This was particularly true in the South, because slavery was the only sort of black-white relationship that many Southerners had ever known. Under slavery, black people were considered inferior and were forced to work for whites. When slavery was suddenly eliminated, Southerners had to develop a new labor system to take its place. Many former slaves were no longer willing to submit to white rule and wanted equal rights. At the same time, many Southern whites expressed anger and fear about the changes taking place in their society. Some white people took their feelings out on blacks through violence.

"For most practical purposes slavery ended with the war. But emancipation [the freeing of slaves] raised new problems that were fully as great," Allen W. Trelease wrote in his book *Re-construction: The Great Experiment*. "If the Negro freedman was no longer a slave, was he to be a full-fledged citizen with rights and privileges equal to those of any other citizen, or a dependent element in the population, free but not equal? This question was destined to torment the American people for generations to come."

Another problem that arose at the end of the Civil War concerned repairing the physical damage to the nation's cities, ports, railroad lines, bridges, and roads. Since most major battles took place in the South, the Southern states bore most of the physical damage of the war. Some cities— including Richmond, Virginia; Atlanta, Georgia; and Columbia, South Carolina—were devastated. Half of the railroad lines in the South had been destroyed, several ports were damaged, and many people had lost their homes. In fact, nearly every house, barn, and fence had been torn down or burned in parts of Virginia, Georgia, and South Carolina. The federal and state governments had to provide food for hungry people and money to rebuild structures.

The South's main advantage was that its economy had depended on agriculture, and a great deal of land was still available for farming. Most of the physical damage to property was repaired within a few years. In addition, the new state governments in the South undertook many building projects after the war in order to provide people with jobs. As a result, the South actually ended up with more factories, railroads, businesses, and public facilities than it had before the war.

Lincoln's wartime reconstruction policies

Some of the earliest Reconstruction efforts began while the Civil War was still going on. As Union forces conquered Southern territory, they occupied several cities and eventually entire states. President Abraham Lincoln started to implement his own Reconstruction policies in these occupied areas.

Lincoln wanted to restore the Union quickly, so he was willing to be fairly lenient in dealing with the Confederate states. In December 1863, he announced his Ten Percent Plan for readmitting states to the Union. Whenever 10 percent of the citizens of a Southern state declared their loyalty to the Union, that state would be allowed to form a new civilian government. This was the first step toward rejoining the United States. Lincoln was also willing to pardon, or officially forgive, all but the highest Confederate leaders, meaning that they would not be prosecuted (brought to trial) for treason or other crimes committed during the war.

Some Northerners felt that Lincoln's plan was too easy on the Confederates. They worried that the safety of the country would be in jeopardy under his plan, because states could conceivably rejoin the Union even when 90 percent of their citizens still supported the Confederacy. They also worried about the safety of former slaves and Union supporters in Southern states. If the Confederate leaders were not punished, they could soon return to power and cause problems for blacks and Unionists.

The U.S. Congress responded to Lincoln's Ten Percent Plan by passing the Wade-Davis bill in July 1864. This bill required a majority of adult white males in any Southern state to take an oath to support the Constitution before that state could be readmitted to the Union. It also prohibited men who had willingly served the Confederacy from voting, and completely abolished slavery. Lincoln felt that the Wade-Davis bill was too strict and worried that it might prolong the war. He refused to sign it, and it never became law. But Lincoln was assassinated in April 1865, just a few days after the end of the war, so his Reconstruction policies were never implemented fully.

President Johnson's reconstruction policies

Vice President Andrew Johnson took over as president after Lincoln's death. Johnson came from a poor white farming family in Tennessee. Even though he was from the South, he was against slavery and did not like wealthy slaveowners. Johnson had also opposed the idea of his state seceding from the Union when he was governor of Tennessee before the war (1853–57). But Johnson also supported states' rights to decide for themselves on issues within their borders. He was reluctant to impose the power

President Andrew Johnson. *(Courtesy of the Library of Congress.)*

of the federal government on the South in order to guarantee equality for blacks.

From the beginning of his term of office, Johnson made it clear that he intended to control the process of Reconstruction. He believed that restoring the Union was his job rather than that of the U.S. Congress. He began implementing his own Reconstruction programs during the summer of 1865, while Congress was in recess. (Congress often adjourns to let its members take time off between legislative sessions.)

First, Johnson accepted new state governments that had been formed in Arkansas, Louisiana, Tennessee, and Virginia. He then appointed governors in the other Southern states and required each state to hold a convention to rewrite its constitution. Johnson insisted that these new constitutions meet certain conditions. For example, the states had to admit that they had been wrong to secede from the Union. They also had to abolish slavery and refuse to pay the debts of the Confederate government. Once the states had made these changes to their constitutions, they would be allowed to elect their own representatives to the federal government. Black people would not be allowed to vote or to serve as representatives under the president's plan. Once these steps were complete, Johnson believed that Congress would accept the Southern representatives and readmit their states to the Union.

The president also pardoned all Confederate officials who agreed to take an oath of loyalty to the United States. He made the wealthiest Confederates appear before him personally to plead their cases, and he pardoned the rest all at once as an official act. Once a former Confederate had received a presidential pardon, he regained his rights of citizenship in the United States, and all of his property was returned. Some Northerners wanted to see the Confederate leaders punished for their actions, but Johnson worried that punishing them would only stir up resentment in the South. Confederate president Jefferson Davis

(1808–1889) and vice president Alexander Stephens (1812–1883) both spent some time in prison, but the charges against them were eventually dismissed. The only Confederate leader who was executed was Major Henry Wirz (1823–1865), who had mistreated Union prisoners of war as commander of the Andersonville Prison Camp in Georgia. As Trelease noted, "Very few participants in unsuccessful revolutions were ever treated so leniently as the Southern participants in the Civil War."

Discrimination continues in the South

Within a few months, those Northerners who had complained that Johnson's policies were too lenient had evidence to support their claims. Former Confederates began rising to power again throughout much of the South. In fact, during the first elections after the war, the Southern states elected nine men who had served as officers in the Confederate Army and fifty-eight men who had served in the Confederate Congress to represent them in the U.S. Congress once they were readmitted to the Union. Even Confederate vice president Stephens was elected to represent Georgia in the U.S. Senate (though the U.S. Congress refused to allow him to serve). Many other men who had supported the Confederacy were elected to positions in state and local governments. As people in the North learned of these election results, they began to wonder if the South had learned anything from its defeat.

Shortly after the Southern states established new governments, it became clear that they had no intention of giving black people equal rights as citizens. Instead, most Southern states passed a series of laws known as "Black Codes" to regulate the behavior of blacks and make sure that whites maintained control over them. For example, black people were not allowed to own weapons, purchase land in certain areas, conduct business in some towns, or testify in court. Schools and public transportation were segregated (divided into separate facilities for blacks and whites). Orphaned black children, as well as homeless black adults, could be leased out to work for whites against their will. In effect, the Black Codes often returned black people to a condition very close to slavery in Southern society.

"Slavery disappeared much faster than the race prejudice which had grown up with it," Trelease explained. "The firm conviction that God had created black men as an inferior race—possibly for the very purpose of serving white men—did not die so easily. . . . White supremacy reigned in every area of life, so far as the new state governments were concerned. There was no desire to help the former slaves make even a gradual transition to equality. The only significant help extended to the Negro was the aid coming from Northern charitable organizations and the Freedman's Bureau."

Southern farmers and plantation owners continued to depend on black laborers to work their fields.

The Freedmen's Bureau

There were some positive developments in race relations in the South immediately after the Civil War. Many of these changes took place under the guidance of the Freedmen's Bureau, a federal government agency formed in 1865 and led by General Oliver O. Howard (1830–1909). The mission of the Freedmen's Bureau was to help former slaves make the transition to freedom. The bureau provided food, clothing, and other assistance to former slaves until they were able to provide for themselves. It also set up fair labor contracts between blacks and whites and tried legal cases.

Education was one of the most successful activities of the Freedmen's Bureau. It created over 4,300 schools, hired ten thousand teachers, and educated nearly 250,000 students throughout the South after the war. The bureau's efforts led to the founding of several prominent black universities that still exist today, including Howard and Fisk universities.

Probably the least successful efforts of the Freedmen's Bureau involved distributing land to former slaves. Many people believed that Southern blacks needed land of their own if they were to become independent and self-sustaining

General Oliver O. Howard, head of the Freedmen's Bureau.

members of society. They wanted to provide "forty acres and a mule" to each black family so that they could grow their own food. Some Northerners wanted to take away the property of Confederate leaders and give it to former slaves. The Freedmen's Bureau did give out some land in the South, but much of it was later taken back when President Andrew Johnson pardoned, or officially forgave, Confederate leaders and returned their property after the war.

They replaced the old system of slavery with a new system called sharecropping. Most black people could not afford to buy land to start their own farms, so they arranged to use land that belonged to white people. In exchange for use of the land and farming equipment, the black laborers gave

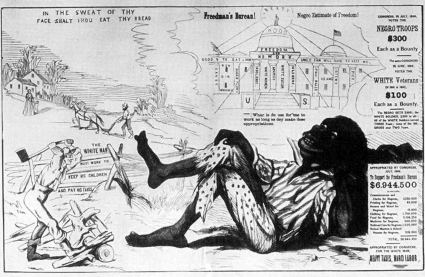

A handbill displays opposition to the Freedmen's Bureau. *(Courtesy of the Library of Congress.)*

the white landowners a portion (or "share") of the crops they grew. Although sharecropping might seem like a fair arrangement, most black families ended up owing the landowners more than they were able to pay each year. They were forced to continue farming the same land year after year in order to pay their debts to the landowners. The landowners often used these debts as a way to control blacks and prevent them from exercising their rights. In some cases, therefore, sharecropping became like a new form of slavery.

As news of the Black Codes spread to the North, many Northern-ers became more convinced than ever that the South was not willing to change on its own. They believed that black people would never achieve equal rights without help from the federal government. Members of the U.S. Congress, particularly those belonging to the Republican Party, became determined to make changes in President Johnson's Reconstruction policies.

Congress takes control of Reconstruction

Congress came back in session in December 1865, more than six months after President Johnson had begun implementing his Reconstruction policies. Many members were not pleased that the president had proceeded without them. They believed that Congress should control Reconstruction rather than the president. After all, only Congress had the power to admit new states to the Union under the U.S. Constitution.

Republican members of Congress, in particular, worried that Johnson's soft policies toward the Southern states might be dangerous for the country. Their feelings grew stronger as many former Confederate leaders returned to power in the South and began passing laws that discriminated against blacks. They began to think that the president's plan was allowing the Union victory to slip away. "Northerners resented the South's cockiness," Trelease wrote. "Right after the war, Southerners, still dazed from their defeat, seemed ready to accept any peace terms the North might offer. But once Andrew Johnson became lenient, they began sitting up and demanding favorable treatment as their right. . . . Who won the war after all? Northerners demanded. And what was it all for? With unrepentant [without regret for past actions] rebels still in the saddle, what had four long years of death and sacrifice achieved?"

As fears increased that the South seemed to be returning to its pre-Civil War attitudes, Congress decided to take over control of Reconstruction from the president. First, Congress refused to allow any representatives from Southern states to take their seats until their states were formally readmitted to the Union. Next, they passed the Civil Rights Act of 1866. This act, which granted citizenship and equal rights to black people, was designed to put an end to the Black Codes. President Johnson vetoed the Civil Rights Act because he felt it invaded the states' rights. But Congress overrode his veto, and the measure became law in 1866. (The president of the United States must sign bills passed by Congress before they can become laws. When the president refuses to approve a bill, he is exercising his veto power. A bill can become law without the president's signature if two-thirds of each chamber of Congress vote in favor of it. Such a vote is known as overriding the president's veto.)

Radical Republican members of Congress, led by Representative Thaddeus Stevens (1792–1868) of Pennsylvania and Senator Charles Sumner (1811–1874) of Massachusetts, wanted to place harsh restrictions on Southern states. But more moderate Republicans wanted to compromise with the president. Congress ended up forming a committee of fifteen members to examine the situation in the South. Dozens of witnesses appeared before the Joint Committee on Reconstruction and told them about discrimination and mistreatment of blacks and loyal Unionists in Southern states.

The Fourteenth Amendment

The committee eventually decided to prepare an amendment to the

U.S. Constitution in order to protect the rights of blacks forever. The Fourteenth Amendment granted equal rights to former slaves and protected them against discrimination by the states. Although the amendment expanded Johnson's Reconstruction policies to include protection for blacks, it left the state governments that he had formed intact. It also accepted nearly all of the pardons the president had granted to former Confederates. The amendment did not force the Southern states to grant blacks the right to vote. Instead, it allowed voting rights to be determined by the states. But the amendment limited each state's representation in Congress to a percentage of the total number of voters, rather than the total population, in that state. This way, Southern states that did not allow blacks to vote, or imposed restrictions that limited the number of black voters, would not have as much influence in the federal government.

In order to be ratified (approved), the Fourteenth Amendment needed the votes of three-fourths of the state governments. All twenty-five of the states that had supported the Union approved it, as did Tennessee. But the remaining ten Southern states did not. As a result, the amendment failed to be ratified by one vote. Since the Southern state governments that had been set up under President Johnson's Reconstruction plan refused to ratify the amendment and give basic rights to black people, the Republican-controlled U.S. Congress did not readmit these states to the Union. The failure to pass the Fourteenth Amendment ended up being a major turning point in the Reconstruction process, because it forced Congress to take more radical action toward the South.

New hopes of equality

Several other factors helped drive Congress toward a stricter Reconstruction policy. The growing tension between blacks and whites erupted into race riots in the Southern cities of Memphis and New Orleans during the summer of 1866. These riots received a great deal of publicity in the North and convinced many people that stronger action against Southern leaders was needed.

In addition, Congress held its regular midterm elections in the fall of 1866. The entire House of Representatives and one-third of the Senate was up for reelection. Reconstruction policy became the main issue of debate among the candidates. President Johnson toured the country making speeches on behalf of the Democrats, who tended to support his lenient policies. But his rambling speeches, which often included personal insults toward his rivals, only made him the subject of ridicule. The Republicans ended up winning the elections in a landslide and increasing their majorities in both houses of Congress.

After the elections, the strongly Republican Congress considered three options for dealing with the South. First, they could refuse to readmit the Southern states to the Union and keep them under federal government control indefinitely. Second, they could take away the voting rights of so many former Confederates that white Union supporters would control the Southern state governments. Or third, they could grant black men the right to vote. All but the most radical members of Congress felt that the first two options were too drastic. But the third option seemed to have several positive elements. If blacks were allowed to vote, they would help organize loyal state governments and ratify the Fourteenth Amendment. Then the Southern states could be readmitted to the Union safely. In addition, many Northerners believed that black people deserved voting rights in a democratic society. Of course, Republicans also had a political motive in granting black men the right to vote—they knew that black voters would be likely to support their party.

In March 1867, the U.S. Congress passed its Reconstruction Act over President Johnson's veto. This act separated the defeated Southern states into five military districts and sent federal troops to maintain order in each one. It also required each state to hold a new convention to rewrite the basic laws in its constitution. This time, however, all adult men—black and white—were allowed to vote for and serve as delegates (representatives) to the constitutional conventions. Congress did make an exception for former Confederate leaders, who were denied the right to vote or hold office. Under the new Congressional plan, the Southern states had to ratify the Fourteenth Amendment and guaran-

tee black voting rights in order to be readmitted to the Union.

"Radical Reconstruction"

The policies set in motion by the Reconstruction Act of 1867, which came to be known as "Radical Reconstruction," led to a social revolution in the South. Black men jumped at the chance to vote and have a say in their state governments. In fact, more blacks than whites registered to vote in five Southern states. But many of these new voters showed a willingness to vote for white candidates. South Carolina was the only Southern state in which black delegates outnumbered white delegates at the constitutional convention.

In general, the delegates in the Southern states cooperated in making their constitutions more fair for all citizens. Most states guaranteed equal civil rights for whites and blacks, established fairer tax systems, reformed prisons and reduced the sentences for certain crimes, granted greater rights to women, reformed hospitals and institutions for the insane, and increased assistance for the poor. Every new state constitution created a public school system that was open to children of both races, although schools were still segregated. The Southern states also eliminated laws that required people to own property in order to vote or hold public office. Historians have remarked on the fairness of the new constitutions created by the delegates. "The constitutions drawn up by these bodies were revolutionary only by the standards of conservative white supremacy which had prevailed in the South," Trelease wrote. "Most of them were modeled on Northern state constitutions and, in many aspects, on earlier Southern documents."

According to Congress's formula, a majority of registered voters in each state had to approve the new constitution in order for it to take effect. Alabama was the first state to hold its election. Many white voters who opposed the changes decided not to vote as a form of protest. As a result, the new constitution was approved by a majority of the people who actually voted, but not by enough people to pass. Congress quickly changed its rule so that the new constitutions could take effect when they were approved by a majority of the people who cast votes. Elections for the new state governments were held at the same time as the votes on the new constitutions. Once again, the changes were less radical than some people anticipated. Black men played a role in the government of each state, but usually a minor one. Blacks became school principals, sheriffs, mayors, and legislators for the first time in much of the South. But there were still no black governors, only two black U.S. senators, and twenty black U.S. representatives during Reconstruction.

Most of the Southern states—with their new governments and constitutions—were readmitted to the Union in 1868. (Tennessee had been readmitted in 1866, after it had ratified the Fourteenth Amendment. Georgia, Mississippi, Virginia, and Texas had trouble passing their new constitutions and were not readmitted until 1870.) To ensure that the new state governments would remain in power, the U.S. Congress passed the Fifteenth Amendment to the Constitution in 1868. This amendment guaranteed black voting rights and prohibited the states from restricting them. It was ratified by the states two years later.

Black people still lacked economic and social power in the South. For example, many black families could not afford land of their own and remained sharecroppers. But they finally held some political power. "For the first time in their lives, many felt they had a place in their state. They could vote for their leaders and thus have a say in laws and taxes," William Loren Katz wrote in his book *An Album of Reconstruction*. "But this democracy depended on cooperation between whites who had always been told they were superior, and black people who had always been told they were inferior. How long would it hold up?"

President Johnson faces impeachment

As Congress began implementing its Reconstruction program, some members were willing to compromise with President Johnson. But Johnson refused to accept any changes to his lenient policies toward the South. He believed that some of his Republican opponents were engaged in a conspiracy

The Impeachment of President Bill Clinton

For more than one hundred years, Andrew Johnson was the only American president to be impeached. The U.S. Congress put Johnson on trial in an attempt to remove him from office in 1868. In 1998, Bill Clinton (1946–) became the second president ever to face impeachment. After a lengthy investigation into Clinton's financial dealings and personal life, the U.S. House of Representatives passed two articles of impeachment against the president. They charged him with perjury (lying while under oath to tell the truth) and obstruction of justice (interfering with an official investigation). These charges had to do with Clinton's sexual relationship with a White House intern named Monica Lewinsky (1973–), and his alleged attempts to prevent information about that relationship from becoming public.

Throughout the impeachment hearings and Senate trial, Clinton remained popular with the public. Many Americans felt that the Republican-controlled Congress simply did not like the Democratic president and wanted any excuse to remove him from office. Most people agreed that Clinton was wrong to have an affair and to lie about it. But they also felt that the president's personal life should remain private and should not be used as grounds for impeachment.

In 1998, President Bill Clinton became the first president since Andrew Johnson to be impeached. *(Courtesy of the Library of Congress.)*

Clinton's trial before the Senate lasted for several weeks and attracted a great deal of news coverage. The Senate finally voted on the two articles of impeachment in February 1999. The vote on the perjury charge was 55–45 in favor of acquittal (finding the president not guilty). The vote on the obstruction of justice charge was 50–50, far short of the two-thirds majority (67 votes) needed to convict Clinton. Like President Johnson before him, Clinton survived impeachment and remained in office.

(plot) to overthrow him, and he grew more and more determined to resist. "Ironically, the conspiracy he feared was almost nonexistent until he fanned it to life by his own stubbornness," Trelease noted. Johnson used his veto power to fight Congress's Reconstruction efforts every step of the way. Over time, even the more moderate members of Congress began to believe that the president would do anything to destroy their plans.

Even though the Republicans increased their majority in Congress after the midterm elections of 1866—meaning that they could easily override Johnson's veto—they could not afford to ignore the president completely. Johnson remained the chief executive of the federal government. It was his job to carry out and enforce the laws made by Congress, and he could potentially refuse to do this. So Congress took steps to limit the president's ability to interfere with their plans. One of these steps was passing the Tenure of Office Act in March 1867. This act prevented the president from replacing federal officials without the consent of Congress. It was specifically designed to prevent Johnson from replacing Secretary of War Edwin Stanton (1814–1869), who was the only member of the cabinet who favored Congress's Reconstruction plans. Stanton basically acted like a spy, letting Congress know the president's next move. Congress also passed a law that required the president to issue all orders to the army through its commanding general, Ulysses S. Grant.

Johnson believed that the Tenure of Office Act was unconstitutional, meaning that it conflicted with laws set forth in the U.S. Constitution and would not hold up in court. He fired Stanton in August 1867, shortly after Congress had adjourned. He then dismissed four of the five commanders that Congress had placed in charge of the military districts in the South. Johnson's actions infuriated the Republican-led Congress. Tired of arguing with Johnson, the Republicans decided to impeach the president.

The Constitution says that all federal officials can be impeached (brought up on legal charges) and removed from elected office if they are found guilty of "treason, bribery, or other high crimes and misdemeanors." All of the branches of the federal government have roles in an impeachment trial. The House of Representatives brings the charges and acts as prosecutor. The chief justice of the Supreme Court presides over the trial as a judge. The Senate hears the case and votes as a jury. Two-thirds of the senators present must vote to convict in order to remove the impeached official from office.

Congress began the process of impeachment on February 22, 1868. It marked the first time in history that an American president had been impeached. Johnson was charged with violating the Tenure of Office Act and disgracing the office of the president. Even though the charges did not really meet the conditions for impeachment, Johnson was so unpopular that the outcome of the trial was uncertain. "Many Americans had such hatred for Andrew Johnson as a defender of the rebel South and a persistent thwarter [obstructer] of majority will that they had come to regard him as Public Enemy No. 1," Trelease explained. "In this outraged state of mind, the public good seemed to them to require that he be driven from office by any means legal." The trial before the Senate continued for more than two months and captured the attention of the entire country. Finally, the senators voted on the charges on May 16. Johnson was found not guilty by one vote and remained in office.

Reconstruction unravels

The remainder of Johnson's term in office was uneventful. Union general Ulysses S. Grant was elected to replace him as president later in 1868. By this time, Congress's Reconstruction program had been in place for two years. It was very unpopular among white Southerners. Many white people in the South hated the Reconstruction policies that allowed blacks to vote and hold positions in the government. They still believed that black people were inferior and should submit to white rule. White Southerners also resented the presence of federal troops in the South. They complained that the military rule violated their rights. But in most cases, the Northern troops did not use their full authority. "Military tyranny, against which Southerners protested so loudly and so often, simply did not

exist," Trelease wrote. "It was nothing compared with the tyranny which Southerners continued to exercise over Negroes and Unionists, despite military efforts to prevent it. There were too few soldiers available and the commanders were too reluctant to interfere on the massive scale required to ensure really equal protection of the laws for all persons."

Anger over Congress's Reconstruction policies convinced many white Southerners to use any means necessary to reclaim control of their governments and society. Some people—known as "white supremacists" due to their belief that blacks were inferior—used violence and terrorism to intimidate blacks and any whites who helped them. These people bombed or set fire to black schools and churches. They terrorized black officeholders, successful black farmers and businessmen, and white teachers who worked at black schools. They were rarely punished for these crimes because juries were afraid to convict them.

One of the worst white supremacist groups was the Ku Klux Klan. This group was formed in 1866 by young Confederate veterans. They started out by playing practical jokes on each other, and later on black people. They rode around on horseback, dressed in white sheets, pretending to be the ghosts of dead Confederate soldiers. Before long, however, the Klan began using threats and violence to frighten their enemies and control their behavior. By 1868, Klan activities had spread throughout the South. Several states passed laws against them, but in most places the laws were not well enforced. The only state that waged a successful fight against the Klan was Arkansas, where Governor Powell Clayton (1833–1914) called out the state militia to restore order.

Violence against blacks increases

By 1870, violence against black people had increased to extreme levels in the South. Elected black members of the state governments were forced out of office in Virginia, North Carolina, Tennessee, and Georgia. The new, white-controlled governments again began passing laws that discriminated against blacks. For example, one law prohibited black people from shopping at white stores. Another law required black workers to sign employment contracts in which they agreed not to participate in various political groups.

The federal government made a few attempts to restore order in the South and protect the rights of black citizens. Congress conducted an investigation of the Ku Klux Klan and similar organizations in 1871. Afterward, it passed several new laws designed to suppress the groups' terrorist activities. Racially motivated violence became a federal offense. This meant that anyone accused of such crimes would be put on trial in federal courts, where they would be more likely to be convicted than in Southern state and local courts. As a result, most white supremacist organizations disappeared

by 1872, although less-organized violence continued.

As the situation in the South spun out of control, many people in the North became disgusted. They began pressuring President Grant to remove the remaining federal troops from the South. Some Northerners were willing to allow the South to return to white rule if it would put an end to the violence. Southern whites took advantage of this change in public opinion in the North. They used a variety of illegal methods to prevent black people from voting. As a result, the Democratic Party took control of many Southern state governments. In 1874, the Democrats captured a majority of seats in the U.S. House of Representatives for the first time since before the Civil War. The Republicans still held the presidency and a majority of the U.S. Senate, but they had considerably less power to protect the rights of blacks in the South.

Prior to the elections of 1875, white people in Mississippi openly admitted that they planned to use force to regain control of their state government from blacks. This announcement became known as the "Mississippi Plan." Democrats in the state formed armed militias (armies of regular citizens) and marched through black areas. They broke up meetings of Republican supporters and provoked riots with blacks. By the time the election took place, thousands of black voters were too afraid to go to the polls. White supremacists took over the government of Mississippi that

Samuel J. Tilden (above) lost to Rutherford B. Hayes by one electoral vote. *(Courtesy of the Library of Congress.)*

year, and a similar pattern occurred in other Southern states in later years.

The election of 1876 ends Reconstruction

The presidential election of 1876 was a hotly contested one. Rutherford B. Hayes was the Republican candidate, and Samuel J. Tilden (1814–1886) was the Democratic candidate. Most people in the North voted for Hayes, and most people in the South voted for Tilden. The election ended up being the closest in history. Tilden won the popular vote— 4,284,020 people who submitted ballots voted for him, compared to 4,036,572 for Hayes. But the actual winner of presidential elections is determined by an institution known as the electoral college. Each state receives a certain number of electoral votes depending on its population. When the electoral votes were counted, Tilden had 184 and Hayes had 165, and 20 votes were in dispute. A candidate needed 185 electoral votes to win the presidency, so neither man could be declared the winner.

The controversy came down to three Southern states that still had their black-white Reconstruction governments intact—South Carolina, Florida, and Louisiana. Hayes needed the electoral votes of all three states in order to become president. Congress set up a special committee to examine the election results in these states. But it was difficult to tell for certain which candidate had won because the elections had caused widespread violence.

Eventually, the two main political parties arranged a compromise. The Democrats would allow Hayes to become president if he agreed to remove federal troops from the South. This meant that Republicans would lose control of the last three Southern states to white supremacists. The arrangement became known as the Compromise of 1877. "In perspective, it appears that the Democrats first stole the election of 1876 by a systematic and deliberate campaign of terrorism and violence in the South. Then, as a result of the compromise between Republicans and Southern whites, the Republicans stole back the Presidency but allowed the Democrats to keep the South," Trelease explained.

Hayes became the nineteenth president of the United States in March 1877 and immediately removed federal troops from the South. This marked the end of the period of American history known as Reconstruction. From this time onward, the North left the South to settle its own racial issues. Unfortunately, many issues remained unresolved for generations. Discrimination against blacks was a way of life in much of the South for many years. The South was not completely to blame for the failure of Reconstruction, however. Some Northerners had never felt strongly about black equality in the first place. They had supported black voting rights primarily because it would help the Republican Party maintain power in the federal government. Republican policies had forced the South to give blacks greater political and legal rights, but had stopped short of providing former slaves with land, education, and jobs.

Without these things, black people never had an opportunity to make political and legal rights permanent.

Even though Reconstruction failed to ensure equality for black citizens in the United States, it set the stage for the Civil Rights Movement that would take place nearly a century later. "To say that Reconstruction was a complete and utter failure would be a mistake," Trelease noted. "For one thing, it remained in the memories of Negroes and a minority of whites; they might be outnumbered and silenced for the present, but they would not always be. When the same dedication to equal rights arose in a later day, Reconstruction remained as a precedent and stimulus to further progress. For another thing, some of the enactments of the Reconstruction period were so basic and so fully accepted that they could never be entirely repealed or ignored. Three constitutional amendments remained as part of the basic law of the land; however neglected or nullified they might have been in practice, they were never abandoned in theory and they were later to be enforced again."

Where to Learn More

The following list of resources focuses on material appropriate for middle school or high school students. Please note that the web site addresses were verified prior to publication, but are subject to change.

Books

Anders, Curt. *Hearts in Conflict: A One-Volume History of the Civil War.* Secaucus, NJ: Carol Pub. Group, 1994.

Anderson, Nancy Scott, and Dwight Anderson. *The Generals—Ulysses S. Grant and Robert E. Lee.* New York: Knopf, 1988.

Aptheker, Herbert. *Abolitionism: A Revolutionary Movement.* Boston: Twayne, 1989.

Basler, Roy P., ed. *The Collected Works of Abraham Lincoln.* New Brunswick, NJ: Rutgers University Press, 1953.

Berlin, Ira, Joseph P. Reidy, and Leslie S. Rowland, eds. *Freedom's Soldiers: The Black Military Experience in the Civil War.* New York: Cambridge University Press, 1998.

Blight, David W. *Frederick Douglass's Civil War: Keeping Faith in Jubilee.* Baton Rouge: Louisiana State University Press, 1989.

Bradford, Ned, ed. *Battles and Leaders of the Civil War.* New York: New American Library, 1984.

Buell, Thomas B. *The Warrior Generals: Combat Leadership in the Civil War.* New York: Crown, 1997.

Carter, Alden R. *The Civil War: American Tragedy.* New York: Franklin Watts, 1992.

Carter, Samuel. *The Last Cavaliers: Confederate and Union Cavalry in the Civil War.* St. Martin's Press, 1980.

Catton, Bruce. *The Centennial History of the Civil War.* 3 vols. Garden City, NY: Doubleday, 1961–65.

Catton, Bruce. *The Civil War.* Boston: Houghton Mifflin, 1960.

Chadwick, Bruce. *The Two American Presidents: A Dual Biography of Abraham Lincoln and Jefferson Davis.* Secaucus, NJ: Carol, 1999.

Chang, Ina. *A Separate Battle: Women and the Civil War.* New York: Scholastic, 1994.

Civil War Generals: An Illustrated Encyclopedia. New York: Gramercy, 1999.

Commager, Henry Steele. *The Blue and the Gray.* Indianapolis: Bobbs-Merrill, 1950.

Davis, William C. *The Commanders of the Civil War.* San Diego: Thunder Bay Press, 1999.

Davis, William C. *Jefferson Davis: The Man and His Hour.* New York: HarperCollins, 1991.

Donald, David Herbert. *Lincoln.* New York: Simon & Schuster, 1995.

Dowdey, Clifford. *Lee's Last Campaign: The Story of Lee and His Men against Grant.* Lincoln: University of Nebraska Press, 1993.

Foote, Shelby. *The Civil War: A Narrative.* 3 vols. New York: Random House, 1958–74.

Freeman, Douglas S. *Lee's Lieutenants.* 3 vols. New York: Scribner's, 1942–44.

Goen, C. C. *Broken Churches, Broken Nation.* Macon, GA: Mercer University Press, 1985.

Grant, Ulysses S. *Personal Memoirs of U. S. Grant.* New York: Library of America, 1990.

Green, Carl R., and William R. Sanford. *Confederate Generals of the Civil War.* Springfield, NJ: Enslow, 1998.

Green, Carl R., and William R. Sanford. *Union Generals of the Civil War.* Springfield, NJ: Enslow, 1998.

Grimsley, Mark. *The Hard Hand of War, Union Military Policy Toward Southern Civilians, 1861-1865.* New York: Cambridge University Press, 1995.

Gutman, Herbert G. *The Black Family in Slavery and Freedom.* New York: Pantheon, 1976.

Hargrove, Hondon B. *Black Union Soldiers in the Civil War.* Jefferson, NC: McFarland, 1988.

Harmon, Dan. *Civil War Generals.* Philadelphia: Chelsea House, 1997.

Harrell, Carolyn L. *When the Bells Tolled for Lincoln*. Macon, GA: Mercer University Press, 1997.

Haskins, J. *The Day Fort Sumter Was Fired On: A Photo History of the Civil War*. New York: Scholastic, 1995.

Hattaway, Herman. *Shades of Blue and Gray: An Introductory Military History of the Civil War*. Columbia: University of Missouri Press, 1997.

Hendrickson, Robert. *The Road to Appomattox*. New York: John Wiley & Sons, 1998.

Hennessey, John. *Return to Bull Run: The Campaign and Battle of Second Manassas*. New York: Simon & Schuster, 1992.

Holt, Michael F. *The Political Crisis of the 1850s*. New York: John Wiley & Sons, 1978.

Kunhardt, Philip B., Jr. *A New Birth of Freedom: Lincoln at Gettysburg*. Boston: Little, Brown, 1983.

Leonard, Elizabeth D. *All the Daring of the Soldier: Women of the Civil War Armies*. New York: W. W. Norton, 1999.

Lincoln, Abraham. *Abraham Lincoln: Speeches and Writings*. 2 vols. New York: Library of America, 1989.

Linderman, Gerald. *Embattled Courage: The Experience of Combat in the American Civil War*. New York: Free Press, 1987.

Litwack, Leon. *Been in the Storm So Long: The Aftermath of Slavery*. New York: Alfred A. Knopf, 1979.

Macdonald, John. *Great Battles of the Civil War*. New York: Macmillan, 1988.

Macmillan Encylopedia of the Confederacy. New York: Macmillan, 1998.

Massey, Mary Elizabeth. *Women in the Civil War*. Lincoln: University of Nebraska Press, 1966.

McFeely, William S. *Grant: A Biography*. New York: Norton, 1981.

McPherson, James M. *Battle Cry of Freedom*. New York: Oxford University Press, 1988.

McPherson, James M. *For Cause and Comrades: Why Men Fought in the Civil War*. New York: Oxford University Press, 1997.

McPherson, James M. *Ordeal by Fire: The Civil War and Reconstruction*. New York: Alfred A. Knopf, 1982.

McPherson, James M., ed. *Encyclopedia of Civil War Biographies*. Armonk, NY: Sharpe Reference, 2000.

Mitchell, Joseph B. *Military Leaders in the Civil War*. New York: Putnam, 1972.

Mitchell, Reid. *Civil War Soldiers: Their Expectations and Their Experiences*. New York: Viking, 1988.

Morris, Roy, Jr. *Sheridan: The Life and Wars of General Phil Sheridan*. New York: Crown, 1992.

Murphy, Jim. *The Long Road to Gettysburg*. New York: Scholastic, 1995.

Nolan, Alan T. *Lee Considered: General Robert E. Lee and Civil War History.* Chapel Hill: University of North Carolina Press, 1991.

Oates, Stephen B. *With Malice Toward None: The Life of Abraham Lincoln.* New York: Harper & Row, 1977.

Paludan, Phillip S. *The Presidency of Abraham Lincoln.* Lawrence: University Press of Kansas, 1994.

Potter, David M. *The Impending Crisis, 1848–1861.* New York: Harper & Row, 1976.

Ritter, Charles F., and Jon L. Wakelyn. *Leaders of the American Civil War.* Westport, CT: Greenwood Press, 1998.

Royster, Charles. *The Destructive War: William Tecumseh Sherman, Stonewall Jackson, and the Americans.* New York: Alfred A. Knopf, 1991.

Sandburg, Carl. *Abraham Lincoln: The War Years.* 4 vols. New York: Harcourt Brace, 1939.

Sifakis, Stewart. *Who Was Who in the Civil War.* New York: Facts on File, 1988.

Stewart, James Brewer. *Holy Warriors: The Abolitionists and American Slavery.* New York: Hill & Wang, 1976.

Stokesbury, James L. *A Short History of the Civil War.* New York: William Morrow, 1995.

Thomas, Emory. *The Confederate Nation, 1861–1865.* New York: Harper & Row, 1979.

Tracey, Patrick Austin. *Military Leaders of the Civil War.* New York: Facts on File, 1993.

Trelease, Allen W. *Reconstruction: The Great Experiment.* New York: Harper & Row, 1971.

Trudeau, Noah Andre. *Like Men of War: Black Troops in the Civil War, 1862–1865.* Boston: Little, Brown, 1998.

Venet, Wendy Hamand. *Neither Ballots Nor Bullets: Women Abolitionists and the Civil War.* Charlottesville: University Press of Virginia, 1991.

Ward, Geoffrey C. *The Civil War: An Illustrated History.* New York: Alfred A. Knopf, 1990.

Woodworth, Steven E. *Jefferson Davis and His Generals.* Lawrence: University Press of Kansas, 1990.

World Wide Web

American Civil War/Conflict Between the States. http://americanhistory.miningco.com/education/history/americanhistory/msub13.htm (accessed on October 20, 1999).

American Civil War Homepage. http://sunsite.utk.edu/civil-war (accessed on October 20, 1999).

American Civil War Resources on the Internet. http://www.janke.washcoll. edu/civilwar/civilwar.htm (accessed on October 20, 1999).

Civil War Music and Poetry and Music of the War Between the States. http://users.erols.com/kfraser/ (accessed on October 20, 1999).

Library of Congress. *Gettysburg Address Exhibit.* www.lcweb.loc.gov/ex-hibits/gadd (accessed on October 20, 1999).

Library of Congress, American Memory. *Selected Civil War Photographs.* lcweb2.loc.gov/ammem/cwphome.html (accessed on October 20, 1999).

Rutgers University Libraries. *Civil War Resources on the Internet.* http:// www.libraries.rutgers.edu/rulib/socsci/hist/civwar-2.html (accessed on October 20, 1999).

Index

A

Abolitionist movement, 4, 15–29, 36, 44, 53; opposition to, 20; ties to religion, 18
Abolitionists, 15–29, 42, 71
Adams, Charles Francis, 94–96, 95 (ill.)
Adams, John, 95
Adams, John Quincy, 21, 36, 63, 95
African colonization, 16–17
Alabama, Reconstruction in, 245; secession of, 68
Allen, Richard, 16
American Anti-Slavery Society, 21
American Colonization Society, 16–17
American Revolution, 3, 204
American Slavery as It Is, 22–23
Anaconda Plan, 108–9
Anderson, Robert, 76, 76 (ill.), 77, 80, 81, 228
Andrew, John, 212
Antietam, Battle of, 97, 117, 133–34, 133 (map), 135, 135 (ill.)

Antislavery movement, 3. *See also* Abolitionist movement
Appeal of the Independent Democrats, The, 45
Arkansas, Reconstruction in, 249; secession of, 70, 83
Articles of Confederation, 32
Atchison, David, 45, 46
Atlanta, capture of, 191 (ill.); eviction of population from, 191–92; siege of, 187

B

Barton, Clara, 166
Battle of Antietam, 117, 133–34, 135
Battle of Chancellorsville, 145, 148–49
Battle of Chattanooga, 140, 160, 162
Battle of Chickamauga, 140, 160
Battle of Cold Harbor, 183–84
Battle of Five Forks, 224

Battle of Fredericksburg, 136–38
Battle of Gettysburg, 139, 149–52, 151 (map)
Battle of Jonesboro, 191
Battle of Mobile Bay, 189–90, 192
Battle of New Orleans, 122–24
Battle of Perryville, 140
Battle of Shiloh, 120–21, 124
Battle of Spotsylvania, 181
Battle of Stones River, 142
Battle of the Wilderness, 179, 181
Beauregard, Pierre Gustave Toutant, and attack on Fort Sumter, 77, 80, 81; and Battle of Shiloh, 121; and First Battle of Bull Run, 112–14, 226
Beecher, Henry Ward, 46
Beecher's Bibles, 46
Bell, John, 65
Benezet, Anthony, 4
Benjamin, Judah P., 68
Black Codes, 239, 241, 242
Black soldiers, admittance into Union Army, 210–15; Confederate treatment of, 211; discrimination against, 214
Blacks, efforts to join Union Army, 203–4; receive the right to vote, 244, 251; role in the Civil War, 201–15
Bleeding Kansas, 45–46
Booth, John Wilkes, 227–28, 229 (ill.), 230, 231
Border ruffians, 46
Bowser, Mary Elizabeth, 174
Bragg, Braxton, 140, 142–43, 158–60, 162–63
Breckinridge, John C., 64, 64 (ill.), 65
Brooks, Preston, 46–47
"Brother Jonathan's Lament for Sister Caroline," 66–67
Brown, John, 46, 59–61, 60 (ill.); activities in Kansas, 59; execution of, 61; raid on Harpers Ferry, 59–61
Buchanan, James, 47, 48, 55, 70, 76–77, 78–79, 79 (ill.)
Buell, Don Carlos, 120, 121
Bull, Rice C., 144
Bull Run, First Battle of, 111–16, 113 (ill.), 116 (ill.), 174

Bull Run, Second Battle of, 130–31
Burnside, Ambrose, 136, 137, 138, 143; and "Mud March," 143
Butler, Benjamin F., 84, 106, 124, 208, 208 (ill.)

C

C.S.S. Virginia, 122
Caldera, Louis, 231
Calhoun, James, 192
Calhoun, John C., 33, 37, 38–39, 39 (ill.), 41
California, 41
Cameron, Simon, 103
Carter, Jimmy, 231
Cass, Lewis, 41
Chamberlain, Joshua L., 151
Chancellorsville, Battle of, 145, 148–49
Chase, Salmon P., 45
Chattanooga, Battle of, 140, 160, 162; Southern abandonment of, 158–59
Chesnut, Mary Boykin, 166; and Southern view of war, 101
Chickamauga, Battle of, 140, 160
Child, Lydia Maria, 17
Civil Rights Act of 1875, 242
Civil rights movement, 235, 251
Civil War songs. See Songs of the Civil War
Clay, Henry, 35, 40 (ill.), 40–41, 85
Clayton, Powell, 249
Cleveland, Grover, 63
Clinton, Bill, 246, 246 (ill.)
Cold Harbor, Battle of, 183–84
Colonization. See African colonization
Compromise of 1850, 28, 41, 42–44, 57
Compromise of 1877, 250–51
Confederate Army, experiences of soldiers in, 146–47; illness and disease suffered by soldiers in, 182; uniforms of, 113–14, 115; victories in West, 131–32

Confederate commerce raiders, 91
Confederate Constitution, 72
Confederate States of America, 69–70, 74 (map); formation of, 71–73. *See also* South
Confiscation Act, 208
Conscription Act of 1863 (North), 156–57
Constitutional Union Party, 64–65
Contrabands, 208–10
Copperheads, 187, 197
Cotton, 6; South's decision to withhold from European markets, 90–93
Cotton gin, 2, 6
Crittenden Compromise, 70–71
Crittenden, John, 70, 72 (ill.)
Cuba, 93
Cumming, Kate, 172–73

D

Davis, Jefferson, 73, 79, 87, 104, 106, 109, 124, 129, 174, 175, 238; capture and imprisonment of, 229–30; defiance of, 224, 227; and fight for Chattanooga, 158–59; and flight from Richmond, 224, 227; and Lincoln's reelection, 198; and recruitment of soldiers, 125–26; and relationship with Johnston, 163, 187; and Richmond bread riots, 159; and siege of Vicksburg, 155; and use of black soldiers, 222–23
Declaration of Independence, 8
Delaware, 84
Democratic Party, 48–49, 54, 63–64, 68, 78, 187, 249
Dix, Dorothea Lynde, 170–71, 171 (ill.)
Douglas, Stephen A., 41, 44, 47–48, 55–59, 57 (ill.), 64, 65–66
Douglass, Frederick, 7, 18, 19, 19 (ill.), 21, 25, 135, 203, 204
Dred Scott v. Sandford, 52–54, 55, 56, 57, 215

E

Early, Jubal, 150, 188, 189, 193, 194, 196
Electoral college, 62–63
Emancipation Proclamation, 134–36, 143, 201, 206–7; effect on European neutrality, 97
Emigrant Aid Society, 46
England, 3; reaction to Trent Affair, 94
Europe, neutrality during Civil War, 91–92, 132, 149; reaction to American Civil War, 87–97
Ewell, Richard S., 150

F

Fair Oaks, Battle of. *See* Seven Pines, Battle of
Fairbanks, Calvin, 25
Farragut, David, 190 (ill.), 192; and Battle of Mobile Bay, 188–90; and Battle of New Orleans, 123–24
Female Anti-Slavery Society, 21
Female soldiers. *See* Women soldiers
Fifteenth Amendment, 245
Fifty-Fourth Massachusetts Regiment, 212–13
Fillmore, Millard, 41, 42 (ill.)
Finney, Charles G., 22
First Battle of Bull Run. *See* Bull Run, First Battle of
First Battle of Manassas. *See* Bull Run, First Battle of
First South Carolina Volunteers, 211
Five Forks, Battle of, 224
Florida, Reconstruction in, 250; secession of, 68
Foote, A. H., 120
Forrest, Nathan Bedford, 188, 211, 221
Fort Pillow massacre, 211
Fort Sumter, 75 (map), 100, 228, 228 (ill.); attack on, 69, 76–81; attempts to resupply, 77

Fort Wagner, attack on, 212
Forten, James, 16
Foster, William Lovelace, 155
Fourteenth Amendment, 242–43
Fox, George, 4, 4 (ill.)
Fox, Gustavus, 79
France, 3
Fredericksburg, Battle of, 136–38, 137 (ill.), 138 (ill.)
Free Soil Party, 37, 48
Freedmen's aid societies, 208, 209
Freedmen's Bureau, 240
Freedom of speech, limitations on, 21
Freeport Doctrine, 58
Fugitive Slave Act of 1850, 28, 41, 42–44, 208
Fugitive slave laws, 27–28, 202
Fugitive slaves, Union policy toward, 208

G

Galloway, Edward, 81
Garrison, William Lloyd, 17, 20, 21
Georgia, rejoins the Union, 245; secession of, 68
Gettysburg, Battle of, 139, 149–52, 151 (map)
Glory, 213, 213 (ill.)
Gorgas, Josiah, 156
Grant, Ulysses S., 154 (ill.), 174, 195 (ill.), 225 (ill.), 233, 247; and Battle of Cold Harbor, 183–84; and Battle of Shiloh, 120–21; and Battle of Spotsylvania, 181; and Battle of the Wilderness, 179, 181; and capture of Fort Donelson, 120; and capture of Fort Henry, 120; and capture of Richmond, 224; and Lee's surrender, 225–27; military strategy of, 177, 178–79; and offensive on Petersburg, 185; as president, 248, 249; promoted by Lincoln, 162, 163; reaction to Lincoln's death, 228; and siege of Petersburg, 218–19, 223–24; and siege of Vicksburg, 154–56

Greeley, Horace, 108, 185
Greenhow, Rose O'Neal, 112, 174–75
Grierson, Benjamin, 154
Grimké Angelina Emily, 21, 22, 24, 24 (ill.), 213
Grimké Sarah Moore, 21, 22, 24

H

Habeus corpus, writ of, 84
Halleck, Henry W., 120, 121, 129 (ill.), 130
Harpers Ferry, Virginia, 59
Harrison, Benjamin, 63
Hayes, Rutherford B., 63, 235, 250, 251; removes federal troops from the South, 250–51
Hemings, Sally, 9
Herold, David, 230
Higginson, Thomas Wentworth, 211
Holmes, Oliver Wendell, 66, 67 (ill.)
Hood, John Bell, 160, 187, 191, 199
Hooker, Joseph, 143–45, 145 (ill.), 148–49, 162
Hospital ships, 172
Hough, Daniel, 81
Houston, Sam, 73
Howard, Oliver O., 240, 240 (ill.)

I

Industrial Revolution, 12

J

Jackson, Andrew, 34, 34 (ill.), 63
Jackson, Thomas "Stonewall," and Battle of Antietam, 133, 134; and Battle of Chancellorsville, 148; and First Battle of Bull Run, 114; and Second Battle of Bull Run, 131; and

Shenandoah Campaign, 128–29

Jefferson, Thomas, 5, 7, 8–9, 9 (ill.), 34, 35

Johnson, Andrew, 234, 237–39, 238 (ill.), 240, 242, 243; impeachment of, 245–48; pardons former Confederates, 238; pardons Samuel Mudd, 231; Reconstruction policies of, 238

Johnston, Albert S., 120, 121

Johnston, Joseph E., 112 (ill.), 155, 178, 179, 224; and campaign against Sherman, 185, 187; and First Battle of Bull Run, 112–14; and Peninsula Campaign, 128, 129; and relationship with Davis, 163, 187; and Sherman's March to the Sea, 221–22

Joint Committee on Reconstruction, 242

Joint Committee on the Conduct of the War, 126

Jones, Absalom, 16

Jones, John, 21

Jonesboro, Battle of, 191

K

Kansas, 45, 47–48, 59

Kansas-Nebraska Act, 44–46, 48, 57

Kate: The Journal of a Confederate Nurse, 172

Kennedy, Jihmi, 213 (ill.)

Kentucky, 84, 85

Kirkland, Richard R., 137

Ku Klux Klan, 248–49

L

Labor unions, 204

Lecompton Constitution, 47–48, 58, 64

Lee, Robert E., 60, 107 (ill.), 111, 117, 177, 178, 184 (ill.), 185, 225 (ill.), 233; and 1862 invasion of the North, 132–34; and 1863 invasion of the North, 149–52; and Battle of Antietam, 133–34; and Battle of Chancellorsville, 139, 145, 148–49; and Battle of Cold Harbor, 183–84; and Battle of Fredericksburg, 136, 138; and Battle of Gettysburg, 149–52; and Battle of Spotsylvania, 181; and Battle of the Wilderness, 179, 181; decision to join Confederacy, 107; and defense of Richmond, 179, 218–19, 224; and evacuation of Richmond, 224; and Peninsula Campaign, 129–30; and Second Battle of Bull Run, 130–31; and siege of Petersburg, 218–19, 223–24; surrender of, 217, 225–27; takes command of Army of Northern Virginia, 129; and use of black soldiers, 222–23; views on slavery, 107

Letcher, John, 158

Levin, Carl, 231

Lewinsky, Monica, 246

Liberia, 17

Lincoln, Abraham, 29, 55–59, 63, 64, 65, 65 (ill.), 69, 70, 71, 74, 80 (ill.), 87, 101, 102, 103, 106, 107, 112, 125 (ill.), 145, 185, 229 (ill.), 234; and 1860 election, 67–68; and 1864 election, 177–78, 187–88, 192, 196–97; assassination of, 227–29; call for seventy-five thousand volunteers, 82; and creation of West Virginia, 110–11; and efforts to prevent secession of border states, 84–85; and Emancipation Proclamation, 97, 134–36, 143, 201; first inaugural address, 75; at Fort Stevens, 189; handling of Fort Sumter crisis, 77–80; handling of Trent Affair, 94–96; and Northern public opinion, 132, 139, 156–57; political leadership of, 157; and relationship with Mc-

Clellan, 126–27, 129, 130, 132–33, 136; and Sons of Liberty, 197; and Thirteenth Amendment, 223; and Ulysses S. Grant, 163; wartime Reconstruction policies of, 237

Lincoln, Mary Todd, 227, 229 (ill.)

Lincoln-Douglas debates, 56–58

Longstreet, James, 148 (ill.); and Battle of Chancellorsville, 145, 148–49; and Battle of Gettysburg, 150, 152; and Second Battle of Bull Run, 131

Louisiana, Reconstruction in, 250; secession of, 68

Louisiana Purchase, 35

Lovejoy, Elijah P., 21

M

Magruder, John B., 127

Maine, 35

Manassas, First Battle of. *See* Bull Run, First Battle of

Marye's Heights, Battle of. *See* Fredericksburg, Battle of

Maryland, establishment of martial law in, 84–85; suspension of writ of habeus corpus in, 84–85

Mason, James Murray, 93, 93 (ill.), 94, 96

Mayo, Joseph C., 159

McClellan, George, 111, 116, 125 (ill.), 131, 188 (ill.); and 1864 election, 177–78, 187–88, 196–97; administrative and training skills, 118, 120; and Battle of Antietam, 133–34; cautious style of, 126–27; and loss of command, 136; and Peninsula Campaign, 127–28, 129–30; and relationship with Lincoln, 126–27, 129, 130, 132–33, 136

McClernand, John, 106

McDowell, Irvin, 112–14, 116

McLean, Wilmer, 226

Meade, George G., 149–52, 150 (ill.), 178, 179

Mexican War, 36–37

Mexico, 89

Mississippi, Reconstruction in, 249; rejoins the Union, 245; secession of, 68

Mississippi Plan, 249

Mississippi River, 153 (map), 154–55

Missouri, 35, 84, 85

Missouri Compromise of 1820, 17, 35–36, 37, 44, 45; United States after, 18 (map)

Mobile Bay, Battle of, 189–90, 192

Montgomery, James, 211

Mott, Lucretia Coffin, 21

Mudd, Richard, 231

Mudd, Samuel, 230–31

Mudd, Sarah Frances, 231

Murfreesboro, Battle of. *See* Stones River, Battle of

N

Napolean III, 88, 89, 90 (ill.), 91

Nebraska, 45

Negro Soldier Law, 215

Neutrality, European announcements of, 91–92

New Orleans, Battle of, 122–24

New York draft riots, 157

Nightingale, Florence, 169, 170

North, celebrations of victory in, 217, 227; industrialization in, 103; military leadership of, 104–8; military strategy of, 108–9; naval blockade of South, 109, 122–23, 188–90; naval forces of, 102; opinion of Lincoln in, 132, 139; prejudice against blacks in, 157; reaction to Lincoln's death in, 228–29; recruitment of soldiers in, 100–101, 102, 103, 116, 156–57; transportation systems of, 104; view of war in, 99–101, 115–16, 139, 149, 152, 156–57, 162, 177, 185, 192, 196–97. *See also* Union Army

North Carolina, secession of, 70, 83
Northwest Territory, 5
Nurses, 169–71, 172

O

Ordinance of Nullification, 33

P

Palmerston, Lord, 94
Panic of 1857, 55
Parker, Theodore, 43
Patterson, Robert, 112, 114
Pemberton, John C., 154, 155, 156
Penn, William, 4
Perryville, Battle of, 140
Petersburg, Virginia, fall of, 217; siege of, 218–19
Pettigrew, James, 151–52
Phillips, Wendell, 18
Pickens, Francis, 79
Pickett, George, 151–52, 224
Pickett's Charge, 151–52, 151 (map)
Pierce, Franklin, 73
Pope, John, 128 (ill.), 130, 131
Popular sovereignty, 45, 47–48, 54, 55, 56, 64
Prigg v. Pennsylvania, 27
Prosser, Gabriel, 10

Q

Quakers, 3, 4, 16

R

Race relations, following the Civil War, 236
Race riots, 204–5, 243
Radical Republicans, 242, 247
Reconstruction, 233–51; Congressional, 235, 242–45, 248; end of, 250–51; Joint Committee on, 242; Lincoln's wartime policies, 237; physical damage to property, 236; Radical, 244; removal of federal troops from the South, 250–51; violence and intimidation in the South during, 248–50
Reconstruction Act, 244
Refugees, 167
Republican Party, 48, 59, 62–63, 70, 234, 241, 243, 251
Revolutionary War. *See* American Revolution
Richmond bread riots, 158–59
Richmond, Virginia, defense of, 179, 218–19; fall of, 224
Rock, John S., 215
Rosecrans, William, 111, 142–43, 157–60, 162
Russell, John, 95, 96

S

Schofield, John M., 199, 221, 222 (ill.)
Schurz, Carl, 106
Scott, Dred, 52–54
Scott, Winfield, 107, 108, 111, 116
Secession, 34, 67–68, 70; Northern opposition to, 72; Southern threats of, 37–38, 39, 61–62, 65
Second Battle of Bull Run. *See* Bull Run, Second Battle of
Second Battle of Manassas. *See* Bull Run, Second Battle of
Second Great Awakening, 18
Secret Six, 59
Semmes, Raphael, 91
Seven Days' Battles, 129–30
Seward, William, 41, 45, 61, 77, 94–96, 135; relationship with Lincoln, 77
Shadrach, 43
Sharecropping, 240–41
Sharpsburg, Battle of. *See* Antietam, Battle of
Shaw, Robert Gould, 212–13
Sheridan, Philip H., 221, 221 (ill.), 224; and Battle of Five

Forks, 224; and Battle of Stones River, 142; and death of Jeb Stuart, 182; and Shenandoah Valley, 192–94, 196

Sherman, William T., 162, 177, 178, 179, 220 (ill.); and campaign against Johnston, 185, 187; and capture of Savannah, 198; and "March to the Sea," 198, 218, 219–22, 223; and policies toward South, 191–92; and siege of Atlanta, 187, 190–91, 192; and total warfare, 193–94, 196

Shiloh, Battle of, 120–21, 124

Sickles, Daniel, 106

Slave rebellions, 10, 19, 59, 61, 202, 205, 207

Slavecatchers, 42

Slavery, 1–14, 51, 56, 89, 97, 207; abolition of, in other countries, 22–23; as cause of the Civil War, 203; compromises on the issue of, 31–49; efforts to abolish, in the United States, 15, 29, 235; expansion into new states and territories, 31–32, 35–36, 37–41, 44–46, 71; growth of, 6, 202; laws limiting, 5; laws supporting, 2, 27–28; and the Southern economy, 2, 3, 6, 11–12

Slaves, role in Confederacy during Civil War, 205–6; runaway, 25–28, 42; treatment of, 7–10, 12–13

Slidell, John, 92 (ill.), 93, 94, 96

Society of Friends. See Quakers

Songs of the Civil War, 186

Sons of Liberty, 197

South, and Conscription Act, 124–26; considers using black soldiers, 222–23; economy of, 218, 222; efforts to win support of Europe, 89–93; industrialization in, 103; military leadership of, 104–8; military strategy of, 109–10; naval forces of, 103–4; opinion of North in, 110; racism toward blacks in,

222–23; recruitment of soldiers in, 100–101, 102, 103–4, 124–26, 152; shortages in, 158–59; and states' rights, 125–26; supplies of, 194–95; transportation systems of, 104; view of Lee in, 129–30; view of war in, 99–101, 115–16, 156, 160, 198, 217–18, 220. See also Confederate Army

South Carolina, 33–34, 66, 69, 76; Reconstruction in, 244, 250; secession of, 68

Southern states, rejoin the Union, 245

Spies, 173–75

Spotsylvania, Battle of, 181

Stanton, Edwin, 103, 122, 130, 247

Stanton, Elizabeth Cady, 21

States' rights, 32–34, 37, 38, 54, 58, 125–26

Stephens, Alexander H., 72, 73 (ill.), 239

Stevens, Thaddeus, 242

Stones River, Battle of, 142, 142 (ill.)

Stowe, Harriet Beecher, 28–29, 44

Stuart, Jeb, 114, 148, 149, 182

Sumner, Charles, 46–47, 47 (ill.), 242

T

Taney, Roger B., 52–53, 54, 84

Tappan, Arthur, 18

Tappan, Lewis, 18

Tariffs, 33, 55

Taylor, Zachary, 41

"Tell Me, Is My Father Coming Back?" 186

Ten Percent Plan, 237

Tennessee, rejoins the Union, 245; secession of, 70, 83

"Tenting on the Old Camp Ground," 186

Tenure of Office Act, 247

Texas, 36, 37, 41; rejoins the Union, 245; secession of, 69, 73

Thirteenth Amendment, 223

Thomas, George Henry, 142, 160, 162, 199
Thoreau, Henry David, 61
Tilden, Samuel J., 63, 250, 250 (ill.)
Toombs, Robert, 37–38, 80
Torrey, Charles T., 25
Total warfare, 193–94, 196
Transcontinental railroad, 44
Trent Affair, 93–96
Tubman, Harriet, 25, 26 (ill.)
Turner, Henry McNeal, 209, 209 (ill.)
Turner, Nat, 11, 11 (ill.), 61

U

U.S. Constitution, 1, 3–5, 32
U.S. Sanitary Commission, 170–72
U.S.S. Merrimac, 122
U.S.S. Monitor, 122
U.S.S. Tecumseh, 190
Uncle Tom's Cabin, 28–29, 44
Underground Railroad, 25–28, 36
Union Army, admittance of black soldiers, 210–15; experiences of soldiers in, 146–47; illness and disease suffered by soldiers in, 182; uniforms of, 113–14, 115
Union Navy, blockades of Confederate ports, 91, 92–93, 109, 122–23, 188–90

V

Van Lew, Elizabeth, 174
Vesey, Denmark, 10
Vicksburg, Mississippi, siege of, 139, 154–56
Victoria, Queen of England, 88, 91, 96 (ill.)
Virginia, rejoins the Union, 245; secession of, 70, 83

W

Wade-Davis Bill, 237
Walker, David, 17
War, American conceptions of, 99
War for Independence. *See* American Revolution
War of 1812, 204
Washington, Booker T., 207, 207 (ill.)
Washington, D.C., 84; abolition of slave trade in, 41
Washington, Denzel, 213 (ill.)
Washington, George, 5
Weld, Theodore Dwight, 18, 20, 22–23, 23 (ill.), 24
Welles, Gideon, 102
West Point Military Academy, 106–8
West Virginia, creation of, 110–11
Westward expansion, 31, 34–35, 36–37
"When This Cruel War Is Over," 186
Whig Party, 48, 64
White supremacists, 248
Whitney, Eli, 2, 6, 7 (ill.)
Wigfall, Louis, 126
Wilderness, Battle of the, 179, 181
Wilkes, Charles, 93–94, 94 (ill.)
Williams, Peter, Jr., 17
Wilmington, Delaware, capture of, 221
Wilmot, David, 37
Wilmot Proviso, 37
Wilson, James H., 221
Wirz, Henry, 239
Women, role in Civil War, 165–75
Women nurses, qualifications and rules for, 170–71
Women soldiers, 169
Women spies, 173–75
Women's rights movement, 24

Y

"Yes, I Would the War Were Over," 186